MznLnx

Missing Links Exam Preps

Exam Prep for

MP Principles of Auditing and Other Assurance Services

Whittington & Panny, 15th Edition

The MznLnx Exam Prep is your link from the texbook and lecture to your exams.
The MznLnx Exam Preps are unauthorized and comprehensive reviews of your textbooks.

All material provided by MznLnx and Rico Publications (c) 2010
Textbook publishers and textbook authors do not particpate in or contribute to these reviews.

MznLnx

Rico
Publications

Exam Prep for MP Principles of Auditing and Other Assurance Services
15th Edition
Whittington & Panny

Publisher: Raymond Houge
Assistant Editor: Michael Rouger
Text and Cover Designer: Lisa Buckner
Marketing Manager: Sara Swagger
Project Manager, Editorial Production: Jerry Emerson
Art Director: Vernon Lowerui

Product Manager: Dave Mason
Editorial Assitant: Rachel Guzmanji
Pedagogy: Debra Long
Cover Image: Jim Reed/Getty Images
Text and Cover Printer: City Printing, Inc.
Compositor: Media Mix, Inc.

(c) 2010 Rico Publications
ALL RIGHTS RESERVED. No part of this work covered by the copyright may be reproduced or used in any form or by an means--graphic, electronic, or mechanical, including photocopying, recording, taping, Web distribution, information storage, and retrieval systems, or in any other manner--without the written permission of the publisher.

Printed in the United States
ISBN:

For more information about our products, contact us at:
Dave.Mason@RicoPublications.com

For permission to use material from this text or product, submit a request online to:
Dave.Mason@RicoPublications.com

Contents

CHAPTER 1
The Role of the Public Accountant in the American Economy   1

CHAPTER 2
Professional Standards   13

CHAPTER 3
Professional Ethics   24

CHAPTER 4
Legal Liability of CPAs   33

CHAPTER 5
Audit Evidence and Documentation   38

CHAPTER 6
Planning the Audit; Linking Audit Procedures to Risk   50

CHAPTER 7
Internal Control   65

CHAPTER 8
Consideration of Internal Control in an Information Technology Environment   75

CHAPTER 9
Audit Sampling   82

CHAPTER 10
Cash and Financial Investments   86

CHAPTER 11
Accounts Receivable, Notes Receivable, and Revenue   96

CHAPTER 12
Inventories and Cost of Goods Sold   107

CHAPTER 13
Property, Plant, and Equipment: Depreciation and Depletion   117

CHAPTER 14
Accounts Payable and Other Liabilities   126

CHAPTER 15
Debt and Equity Capital   135

CHAPTER 16
Auditing Operations and Completing the Audit   148

CHAPTER 17
Auditors' Reports   161

CHAPTER 18
Integrated Audits of Public Companies   168

CHAPTER 19
Additional Assurance Services: Historical Financial Information   174

CHAPTER 20
Additional Assurance Services: Other Information   181

Contents (Cont.)

CHAPTER 21
  Internal, Operational, and Compliance Auditing   186
ANSWER KEY   192

TO THE STUDENT

COMPREHENSIVE

The *MznLnx* Exam Prep series is designed to help you pass your exams. Editors at MznLnx review your textbooks and then prepare these practice exams to help you master the textbook material. Unlike study guides, workbooks, and practice tests provided by the texbook publisher and textbook authors, *MznLnx* gives you **all** of the material in each chapter in exam form, not just samples, so you can be sure to nail your exam.

MECHANICAL

The MznLnx Exam Prep series creates exams that will help you learn the subject matter as well as test you on your understanding. Each question is designed to help you master the concept. Just working through the exams, you gain an understanding of the subject--its a simple mechanical process that produces success.

INTEGRATED STUDY GUIDE AND REVIEW

MznLnx is not just a set of exams designed to test you, its also a comprehensive review of the subject content. Each exam question is also a review of the concept, making sure that you will get the answer correct without having to go to other sources of material. You learn as you go! Its the easiest way to pass an exam.

HUMOR

Studying can be tedious and dry. MznLnx's instructional design includes moderate humor within the exam questions on occassion, to break the tedium and revitalize the brain

Chapter 1. The Role of the Public Accountant in the American Economy

1. _____ is the statutory title of qualified accountants in the United States who have passed the Uniform _____ Examination and have met additional state education and experience requirements for certification as a _____. Individuals who have passed the Exam but have not either accomplished the required on-the-job experience or have previously met it but in the meantime have lapsed their continuing professional education are, in many states, permitted the designation '_____ Inactive' or an equivalent phrase. In most U.S. states, only _____s who are licensed are able to provide to the public attestation (including auditing) opinions on financial statements.
   a. Certified public accountant
   b. Chartered Accountant
   c. Chartered Certified Accountant
   d. Certified General Accountant

2. The U.S. _____ is an independent agency of the United States government which holds primary responsibility for enforcing the federal securities laws and regulating the securities industry, the nation's stock and options exchanges, and other electronic securities markets. The SEC was created by section 4 of the Securities Exchange Act of 1934 (now codified as 15 U.S.C. ÂÂ§ 78d and commonly referred to as the 1934 Act.)
   a. Securities and Exchange Commission
   b. BMC Software, Inc.
   c. BNSF Railway
   d. 3M Company

3. An _____ is a practitioner of accountancy, which is the measurement, disclosure or provision of assurance about financial information that helps managers, investors, tax authorities and other decision makers make resource allocation decisions.

The word '_____' is derived from the French 'Compter' which took its origin from the Latin 'Computare'. The word was formerly written in English as 'Accomptant', but in process of time the word, which was always pronounced by dropping the 'p', became gradually changed both in pronunciation and in orthography to its present form.

   a. ABC Television Network
   b. AIG
   c. Accountant
   d. AMEX

4. The _____ is the national, professional association of CPAs in the United States, with more than 330,000 members, including CPAs in business and industry, public practice, government, and education; student affiliates; and international associates. It sets ethical standards for the profession and U.S. auditing standards for audits of private companies; federal, state and local governments; and non-profit organizations.

Approximately 40% of its members are engaged in the practice of public accounting, in areas such as auditing, accounting, taxation, general business consulting, business valuation, personal financial planning and business technology.

   a. American Institute of Certified Public Accountants
   b. AIG
   c. ABC Television Network
   d. Other postemployment benefits

5. _____s have been defined by the American Institute of Certified Public Accountants (AICPA) as 'Independent Professional Services that improve information quality or its context'. _____s reduce the information risk; risk that the information provided is incorrect, on more than just financial data. The major purpose of _____s is to provide independent and professional opinions that improve the quality of information to management as well as other decision makers within a given firm.

Chapter 1. The Role of the Public Accountant in the American Economy

a. ITGCs
b. Assurance service
c. Auditor independence
d. Institute of Chartered Accountants of India

6. The general definition of an _____ is an evaluation of a person, organization, system, process, project or product. _____s are performed to ascertain the validity and reliability of information; also to provide an assessment of a system's internal control. The goal of an _____ is to express an opinion on the person/organization/system (etc) in question, under evaluation based on work done on a test basis.

a. Audit regime
b. Audit
c. Institute of Chartered Accountants of India
d. Assurance service

7. The _____ was established as the _____ by the Budget and Accounting Act of 1921 (Pub.L. 67-13, 42 Stat. 20, June 10, 1921.)

a. General Accounting Office
b. BMC Software, Inc.
c. GAO
d. 3M Company

8. _____ is an umbrella term which refers to the various accounting systems used by various public sector entities. In the United States, for instance, there are two levels of government which follow different accounting standards set forth by independent, private sector boards. At the federal level, the Federal Accounting Standards Advisory Board (FASAB) sets forth the accounting standards to follow.

a. Nonassurance services
b. Product control
c. Management accounting
d. Governmental Accounting

9. The _____ is currently the source of generally accepted accounting principles (GAAP) used by State and Local governments in the [[United States of America]]. As with most of the entities involved in creating GAAP in the United States, it is a private, non-governmental organization.

The _____ is subject to oversight by the Financial Accounting Foundation (FAF), which selects the members of the _____ and the Financial Accounting Standards Board, and funds both organizations.

a. National Conference of Commissioners on Uniform State Laws
b. Multinational corporation
c. Governmental Accounting Standards Board
d. Fannie Mae

10. Established in 1941, The _____ is internationally recognized as a trustworthy guidance-setting body. Serving members in 165 countries, The IIA is the internal audit profession's global voice, chief advocate, recognized authority, acknowledged leader, and principal educator, with global headquarters in Altamonte Springs, Fla., United States.

The stated mission of The _____ is to provide dynamic leadership for the global profession of internal auditing.

a. Event data
b. Auditor independence
c. Institute of Internal Auditors
d. Audit regime

Chapter 1. The Role of the Public Accountant in the American Economy

11. An _____ is a term used in behavioral economics to describe those types of behaviors that impose costs on a person in the long-run that are not taken into account when making decisions in the present. Classical Economics discourages government from creating legislation that targets internalities, because it is assumed that the consumer takes these personal costs into account when paying for the good that causes the _____. For example, cigarettes should be taxed because of the negative consumption externalities that they impose, such as second-hand smoke, not because the smoker harms him or herself by smoking.
   a. Authorised capital
   b. Internality
   c. Inventory turnover ratio
   d. Operating budget

12. Internal auditing is a profession and activity involved in helping organisations achieve their stated objectives. It does this by utilizing a systematic methodology for analyzing business processes, procedures and activities with the goal of highlighting organizational problems and recommending solutions. Professionals called _____ are employed by organizations to perform the internal auditing activity.
   a. Auditor independence
   b. Auditing Standards Board
   c. Internal Auditing
   d. Internal auditors

13. In accounting and organizational theory, _____ is defined as a process effected by an organization's structure, work and authority flows, people and management information systems, designed to help the organization accomplish specific goals or objectives. It is a means by which an organization's resources are directed, monitored, and measured. It plays an important role in preventing and detecting fraud and protecting the organization's resources, both physical (e.g., machinery and property) and intangible (e.g., reputation or intellectual property such as trademarks.)
   a. Auditor independence
   b. Audit committee
   c. Audit risk
   d. Internal control

14. The term _____ usually refers to a company that is permitted to offer its registered securities (stock, bonds, etc.) for sale to the general public, typically through a stock exchange, or occasionally a company whose stock is traded over the counter (OTC) via market makers who use non-exchange quotation services.

The term '_____' may also refer to a company owned by the government.

   a. Governmental Accounting Standards Board
   b. MicroStrategy
   c. Professional association
   d. Public Company

15. The _____ (sometimes called 'Peekaboo') is a private-sector, non-profit corporation created by the Sarbanes-Oxley Act, a 2002 United States federal law, to oversee the auditors of public companies. Its stated purpose is to 'protect the interests of investors and further the public interest in the preparation of informative, fair, and independent audit reports'. Although a private entity, the _____ has many government-like regulatory functions, making it in some ways similar to the private Self Regulatory Organizations (SROs) that regulate stock markets and other aspects of the financial markets in the United States.
   a. Pension Benefit Guaranty Corporation
   b. 3M Company
   c. Financial Crimes Enforcement Network
   d. Public Company Accounting Oversight Board

16. A _____ is a fungible, negotiable instrument representing financial value. they are broadly categorized into debt securities (such as banknotes, bonds and debentures), and equity securities; e.g., common stocks. The company or other entity issuing the _____ is called the issuer.

a. Tracking stock
b. BMC Software, Inc.
c. 3M Company
d. Security

17. _____ is the term used to refer to the standard framework of guidelines for financial accounting used in any given jurisdiction. _____ includes the standards, conventions, and rules accountants follow in recording and summarizing transactions, and in the preparation of financial statements.

Financial accounting information must be assembled and reported objectively.

a. Current asset
b. General ledger
c. Long-term liabilities
d. Generally accepted accounting principles

18. Accounting _____ define the basic standards for representing attestation engagements. Attestation is defined as an engagement in which a practitioner is hired to issue written communication that expresses a conclusion about the reliability of written assertions prepared by a separate party. The American Institute of Certified Public Accountants identified a number of different engagements that fall under the scope of _____, including: examining financial forecasts and projections, examining pro forma financial statements, evaluating internal control, assessing compliance with rules, regulations, and contractual obligations, as well as evaluating management discussions and analysis of financial results.

a. Audit working paper
b. Audit management
c. Institute of Chartered Accountants of India
d. Attestation standards

19. _____ is that part of statistical practice concerned with the selection of individual observations intended to yield some knowledge about a population of concern, especially for the purposes of statistical inference. Each observation measures one or more properties (weight, location, etc.) of an observable entity enumerated to distinguish objects or individuals.

a. Abby Joseph Cohen
b. Alan Greenspan
c. Sampling
d. Arthur Betz Laffer

20. _____ is the recording of the value of assets, liabilities, income, and expenses in the daybooks, journals, and ledgers, in which debit and credit entries are chronologically posted to record changes in value. _____ is often mistaken for accounting, which is the system of recording, verifying, and reporting such information. Practitioners of accounting are called accountants.

a. Controlling account
b. Double-entry bookkeeping
c. Debit and credit
d. Bookkeeping

21. _____ provided by CPAs include accounting and bookkeeping services, tax services, and management consulting services. _____ differ from assurance services. Most accounting and bookkeeping services, tax services, and management consulting services fall outside the scope of assurance services, although there is some common area of overlap between consulting and assurance services.

a. Grenzplankostenrechnung
b. Management accounting
c. Product control
d. Nonassurance services

22. _____ is a concept that denotes the precise probability of specific eventualities. Technically, the notion of _____ is independent from the notion of value and, as such, eventualities may have both beneficial and adverse consequences. However, in general usage the convention is to focus only on potential negative impact to some characteristic of value that may arise from a future event.

a. Discounting
c. Discount factor
b. Risk adjusted return on capital
d. Risk

23. In business and accounting, _____ are everything of value that is owned by a person or company. It is a claim on the property your income of a borrower. The balance sheet of a firm records the monetary value of the _____ owned by the firm.

a. Accrual basis accounting
c. Accounts receivable
b. Earnings before interest, taxes, depreciation and amortization
d. Assets

24. _____ means the giving out of information, either voluntarily or to be in compliance with legal regulations or workplace rules.

- In Computer security, full _____ means disclosing full information about vulnerabilities.
- In computing, _____ widget
- Journalism, full _____ refers to disclosing the interests of the writer which may bear on the subject being written about, for example, if the writer has worked with an interview subject in the past.

- In law:
    - The law of England and Wales, _____ refers to a process that may form part of legal proceedings, whereby parties inform to other parties the existence of any relevant documents that are, or have been, in their control. This compares with the process known as discovery in the course of legal proceedings in the United States.
    - In U.S. civil procedure (litigation rules for civil cases), _____ is a stage prior to trial. In civil cases, each party must disclose to the opposing party the following: names of witnesses which it may use to support its side, copies of documents (or mere description of these documents) in its control which it may use to support its side, computation of damages claimed, and certain insurance information. _____ is related to, but technically prior to, the discovery stage.
    - In Company law (known as 'corporate law' in the United States), _____ refers to giving out information about public or limited companies or their officers, which might be kept secret if the company was a private company or a partnership.

- In real property transactions, _____ refers to providing to a buyer information known to the seller or broker/agent concerning the condition or other aspects of real property that would affect the property's value or desirability. These rules regarding what information must be disclosed, and whether the information must be disclosed even if a buyer does not ask, vary from one jurisdiction to the next.

a. Disclosure
c. Trailing
b. Tax harmonisation
d. Controlled Foreign Corporations

25. In financial accounting, a _____ or statement of financial position is a summary of a person's or organization's balances. Assets, liabilities and ownership equity are listed as of a specific date, such as the end of its financial year. A _____ is often described as a snapshot of a company's financial condition.

a. Balance sheet
c. 3M Company
b. Statement of retained earnings
d. Financial statements

26. _____ is a company's financial statement that indicates how the revenue is transformed into the net income The purpose of the _____ is to show managers and investors whether the company made or lost money during the period being reported.

The important thing to remember about an _____ is that it represents a period of time.

a. Income statement
c. AIG
b. AMEX
d. ABC Television Network

27. _____ are formal records of a business' financial activities.

In British English, including United Kingdom company law, _____ are often referred to as accounts, although the term _____ is also used, particularly by accountants.

_____ provide an overview of a business' financial condition in both short and long term.

a. Notes to the financial statements
c. Statement of retained earnings
b. 3M Company
d. Financial statements

28. A _____ is a type of debt Like all debt instruments, a _____ entails the redistribution of financial assets over time, between the lender and the borrower.

a. Lender
c. Loan to value
b. Debenture
d. Loan

29. The _____ is the United States federal government agency that collects taxes and enforces the internal revenue laws. It is an agency within the U.S. Dept of the treasury responsible for interpretation and application of Federal tax law. The official U.S. Treasury regulations provide (in part):

The _____ is a bureau of the Department of the Treasury under the immediate direction of the Commissioner of Internal Revenue.

a. Use tax
c. Internal Revenue Service
b. Indirect tax
d. Income tax

30. _____, in law and economics, is a form of risk management primarily used to hedge against the risk of a contingent loss. _____ is defined as the equitable transfer of the risk of a loss, from one entity to another, in exchange for a premium, and can be thought of as a guaranteed small loss to prevent a large, possibly devastating loss. An insurer is a company selling the _____; an insured is the person or entity buying the _____.

a. AIG
c. Insurance
b. ABC Television Network
d. AMEX

Chapter 1. The Role of the Public Accountant in the American Economy 7

31. _____, commonly abbreviated as SAS, provide guidance to external auditors on generally accepted auditing standards in regards to auditing an entity and issuing a report. They are usually issued by the certified public accountant authoritative body in the region where the standards apply, such as the American Institute of Certified Public Accountants in the United States.

- _____
- _____ (Taiwan)

a. GASB 45
c. Financial Instruments and Exchange Law
b. RSM International
d. Statements on Auditing Standards

32. In accounting/accountancy, _____ are journal entries usually made at the end of an accounting period to allocate income and expenditure to the period in which they actually occurred. The revenue recognition principle is the basis of making _____ that pertain to unearned and accrued revenues under accrual-basis accounting. They are sometimes called Balance Day adjustments because they are made on balance day.

a. Earnings before interest, taxes, depreciation and amortization
b. Accrual
c. Accrued expense
d. Adjusting entries

33. _____ LLP, based in Chicago, was once one of the 'Big Five' accounting firms among PricewaterhouseCoopers, Deloitte Touche Tohmatsu, Ernst ' Young and KPMG, providing auditing, tax, and consulting services to large corporations. In 2002, the firm voluntarily surrendered its licenses to practice as Certified Public Accountants in the United States after being found guilty of criminal charges relating to the firm's handling of the auditing of Enron, the energy corporation, resulting in the loss of 85,000 jobs. Although the verdict was subsequently overturned by the Supreme Court of the United States, it has not returned as a viable business.

a. AIG
b. Arthur Andersen
c. ABC Television Network
d. AMEX

34. A _____ an audit of financial statements, is the review of the financial statements of a company or any other legal entity (including governments), resulting in the publication of an independent opinion on whether or not those financial statements are relevant, accurate, complete, and fairly presented. _____s are typically performed by firms of practicing accountants due to the specialist financial reporting knowledge they require. The _____ is one of many assurance or attestation functions provided by accounting and auditing firms, whereby the firm provides an independent opinion on published information.

a. Management representation
b. Financial audit
c. Mainframe audit
d. Lead Auditor

35. _____, Quarterly Report Pursuant to Section 13 or 15(d) of the Securities Exchange Act of 1934, is an SEC filing that must be filed quarterly with the US Securities and Exchange Commission. It contains similar information to the annual form 10-K, however the information is generally less detailed, and the financial statements are generally unaudited. Information for the final quarter of a firm's fiscal year is included in the 10-K, so only three 10-Q filings are made each year.

a. Form 20-F
b. Form 10-Q
c. 3M Company
d. Form 8-K

Chapter 1. The Role of the Public Accountant in the American Economy

36. The _____ of 2002 (Pub.L. 107-204, 116 Stat. 745, enacted July 30, 2002), also known as the Public Company Accounting Reform and Investor Protection Act of 2002, is a United States federal law enacted on July 30, 2002 in response to a number of major corporate and accounting scandals including those affecting Enron, Tyco International, Adelphia, Peregrine Systems and WorldCom. The legislation establishes new or enhanced standards for all U.S. public company boards, management, and public accounting firms. It does not apply to privately held companies.
   a. FCPA
   b. Lease
   c. Fair Labor Standards Act
   d. Sarbanes-Oxley Act

37. In a publicly-held company, an _____ is an operating committee of the Board of Directors, typically charged with oversight of financial reporting and disclosure. Committee members are drawn from members of the Company's board of directors, with a Chairperson selected from among the members. An _____ of a publicly-traded company in the United States is composed of independent and outside directors referred to as non-executive directors, at least one of which is typically a financial expert.
   a. Audit committee
   b. Event data
   c. Audit working paper
   d. External auditor

38. A _____ is a body of elected or appointed members who jointly oversee the activities of a company or organization. The body sometimes has a different name, such as board of trustees, board of governors, board of managers, or executive board. It is often simply referred to as 'the board.'

A board's activities are determined by the powers, duties, and responsibilities delegated to it or conferred on it by an authority outside itself.

   a. Hospital Survey and Construction Act
   b. Consumer protection laws
   c. Chief Financial Officers Act of 1990
   d. Board of directors

39. Project _____: The project _____ is a prediction of the costs associated with a particular company project. These costs include labor, materials, and other related expenses. The project _____ is often broken down into specific tasks, with task _____s assigned to each.
   a. 3M Company
   b. Budget
   c. BNSF Railway
   d. BMC Software, Inc.

40. The _____ is a Cabinet-level office, and is the largest office within the Executive Office of the President of the United States (EOP.) It is an important conduit by which the White House oversees the activities of federal agencies. OMB is tasked with giving expert advice to senior White House officials on a range of topics relating to federal policy, management, legislative, regulatory, and budgetary issues.
   a. Analysis of variance
   b. Office of Management and Budget
   c. Alaska Air Group
   d. AT'T Wireless Services, Inc.

41. _____ is a demonstration of a process -- such as a variable, term, or object -- relative in terms of the specific process or set of validation tests used to determine its presence and quantity. Properties described in this manner must be sufficiently accessible, so that persons other than the definer may independently measure or test for them at will. An _____ is generally designed to model a conceptual definition.
   a. AIG
   b. ABC Television Network
   c. AMEX
   d. Operational definition

Chapter 1. The Role of the Public Accountant in the American Economy 9

42. A _____ has several related meanings:

- a daily record of events or business; a private _____ is usually referred to as a diary.
- a newspaper or other periodical, in the literal sense of one published each day;
- many publications issued at stated intervals, such as magazines, or scholarly academic _____s, or the record of the transactions of a society, are often called _____s. Although _____ is sometimes used, erroneously, as a synonym for 'magazine,' in academic use, a _____ refers to a serious, scholarly publication, most often peer-reviewed. A non-scholarly magazine written for an educated audience about an industry or an area of professional activity is usually called a professional magazine.

The word 'journalist' for one whose business is writing for the public press has been in use since the end of the 17th century.

Open access _____s are scholarly _____s that are available to the reader without financial or other barrier other than access to the internet itself. Some are subsidized, and some require payment on behalf of the author. Subsidized _____s are financed by an academic institution or a government information center.

a. Journal
b. BNSF Railway
c. 3M Company
d. BMC Software, Inc.

43. A _____ is a financial expert especially trained in tax law. Some countries require _____s to verify the balance sheets of companies above a certain size. Individuals usually require _____s to minimize taxation, to avoid learning the details of tax law in complicated financial situations themselves or to learn the details of tax law from a professional advisor.

a. Tax Advisor
b. BMC Software, Inc.
c. BNSF Railway
d. 3M Company

44. The term '_____' refers to the concept of collecting information and attempting to spot a pattern in the information. In some fields of study, the term '_____' has more formally-defined meanings.

In project management _____ is a mathematical technique that uses historical results to predict future outcome.

a. Regression analysis
b. 3M Company
c. Trend analysis
d. Multicollinearity

45. In financial accounting, a _____ is defined as an obligation of an entity arising from past transactions or events, the settlement of which may result in the transfer or use of assets, provision of services or other yielding of economic benefits in the future.

a. False Claims Act
b. Corporate governance
c. Vested
d. Liability

46. The _____ is the former authoritative body of the American Institute of Certified Public Accountants (AICPA.) It was created by the American Institute of Certified Public Accountants in 1959 and issued pronouncements on accounting principles until 1973, when it was replaced by the Financial Accounting Standards Board (FASB).

Chapter 1. The Role of the Public Accountant in the American Economy

The _____ was disbanded in the hopes that the smaller, fully-independent FASB could more effectively create accounting standards.

a. International Federation of Accountants
b. Institute of Management Accountants
c. American Payroll Association
d. Accounting Principles Board

47. The _____ is a private, not-for-profit organization whose primary purpose is to develop generally accepted accounting principles (GAAP) within the United States in the public's interest. The Securities and Exchange Commission (SEC) designated the _____ as the organization responsible for setting accounting standards for public companies in the U.S. It was created in 1973, replacing the Accounting Principles Board and the Committee on Accounting Procedure of the American Institute of Certified Public Accountants. The _____'s mission is 'to establish and improve standards of financial accounting and reporting for the guidance and education of the public, including issuers, auditors, and users of financial information.'

The _____ is not a governmental body.

a. Public company
b. Fannie Mae
c. Governmental Accounting Standards Board
d. Financial Accounting Standards Board

48. Congress enacted the _____, in the aftermath of the stock market crash of 1929 and during the ensuing Great Depression.
a. Securities Act of 1933
b. Bookkeeping
c. Sustainability measurement
d. Monte Carlo methods

49. The _____ of 1934 is a law governing the secondary trading of securities (stocks, bonds, and debentures) in the United States of America. The Act, 48 Stat. 881 (enacted June 6, 1934), codified at 15 U.S.C.
a. BNSF Railway
b. BMC Software, Inc.
c. 3M Company
d. Securities Exchange Act

50. The _____ is a law governing the secondary trading of securities (stocks, bonds, and debentures) in the United States of America. The Act, 48 Stat. 881 (enacted June 6, 1934), codified at 15 U.S.C.
a. BMC Software, Inc.
b. BNSF Railway
c. 3M Company
d. Securities Exchange Act of 1934

51. _____ is the world's largest professional services firm. It was formed in 1998 from a merger between Price Waterhouse and Coopers ' Lybrand, both formed in London.

_____ earned aggregated worldwide revenues of $28 billion for fiscal 2008, and employed over 146,000 people in 150 countries.

a. Serial bonds
b. Daybook
c. PricewaterhouseCoopers
d. Total-factor productivity

Chapter 1. The Role of the Public Accountant in the American Economy

52. Established in 1988 the _____ is the professional organization that governs professional fraud examiners. Its activities include producing fraud information, tools and training. It also governs the professional designation of Certified Fraud Examiner.
   a. AIG
   b. AMEX
   c. ABC Television Network
   d. Association of Certified Fraud Examiners

53. _____ is a designation awarded by the Association of _____s (ACertified Fraud Examiner.) The ACertified Fraud Examiner is a 41,000 member-based global association dedicated to providing anti-fraud education and training.

    In order to become a _____ one must meet the following requirements:

    - Be an Associate Member of the ACertified Fraud Examiner in good standing
    - Meet minimum academic and professional requirements
    - Be of high moral character
    - Agree to abide by the Bylaws and Code of Professional Ethics of the Association of _____s

    Generally, applicants for _____ certification have a minimum of a bachelor's degree or equivalent from an institution of higher education. Two years of professional experience related to fraud can be substituted for each year of college.

    a. Chartered Accountant
    b. Certified public accountant
    c. Chartered Certified Accountant
    d. Certified Fraud Examiner

54. _____ is a concept whereby a person's financial liability is limited to a fixed sum, most commonly the value of a person's investment in a company or partnership with _____. A shareholder in a limited company is not personally liable for any of the debts of the company, other than for the value of his investment in that company. The same is true for the members of a _____ partnership and the limited partners in a limited partnership.
    a. Due diligence
    b. Burden of proof
    c. Joint venture
    d. Limited liability

55. A _____ in the law of the vast majority of United States jurisdictions is a legal form of business company that provides limited liability to its owners. Often incorrectly called a 'limited liability corporation' (instead of company), it is a hybrid business entity having certain characteristics of both a corporation and a partnership. The primary characteristic an _____ shares with a corporation is limited liability, and the primary characteristic it shares with a partnership is the availability of pass-through income taxation.
    a. Bond market
    b. Limited liability company
    c. Consumer protection laws
    d. Data protection

56. A _____ is a partnership in which some or all partners (depending on the jurisdiction) have limited liability. It therefore exhibits elements of partnerships and corporations. In an _____ one partner is not responsible or liable for another partner's misconduct or negligence.
    a. Financial Accounting Standards Board
    b. Dow Jones ' Company
    c. Privately held
    d. Limited liability partnership

Chapter 1. The Role of the Public Accountant in the American Economy

57. A _____ is a type of business entity in which partners (owners) share with each other the profits or losses of the business undertaking in which all have invested. _____s are often favored over corporations for taxation purposes, as the _____ structure does not generally incur a tax on profits before it is distributed to the partners (i.e. there is no dividend tax levied.) However, depending on the _____ structure and the jurisdiction in which it operates, owners of a _____ may be exposed to greater personal liability than they would as shareholders of a corporation.
   a. National Information Infrastructure Protection Act
   b. Resource Conservation and Recovery Act
   c. Corporate governance
   d. Partnership

58. The _____ is a 'voluntary organization of persons interested in accounting education and research'. It was formed in 1916. Its main publication, the The Accounting Review, was first published in 1926.
   a. Institute of Management Accountants
   b. American Accounting Association
   c. Australian Accounting Standards Board
   d. International Accounting Standards Board

59. _____s are the documents which keeping all audit evidences obtained during financial statements auditing. _____ is to be able to support the audit works done in order, sufficient and assurance audit evidences have been obtained and reasonable assurance audit conclusion can be made in due course.

   _____s are the property of the auditor.

   a. Auditor independence
   b. Internal Auditing
   c. Audit working paper
   d. Event data

60. _____ is the amount of time someone works beyond normal working hours. Normal hours may be determined in several ways:

   - by custom (what is considered healthy or reasonable by society),
   - by practices of a given trade or profession,
   - by legislation,
   - by agreement between employers and workers or their representatives.

   Most nations have _____ laws designed to dissuade or prevent employers from forcing their employees to work excessively long hours. These laws may take into account other considerations than the humanitarian, such as increasing the overall level of employment in the economy. One common approach to regulating _____ is to require employers to pay workers at a higher hourly rate for _____ work.

   a. AMEX
   b. AIG
   c. ABC Television Network
   d. Overtime

Chapter 2. Professional Standards

1. _____ are ten auditing standards, developed by the AICPA, consisting of general standards, standards of field work, and standards of reporting, along with interpretations. They were developed by the AICPA in 1947 and have undergone minor changes since then.

The _____ are as follows:

1. The auditor must have adequate technical training and proficiency to perform the audit
2. The auditor must maintain independence in mental attitude in all matters related to the audit.
3. The auditor must use due professional care during the performance of the audit and the preparation of the report.

1. The auditor must adequately plan the work and must properly supervise any assistants.
2. The auditor must obtain a sufficient understanding of the entity and its environment, including its internal control, to assess the risk of material misstatement of the financial statements whether due to error or fraud, and to design the nature, timing, and extent of further audit procedures.
3. The auditor must obtain sufficient appropriate audit evidence by performing audit procedures to afford a reasonable basis for an opinion regarding the financial statements under audit.

The new standards are in effect for audits of financial statements for periods beginning on or after December 15, 2006.

1. The auditor must state in the auditor's report whether the financial statements are in accordance with generally accepted accounting principles (GAAP.)
2. The auditor must identify in the auditor's report those circumstances in which such principles have not been consistently observed in the current period in relation to the preceding period.
3. When the auditor determines that informative disclosures are not reasonably adequate, the auditor must so state in the auditor's report.
4. The auditor must either express an opinion regarding the financial statements, taken as a whole the auditor should state the reasons therefore in the auditor's report. In all cases where the auditor's name is associated with the financial statements, the auditor should clearly indicate the character of the auditor's work, if any, and the degree of responsibility the auditor is taking, in the auditor's report.

a. Continuous auditing
b. Joint audit
c. Negative assurance
d. Generally accepted auditing standards

2. An _____ is a practitioner of accountancy, which is the measurement, disclosure or provision of assurance about financial information that helps managers, investors, tax authorities and other decision makers make resource allocation decisions.

The word '_____' is derived from the French 'Compter' which took its origin from the Latin 'Computare'. The word was formerly written in English as 'Accomptant', but in process of time the word, which was always pronounced by dropping the 'p', became gradually changed both in pronunciation and in orthography to its present form.

a. AMEX
b. AIG
c. ABC Television Network
d. Accountant

3. The _____ is the national, professional association of CPAs in the United States, with more than 330,000 members, including CPAs in business and industry, public practice, government, and education; student affiliates; and international associates. It sets ethical standards for the profession and U.S. auditing standards for audits of private companies; federal, state and local governments; and non-profit organizations.

Approximately 40% of its members are engaged in the practice of public accounting, in areas such as auditing, accounting, taxation, general business consulting, business valuation, personal financial planning and business technology.

a. AIG
b. ABC Television Network
c. American Institute of Certified Public Accountants
d. Other postemployment benefits

4. _____ is the statutory title of qualified accountants in the United States who have passed the Uniform _____ Examination and have met additional state education and experience requirements for certification as a _____. Individuals who have passed the Exam but have not either accomplished the required on-the-job experience or have previously met it but in the meantime have lapsed their continuing professional education are, in many states, permitted the designation '_____ Inactive' or an equivalent phrase. In most U.S. states, only _____s who are licensed are able to provide to the public attestation (including auditing) opinions on financial statements.

a. Chartered Accountant
b. Certified General Accountant
c. Certified Public Accountant
d. Chartered Certified Accountant

5. The term _____ usually refers to a company that is permitted to offer its registered securities (stock, bonds, etc.) for sale to the general public, typically through a stock exchange, or occasionally a company whose stock is traded over the counter (OTC) via market makers who use non-exchange quotation services.

The term '_____' may also refer to a company owned by the government.

a. Public Company
b. Governmental Accounting Standards Board
c. MicroStrategy
d. Professional association

6. The _____ (sometimes called 'Peekaboo') is a private-sector, non-profit corporation created by the Sarbanes-Oxley Act, a 2002 United States federal law, to oversee the auditors of public companies. Its stated purpose is to 'protect the interests of investors and further the public interest in the preparation of informative, fair, and independent audit reports'. Although a private entity, the _____ has many government-like regulatory functions, making it in some ways similar to the private Self Regulatory Organizations (SROs) that regulate stock markets and other aspects of the financial markets in the United States.

a. 3M Company
b. Public Company Accounting Oversight Board
c. Pension Benefit Guaranty Corporation
d. Financial Crimes Enforcement Network

Chapter 2. Professional Standards

7. The _____ of 2002 (Pub.L. 107-204, 116 Stat. 745, enacted July 30, 2002), also known as the Public Company Accounting Reform and Investor Protection Act of 2002, is a United States federal law enacted on July 30, 2002 in response to a number of major corporate and accounting scandals including those affecting Enron, Tyco International, Adelphia, Peregrine Systems and WorldCom. The legislation establishes new or enhanced standards for all U.S. public company boards, management, and public accounting firms. It does not apply to privately held companies.
   a. Sarbanes-Oxley Act
   b. Lease
   c. Fair Labor Standards Act
   d. FCPA

8. The general definition of an _____ is an evaluation of a person, organization, system, process, project or product. _____s are performed to ascertain the validity and reliability of information; also to provide an assessment of a system's internal control. The goal of an _____ is to express an opinion on the person/organization/system (etc) in question, under evaluation based on work done on a test basis.
   a. Institute of Chartered Accountants of India
   b. Audit
   c. Assurance service
   d. Audit regime

9. An _____ is a term used in behavioral economics to describe those types of behaviors that impose costs on a person in the long-run that are not taken into account when making decisions in the present. Classical Economics discourages government from creating legislation that targets internalities, because it is assumed that the consumer takes these personal costs into account when paying for the good that causes the _____. For example, cigarettes should be taxed because of the negative consumption externalities that they impose, such as second-hand smoke, not because the smoker harms him or herself by smoking.
   a. Inventory turnover ratio
   b. Internality
   c. Authorised capital
   d. Operating budget

10. In accounting and organizational theory, _____ is defined as a process effected by an organization's structure, work and authority flows, people and management information systems, designed to help the organization accomplish specific goals or objectives. It is a means by which an organization's resources are directed, monitored, and measured. It plays an important role in preventing and detecting fraud and protecting the organization's resources, both physical (e.g., machinery and property) and intangible (e.g., reputation or intellectual property such as trademarks.)
    a. Audit committee
    b. Internal control
    c. Auditor independence
    d. Audit risk

11. _____ are formal records of a business' financial activities.

In British English, including United Kingdom company law, _____ are often referred to as accounts, although the term _____ is also used, particularly by accountants.

_____ provide an overview of a business' financial condition in both short and long term.

   a. Notes to the financial statements
   b. 3M Company
   c. Financial statements
   d. Statement of retained earnings

12. _____ is evidence obtained during a financial audit and recorded in the audit working papers.

- In the audit engagement acceptance or reappointment stage, _____ is the information that the auditor is to consider for the appointment. For examples, change in the entity control environment, inherent risk and nature of the entity business, and scope of audit work.

- In the audit planning stage, _____ is the information that the auditor is to consider for the most effective and efficient audit approach. For examples, reliability of internal control procedures, and analytical review systems.

- In the control testing stage, _____ is the information that the auditor is to consider for the mix of audit test of control and audit substantive tests.

- In the substantive testing stage, _____ is the information that the auditor is to make sure the appropriation of financial statement assertions. For examples, existence, rights and obligations, occurrence, completeness, valuation, measurement, presentation and disclosure of a particular transaction or account balance.

a. Audit evidence
b. Institute of Chartered Accountants of India
c. ITGCs
d. Audit

13. A _____ proof is a mathematical proof that a particular theory is consistent. The early development of mathematical proof theory was driven by the desire to provide finitary _____ proofs for all of mathematics as part of Hilbert's program. Hilbert's program was strongly impacted by incompleteness theorems, which showed that sufficiently strong proof theories cannot prove their own _____

a. Consistency
b. Monte Carlo methods
c. Daybook
d. Consumption

14. The _____ of 1977 (15 U.S.C. §§ 78dd-1, et seq.) is a United States federal law known primarily for two of its main provisions, one that addresses accounting transparency requirements under the Securities Exchange Act of 1934 and another concerning bribery of foreign officials.

a. Pre-emption right
b. Lease
c. Competition law
d. Foreign Corrupt Practices Act

15. _____, commonly abbreviated as SAS, provide guidance to external auditors on generally accepted auditing standards in regards to auditing an entity and issuing a report. They are usually issued by the certified public accountant authoritative body in the region where the standards apply, such as the American Institute of Certified Public Accountants in the United States.

- _____
- _____ (Taiwan)

a. RSM International
b. GASB 45
c. Statements on Auditing Standards
d. Financial Instruments and Exchange Law

Chapter 2. Professional Standards 17

16. A _____ has several related meanings:

- a daily record of events or business; a private _____ is usually referred to as a diary.
- a newspaper or other periodical, in the literal sense of one published each day;
- many publications issued at stated intervals, such as magazines, or scholarly academic _____s, or the record of the transactions of a society, are often called _____s. Although _____ is sometimes used, erroneously, as a synonym for 'magazine,' in academic use, a _____ refers to a serious, scholarly publication, most often peer-reviewed. A non-scholarly magazine written for an educated audience about an industry or an area of professional activity is usually called a professional magazine.

The word 'journalist' for one whose business is writing for the public press has been in use since the end of the 17th century.

Open access _____s are scholarly _____s that are available to the reader without financial or other barrier other than access to the internet itself. Some are subsidized, and some require payment on behalf of the author. Subsidized _____s are financed by an academic institution or a government information center.

a. Journal
b. BMC Software, Inc.
c. BNSF Railway
d. 3M Company

17. _____ is that part of statistical practice concerned with the selection of individual observations intended to yield some knowledge about a population of concern, especially for the purposes of statistical inference. Each observation measures one or more properties (weight, location, etc.) of an observable entity enumerated to distinguish objects or individuals.
a. Abby Joseph Cohen
b. Sampling
c. Alan Greenspan
d. Arthur Betz Laffer

18. _____ is a term that is commonly used in relation to the audit of the financial statements of an entity. (.
a. Auditor independence
b. Audit Risk
c. Audit working paper
d. Engagement Letter

19. _____ is a concept that denotes the precise probability of specific eventualities. Technically, the notion of _____ is independent from the notion of value and, as such, eventualities may have both beneficial and adverse consequences. However, in general usage the convention is to focus only on potential negative impact to some characteristic of value that may arise from a future event.
a. Discounting
b. Discount factor
c. Risk adjusted return on capital
d. Risk

20. In accounting/accountancy, _____ are journal entries usually made at the end of an accounting period to allocate income and expenditure to the period in which they actually occurred. The revenue recognition principle is the basis of making _____ that pertain to unearned and accrued revenues under accrual-basis accounting. They are sometimes called Balance Day adjustments because they are made on balance day.
a. Accrual
b. Accrued expense
c. Earnings before interest, taxes, depreciation and amortization
d. Adjusting entries

Chapter 2. Professional Standards

21. A _____ is a type of debt Like all debt instruments, a _____ entails the redistribution of financial assets over time, between the lender and the borrower.
   a. Lender
   b. Debenture
   c. Loan to value
   d. Loan

22. _____ is the term used to refer to the standard framework of guidelines for financial accounting used in any given jurisdiction. _____ includes the standards, conventions, and rules accountants follow in recording and summarizing transactions, and in the preparation of financial statements.

   Financial accounting information must be assembled and reported objectively.

   a. Long-term liabilities
   b. General ledger
   c. Current asset
   d. Generally accepted accounting principles

23. _____ means the giving out of information, either voluntarily or to be in compliance with legal regulations or workplace rules.

   - In Computer security, full _____ means disclosing full information about vulnerabilities.
   - In computing, _____ widget
   - Journalism, full _____ refers to disclosing the interests of the writer which may bear on the subject being written about, for example, if the writer has worked with an interview subject in the past.

   - In law:
     - The law of England and Wales, _____ refers to a process that may form part of legal proceedings, whereby parties inform to other parties the existence of any relevant documents that are, or have been, in their control. This compares with the process known as discovery in the course of legal proceedings in the United States.
     - In U.S. civil procedure (litigation rules for civil cases), _____ is a stage prior to trial. In civil cases, each party must disclose to the opposing party the following: names of witnesses which it may use to support its side, copies of documents (or mere description of these documents) in its control which it may use to support its side, computation of damages claimed, and certain insurance information. _____ is related to, but technically prior to, the discovery stage.
     - In Company law (known as 'corporate law' in the United States), _____ refers to giving out information about public or limited companies or their officers, which might be kept secret if the company was a private company or a partnership.

   - In real property transactions, _____ refers to providing to a buyer information known to the seller or broker/agent concerning the condition or other aspects of real property that would affect the property's value or desirability. These rules regarding what information must be disclosed, and whether the information must be disclosed even if a buyer does not ask, vary from one jurisdiction to the next.

   a. Tax harmonisation
   b. Controlled Foreign Corporations
   c. Trailing
   d. Disclosure

Chapter 2. Professional Standards

24. The _____ is the former authoritative body of the American Institute of Certified Public Accountants (AICPA.) It was created by the American Institute of Certified Public Accountants in 1959 and issued pronouncements on accounting principles until 1973, when it was replaced by the Financial Accounting Standards Board (FASB.)

The _____ was disbanded in the hopes that the smaller, fully-independent FASB could more effectively create accounting standards.

   a. International Federation of Accountants
   b. American Payroll Association
   c. Accounting Principles Board
   d. Institute of Management Accountants

25. _____ were documents issued by the Committee on Accounting Procedure between 1938 and 1959 on various accounting problems. They were discontinued with the dissolution of the Committee in 1959 under a recommendation from the Special Committee on Research Program. In all, 51 bulletins were issued, however, the lack of binding authority over AICPA's membership reduced the influence of, and compliance with the content of the bulletins.

   a. Other postemployment benefits
   b. AIG
   c. ABC Television Network
   d. Accounting Research Bulletins

26. The _____ is a private, not-for-profit organization whose primary purpose is to develop generally accepted accounting principles (GAAP) within the United States in the public's interest. The Securities and Exchange Commission (SEC) designated the _____ as the organization responsible for setting accounting standards for public companies in the U.S. It was created in 1973, replacing the Accounting Principles Board and the Committee on Accounting Procedure of the American Institute of Certified Public Accountants. The _____'s mission is 'to establish and improve standards of financial accounting and reporting for the guidance and education of the public, including issuers, auditors, and users of financial information.'

The _____ is not a governmental body.

   a. Public company
   b. Governmental Accounting Standards Board
   c. Fannie Mae
   d. Financial Accounting Standards Board

27. The _____ is currently the source of generally accepted accounting principles (GAAP) used by State and Local governments in the [[United States of America]]. As with most of the entities involved in creating GAAP in the United States, it is a private, non-governmental organization.

The _____ is subject to oversight by the Financial Accounting Foundation (FAF), which selects the members of the _____ and the Financial Accounting Standards Board, and funds both organizations.

   a. Governmental Accounting Standards Board
   b. Multinational corporation
   c. Fannie Mae
   d. National Conference of Commissioners on Uniform State Laws

28. _____ is an umbrella term which refers to the various accounting systems used by various public sector entities. In the United States, for instance, there are two levels of government which follow different accounting standards set forth by independent, private sector boards. At the federal level, the Federal Accounting Standards Advisory Board (FASAB) sets forth the accounting standards to follow.

a. Management accounting
b. Nonassurance services
c. Governmental Accounting
d. Product control

29. _____ is the realization of an application idea, model, design, specification, standard, algorithm an _____ is a realization of a technical specification or algorithm as a program, software component, or other computer system. Many _____s may exist for a given specification or standard.

a. AIG
b. AMEX
c. ABC Television Network
d. Implementation

30. _____ was founded in June 1973 in London and replaced by the International Accounting Standards Board on April 1, 2001. It was responsible for developing the International Accounting Standards and promoting the use and application of these standards.

The _____ was founded as a result of an agreement between accountancy bodies in the following countries:

- Australia (Institute of Chartered Accountants in Australia (ICAA) and the CPA Australia (formerly known as Australian Society of Certified Practising Accountants (ASCPA))

- Canada (Canadian Institute of Chartered Accountants (CICA))

- France (Ordre des Experts Comptable et des Comptables Agrees (Order of Accounting Experts and Qualified Accountants))

- Germany and the Wirtschaftsprüferkammer (WPK) (Chamber of Auditors))

- Japan Nihon Kouninkaikeishi Kyoukai)

- Mexico (Instituto Mexicano de Contadores Publicos (IMCP) (Mexican Institute of Public Accountants)) (removed from the board in 1987 due to non-payment of dues; resumed in 1995.)

- the Netherlands (Nederlands Instituut van Registeraccountants (NIVRA)

(Netherlands Institute of Registered Auditors))

- the United Kingdom and Ireland (counted as one) (Institute of Chartered Accountants in England and Wales (ICAEW), Institute of Chartered Accountants of Scotland (ICAS), Institute of Chartered Accountants in Ireland (ICAI), Association of Certified Accountants, Institute of Cost and Management Accountants, and the Institute of Municipal Treasurers and Accountants)

- the United States of America (American Institute of Certified Public Accountants (AICPA))

The Institute of Chartered Accountants of Nigeria became an associate member in 1976 and a member of the board from 1978 to 1987.

Chapter 2. Professional Standards 21

The National Council of Chartered Accountants (South Africa) became an associate member in 1974 and joined the board in 1978.

a. American Payroll Association
c. American Accounting Association
b. International Accounting Standards Board
d. International Accounting Standards Committee

31. In engineering and manufacturing, _____ and quality engineering are used in developing systems to ensure products or services are designed and produced to meet or exceed customer requirements. Refer to the definition by Merriam-Webster for further information . These systems are often developed in conjunction with other business and engineering disciplines using a cross-functional approach.
a. BMC Software, Inc.
c. 3M Company
b. BNSF Railway
d. Quality Control

32. Accounting _____ define the basic standards for representing attestation engagements. Attestation is defined as an engagement in which a practitioner is hired to issue written communication that expresses a conclusion about the reliability of written assertions prepared by a separate party. The American Institute of Certified Public Accountants identified a number of different engagements that fall under the scope of _____, including: examining financial forecasts and projections, examining pro forma financial statements, evaluating internal control, assessing compliance with rules, regulations, and contractual obligations, as well as evaluating management discussions and analysis of financial results.
a. Attestation standards
c. Institute of Chartered Accountants of India
b. Audit management
d. Audit working paper

33. The _____ is the global organization for the accountancy profession. IFAC has 157 member bodies and associates in 123 countries and jurisdictions, representing more than 2.5 million accountants employed in public practice, industry and commerce, government, and academe. The organization, through its independent standard-setting boards, establishes international standards on ethics,auditing and assurance, education, and public sector accounting.
a. Emerging technologies
c. International Federation of Accountants
b. International Accounting Standards Committee
d. American Payroll Association

34. _____ are professional standards for the performance of financial audit of financial information. These standards are issued by International Federation of Accountants through the International Auditing and Assurance Standards Board.

- ISA 200 Objective and General Principles Governing an Audit of Financial Statements
- ISA 210 Terms of Audit Engagements
- ISA 220 Quality Control for Audits of Historical Financial Information
- ISA 230 Documentation
- ISA 240 The Auditor's Responsibility to Consider Fraud in an Audit of Financial Statements
- ISA 250 Consideration of Laws and Regulations in an Audit of Financial Statements
- ISA 260 Communications of Audit Matters with Those Charged with Governance

- ISA 300 Planning and Audit of Financial Statements
- ISA 310 Knowledge of the Business
- ISA 315 Understanding the Entity and its Environment and Assessing the Risks of Material Misstatement
- ISA 320 Audit Materiality
- ISA 330 The Auditor's Procedures in Response to Assessed Risks

- ISA 400 Risk Assessments and Internal Control
- ISA 401 Auditing in a Computer Information Systems Environment
- ISA 402 Audit Considerations Relating to Entities Using Service Organisations

- ISA 500 Audit Evidence
- ISA 501 Audit Evidence - Additional Considerations for Specific Items
- ISA 505 External Confirmations
- ISA 510 Initial Engagements - Opening Balances
- ISA 520 Analytical Procedures
- ISA 530 Audit Sampling and Other Means of Testing
- ISA 540 Audit of Accounting Estimates
- ISA 545 Auditing Fair Value Measurements and Disclosures
- ISA 550 Related Parties
- ISA 560 Subsequent Events
- ISA 570 Going Concern
- ISA 580 Management Representations

- ISA 600 Using the Work of Another Auditor
- ISA 610 Considering the Work of Internal Auditing
- ISA 620 Using the Work of an Expert

- ISA 700 The Auditor's Report on Financial Statements
- ISA 710 Comparatives
- ISA 720 Other Information in Documents Containing Audited Financial Statements

- ISA 800 The Auditor's Report on Special Purpose Audit Engagements
- ISA 810 The Examination of Prospective Financial Information

a. Event data
b. Auditor independence
c. Attestation Standards
d. International Standards on Auditing

Chapter 3. Professional Ethics

1. _____ can be regarded as an outcome of mental processes (cognitive process) leading to the selection of a course of action among several alternatives. Every _____ process produces a final choice. The output can be an action or an opinion of choice.
   a. Decision making
   b. BNSF Railway
   c. BMC Software, Inc.
   d. 3M Company

2. A _____ is a financial expert especially trained in tax law. Some countries require _____s to verify the balance sheets of companies above a certain size. Individuals usually require _____s to minimize taxation, to avoid learning the details of tax law in complicated financial situations themselves or to learn the details of tax law from a professional advisor.
   a. BMC Software, Inc.
   b. Tax advisor
   c. 3M Company
   d. BNSF Railway

3. Book Value = Original Cost - _____

   Book value at the end of year becomes book value at the beginning of next year. The asset is depreciated until the book value equals scrap value.

   If the vehicle were to be sold and the sales price exceeded the depreciated value (net book value) then the excess would be considered a gain and subject to depreciation recapture.

   a. AIG
   b. ABC Television Network
   c. AMEX
   d. Accumulated depreciation

4. _____ is a term used in accounting, economics and finance to spread the cost of an asset over the span of several years.

   In simple words we can say that _____ is the reduction in the value of an asset due to usage, passage of time, wear and tear, technological outdating or obsolescence, depletion, inadequacy, rot, rust, decay or other such factors.

   In accounting, _____ is a term used to describe any method of attributing the historical or purchase cost of an asset across its useful life, roughly corresponding to normal wear and tear.

   a. Net profit
   b. Current asset
   c. General ledger
   d. Depreciation

5. The general definition of an _____ is an evaluation of a person, organization, system, process, project or product. _____s are performed to ascertain the validity and reliability of information; also to provide an assessment of a system's internal control. The goal of an _____ is to express an opinion on the person/organization/system (etc) in question, under evaluation based on work done on a test basis.
   a. Audit regime
   b. Institute of Chartered Accountants of India
   c. Assurance service
   d. Audit

6. _____ are formal records of a business' financial activities.

   In British English, including United Kingdom company law, _____ are often referred to as accounts, although the term _____ is also used, particularly by accountants.

_____ provide an overview of a business' financial condition in both short and long term.

   a. Statement of retained earnings
   b. Financial Statements
   c. 3M Company
   d. Notes to the financial statements

7. An _____ is a term used in behavioral economics to describe those types of behaviors that impose costs on a person in the long-run that are not taken into account when making decisions in the present. Classical Economics discourages government from creating legislation that targets internalities, because it is assumed that the consumer takes these personal costs into account when paying for the good that causes the _____. For example, cigarettes should be taxed because of the negative consumption externalities that they impose, such as second-hand smoke, not because the smoker harms him or herself by smoking.

   a. Internality
   b. Operating budget
   c. Authorised capital
   d. Inventory turnover ratio

8. In accounting and organizational theory, _____ is defined as a process effected by an organization's structure, work and authority flows, people and management information systems, designed to help the organization accomplish specific goals or objectives. It is a means by which an organization's resources are directed, monitored, and measured. It plays an important role in preventing and detecting fraud and protecting the organization's resources, both physical (e.g., machinery and property) and intangible (e.g., reputation or intellectual property such as trademarks.)

   a. Auditor independence
   b. Audit committee
   c. Audit risk
   d. Internal Control

9. The _____ (sometimes called 'Peekaboo') is a private-sector, non-profit corporation created by the Sarbanes-Oxley Act, a 2002 United States federal law, to oversee the auditors of public companies. Its stated purpose is to 'protect the interests of investors and further the public interest in the preparation of informative, fair, and independent audit reports'. Although a private entity, the _____ has many government-like regulatory functions, making it in some ways similar to the private Self Regulatory Organizations (SROs) that regulate stock markets and other aspects of the financial markets in the United States.

   a. 3M Company
   b. Public Company Accounting Oversight Board
   c. Pension Benefit Guaranty Corporation
   d. Financial Crimes Enforcement Network

10. The term _____ usually refers to a company that is permitted to offer its registered securities (stock, bonds, etc.) for sale to the general public, typically through a stock exchange, or occasionally a company whose stock is traded over the counter (OTC) via market makers who use non-exchange quotation services.

The term '_____' may also refer to a company owned by the government.

   a. Professional association
   b. Governmental Accounting Standards Board
   c. MicroStrategy
   d. Public Company

11. _____ is a fee paid on borrowed assets. It is the price paid for the use of borrowed money , or, money earned by deposited funds .Assets that are sometimes lent with _____ include money, shares, consumer goods through hire purchase, major assets such as aircraft, and even entire factories in finance lease arrangements. The _____ is calculated upon the value of the assets in the same manner as upon money.

a. Interest
b. ABC Television Network
c. AIG
d. Insolvency

12. Employment is a contract between two parties, one being the employer and the other being the _____. An _____ may be defined as: 'A person in the service of another under any contract of hire, express or implied, oral or written, where the employer has the power or right to control and direct the _____ in the material details of how the work is to be performed.' Black's Law Dictionary page 471 (5th ed. 1979.)
   a. Employee
   b. ABC Television Network
   c. AMEX
   d. AIG

13. A _____ is a type of debt Like all debt instruments, a _____ entails the redistribution of financial assets over time, between the lender and the borrower.
   a. Lender
   b. Loan to value
   c. Loan
   d. Debenture

14. _____ LLP, based in Chicago, was once one of the 'Big Five' accounting firms among PricewaterhouseCoopers, Deloitte Touche Tohmatsu, Ernst ' Young and KPMG, providing auditing, tax, and consulting services to large corporations. In 2002, the firm voluntarily surrendered its licenses to practice as Certified Public Accountants in the United States after being found guilty of criminal charges relating to the firm's handling of the auditing of Enron, the energy corporation, resulting in the loss of 85,000 jobs. Although the verdict was subsequently overturned by the Supreme Court of the United States, it has not returned as a viable business.
   a. AMEX
   b. ABC Television Network
   c. Arthur Andersen
   d. AIG

15. A _____ has several related meanings:

   - a daily record of events or business; a private _____ is usually referred to as a diary.
   - a newspaper or other periodical, in the literal sense of one published each day;
   - many publications issued at stated intervals, such as magazines, or scholarly academic _____s, or the record of the transactions of a society, are often called _____s. Although _____ is sometimes used, erroneously, as a synonym for 'magazine,' in academic use, a _____ refers to a serious, scholarly publication, most often peer-reviewed. A non-scholarly magazine written for an educated audience about an industry or an area of professional activity is usually called a professional magazine.

The word 'journalist' for one whose business is writing for the public press has been in use since the end of the 17th century.

Open access _____s are scholarly _____s that are available to the reader without financial or other barrier other than access to the internet itself. Some are subsidized, and some require payment on behalf of the author. Subsidized _____s are financed by an academic institution or a government information center.

a. BNSF Railway
b. 3M Company
c. BMC Software, Inc.
d. Journal

Chapter 3. Professional Ethics

16. _____, Quarterly Report Pursuant to Section 13 or 15(d) of the Securities Exchange Act of 1934, is an SEC filing that must be filed quarterly with the US Securities and Exchange Commission. It contains similar information to the annual form 10-K, however the information is generally less detailed, and the financial statements are generally unaudited. Information for the final quarter of a firm's fiscal year is included in the 10-K, so only three 10-Q filings are made each year.
   a. Form 10-Q
   b. Form 20-F
   c. 3M Company
   d. Form 8-K

17. _____ is the recording of the value of assets, liabilities, income, and expenses in the daybooks, journals, and ledgers, in which debit and credit entries are chronologically posted to record changes in value. _____ is often mistaken for accounting, which is the system of recording, verifying, and reporting such information. Practitioners of accounting are called accountants.
   a. Double-entry bookkeeping
   b. Controlling account
   c. Debit and credit
   d. Bookkeeping

18. The _____ of 2002 (Pub.L. 107-204, 116 Stat. 745, enacted July 30, 2002), also known as the Public Company Accounting Reform and Investor Protection Act of 2002, is a United States federal law enacted on July 30, 2002 in response to a number of major corporate and accounting scandals including those affecting Enron, Tyco International, Adelphia, Peregrine Systems and WorldCom. The legislation establishes new or enhanced standards for all U.S. public company boards, management, and public accounting firms. It does not apply to privately held companies.
   a. Fair Labor Standards Act
   b. Lease
   c. Sarbanes-Oxley Act
   d. FCPA

19. In finance, _____ is the process of estimating the potential market value of a financial asset or liability. They can be done on assets (for example, investments in marketable securities such as stocks, options, business enterprises, or intangible assets such as patents and trademarks) or on liabilities (e.g., Bonds issued by a company.) A _____ is required in many contexts including investment analysis, capital budgeting, merger and acquisition transactions, financial reporting, taxable events to determine the proper tax liability, and in litigation.
   a. Vyborg Appeal
   b. Disclosure
   c. Daybook
   d. Valuation

20. _____ is subcontracting a process, such as product design or manufacturing, to a third-party company. The decision to outsource is often made in the interest of lowering cost or making better use of time and energy costs, redirecting or conserving energy directed at the competencies of a particular business, or to make more efficient use of land, labor, capital, (information) technology and resources. _____ became part of the business lexicon during the 1980s.
   a. Economic Growth and Tax Relief Reconciliation Act of 2001
   b. US Airways, Inc.
   c. USA Today
   d. Outsourcing

21. NYSE Amex Equities, formerly known as the _____ is an _____ situated in New York. AMEX was a mutual organization, owned by its members. Until 1953 it was known as the New York Curb Exchange.
   a. AIG
   b. AMEX
   c. ABC Television Network
   d. American Stock Exchange

22. In a publicly-held company, an _____ is an operating committee of the Board of Directors, typically charged with oversight of financial reporting and disclosure. Committee members are drawn from members of the Company's board of directors, with a Chairperson selected from among the members. An _____ of a publicly-traded company in the United States is composed of independent and outside directors referred to as non-executive directors, at least one of which is typically a financial expert.
   a. Audit working paper
   b. Audit committee
   c. External auditor
   d. Event data

23. The _____ (GAO) is the audit, evaluation, and investigative arm of the United States Congress. It is located in the Legislative branch of the United States government.

The _____ was established as the _____ by the Budget and Accounting Act of 1921 (Pub.L.

   a. BMC Software, Inc.
   b. General Accounting Office
   c. 3M Company
   d. GAO

24. The _____ (acronym of National Association of Securities Dealers Automated Quotations) is an American stock exchange. It is the largest electronic screen-based equity securities trading market in the United States. With approximately 3,800 companies, it has more trading volume per hour than any other stock exchange in the world.
   a. Variance
   b. Sale of goods
   c. Sustainability measurement
   d. NASDAQ

25. _____ is an equity (stock) exchange located at 11 Wall Street in lower Manhattan, New York, USA.) It is the largest stock exchange in the world by dollar value of its listed companies' securities. As of October 2008, the combined capitalization of all domestic _____ listed companies was US$10.1 trillion.
   a. BNSF Railway
   b. BMC Software, Inc.
   c. 3M Company
   d. New York Stock Exchange

26. A _____, (formerly a securities exchange) is a corporation or mutual organization which provides 'trading' facilities for stock brokers and traders, to trade stocks and other securities. _____s also provide facilities for the issue and redemption of securities as well as other financial instruments and capital events including the payment of income and dividends. The securities traded on a _____ include: shares issued by companies, unit trusts, derivatives, pooled investment products and bonds.
   a. BMC Software, Inc.
   b. BNSF Railway
   c. 3M Company
   d. Stock Exchange

27. The _____ is the national, professional association of CPAs in the United States, with more than 330,000 members, including CPAs in business and industry, public practice, government, and education; student affiliates; and international associates. It sets ethical standards for the profession and U.S. auditing standards for audits of private companies; federal, state and local governments; and non-profit organizations.

Approximately 40% of its members are engaged in the practice of public accounting, in areas such as auditing, accounting, taxation, general business consulting, business valuation, personal financial planning and business technology.

Chapter 3. Professional Ethics

a. AIG
b. ABC Television Network
c. Other postemployment benefits
d. American Institute of Certified Public Accountants

28. The _____ is currently the source of generally accepted accounting principles (GAAP) used by State and Local governments in the [[United States of America]]. As with most of the entities involved in creating GAAP in the United States, it is a private, non-governmental organization.

The _____ is subject to oversight by the Financial Accounting Foundation (FAF), which selects the members of the _____ and the Financial Accounting Standards Board, and funds both organizations.

a. Fannie Mae
b. Governmental Accounting Standards Board
c. National Conference of Commissioners on Uniform State Laws
d. Multinational corporation

29. _____ is the term used to refer to the standard framework of guidelines for financial accounting used in any given jurisdiction. _____ includes the standards, conventions, and rules accountants follow in recording and summarizing transactions, and in the preparation of financial statements.

Financial accounting information must be assembled and reported objectively.

a. Generally accepted accounting principles
b. Current asset
c. General ledger
d. Long-term liabilities

30. _____ is an umbrella term which refers to the various accounting systems used by various public sector entities. In the United States, for instance, there are two levels of government which follow different accounting standards set forth by independent, private sector boards. At the federal level, the Federal Accounting Standards Advisory Board (FASAB) sets forth the accounting standards to follow.

a. Management accounting
b. Product control
c. Nonassurance services
d. Governmental Accounting

31. _____, commonly abbreviated as SAS, provide guidance to external auditors on generally accepted auditing standards in regards to auditing an entity and issuing a report. They are usually issued by the certified public accountant authoritative body in the region where the standards apply, such as the American Institute of Certified Public Accountants in the United States.

- _____
- _____ (Taiwan)

a. Statements on Auditing Standards
b. Financial Instruments and Exchange Law
c. GASB 45
d. RSM International

32. In financial accounting, a _____ is defined as an obligation of an entity arising from past transactions or events, the settlement of which may result in the transfer or use of assets, provision of services or other yielding of economic benefits in the future.

a. Liability
b. Corporate governance
c. Vested
d. False Claims Act

33. _____ is a report required to be filed by public companies with the United States Securities and Exchange Commission pursuant to the Securities Exchange Act of 1934, as amended. After a significant event like bankruptcy or departure of a CEO, a public company generally must file a Current Report on _____ within four business days to provide an update to previously filed quartely reports on Form 10-Q and/or Annual Reports on Form 10-K. _____ is a very broad form used to notify investors of any unscheduled material event that is important to shareholders or the SEC.
   a. Form 10-Q
   b. 3M Company
   c. Form 20-F
   d. Form 8-K

34. The U.S. _____ is an independent agency of the United States government which holds primary responsibility for enforcing the federal securities laws and regulating the securities industry, the nation's stock and options exchanges, and other electronic securities markets. The SEC was created by section 4 of the Securities Exchange Act of 1934 (now codified as 15 U.S.C. ÂÂ§ 78d and commonly referred to as the 1934 Act.)
   a. 3M Company
   b. BMC Software, Inc.
   c. Securities and Exchange Commission
   d. BNSF Railway

35. A _____ is a fungible, negotiable instrument representing financial value. they are broadly categorized into debt securities (such as banknotes, bonds and debentures), and equity securities; e.g., common stocks. The company or other entity issuing the _____ is called the issuer.
   a. BMC Software, Inc.
   b. Tracking stock
   c. Security
   d. 3M Company

36. The _____ of 1934 is a law governing the secondary trading of securities (stocks, bonds, and debentures) in the United States of America. The Act, 48 Stat. 881 (enacted June 6, 1934), codified at 15 U.S.C.
   a. BMC Software, Inc.
   b. BNSF Railway
   c. 3M Company
   d. Securities Exchange Act

37. The _____ is a law governing the secondary trading of securities (stocks, bonds, and debentures) in the United States of America. The Act, 48 Stat. 881 (enacted June 6, 1934), codified at 15 U.S.C.
   a. Securities Exchange Act of 1934
   b. BNSF Railway
   c. BMC Software, Inc.
   d. 3M Company

38. Literally, _____ means: 'urgently asking'. It is the action or instance of soliciting; petition; proposal.

In England and Wales, the term soliciting refers to: 'for a common prostitute to loiter or solicit in a street or public place for the purpose of prostitution', under the Street Offences Act 1959.

   a. BNSF Railway
   b. 3M Company
   c. BMC Software, Inc.
   d. Solicitation

39. The _____ is a 'voluntary organization of persons interested in accounting education and research'. It was formed in 1916. Its main publication, the The Accounting Review, was first published in 1926.

Chapter 3. Professional Ethics 31

a. Institute of Management Accountants
c. Australian Accounting Standards Board
b. International Accounting Standards Board
d. American Accounting Association

40. The _____ is an independent agency of the United States government, established in 1914 by the _____ Act. Its principal mission is the promotion of 'consumer protection' and the elimination and prevention of what regulators perceive to be harmfully 'anti-competitive' business practices, such as coercive monopoly.

The _____ Act was one of President Wilson's major acts against trusts.

a. 3M Company
c. BNSF Railway
b. Federal Trade Commission
d. BMC Software, Inc.

41. _____ is a concept whereby a person's financial liability is limited to a fixed sum, most commonly the value of a person's investment in a company or partnership with _____. A shareholder in a limited company is not personally liable for any of the debts of the company, other than for the value of his investment in that company. The same is true for the members of a _____ partnership and the limited partners in a limited partnership.
a. Joint venture
c. Due diligence
b. Burden of proof
d. Limited liability

42. A _____ in the law of the vast majority of United States jurisdictions is a legal form of business company that provides limited liability to its owners. Often incorrectly called a 'limited liability corporation' (instead of company), it is a hybrid business entity having certain characteristics of both a corporation and a partnership. The primary characteristic an _____ shares with a corporation is limited liability, and the primary characteristic it shares with a partnership is the availability of pass-through income taxation.
a. Data protection
c. Bond market
b. Consumer protection laws
d. Limited liability company

43. A _____ is a partnership in which some or all partners (depending on the jurisdiction) have limited liability. It therefore exhibits elements of partnerships and corporations. In an _____ one partner is not responsible or liable for another partner's misconduct or negligence.
a. Limited liability partnership
c. Financial Accounting Standards Board
b. Dow Jones ' Company
d. Privately held

44. A _____ is a type of business entity in which partners (owners) share with each other the profits or losses of the business undertaking in which all have invested. _____s are often favored over corporations for taxation purposes, as the _____ structure does not generally incur a tax on profits before it is distributed to the partners (i.e. there is no dividend tax levied.) However, depending on the _____ structure and the jurisdiction in which it operates, owners of a _____ may be exposed to greater personal liability than they would as shareholders of a corporation.
a. Corporate governance
c. Partnership
b. National Information Infrastructure Protection Act
d. Resource Conservation and Recovery Act

45. The _____ is the United States federal government agency that collects taxes and enforces the internal revenue laws. It is an agency within the U.S. Dept of the treasury responsible for interpretation and application of Federal tax law. The official U.S. Treasury regulations provide (in part):

The _____ is a bureau of the Department of the Treasury under the immediate direction of the Commissioner of Internal Revenue.

a. Use tax
b. Internal Revenue Service
c. Indirect tax
d. Income tax

46. Internal auditing is a profession and activity involved in helping organisations achieve their stated objectives. It does this by utilizing a systematic methodology for analyzing business processes, procedures and activities with the goal of highlighting organizational problems and recommending solutions. Professionals called _____ are employed by organizations to perform the internal auditing activity.

a. Internal auditors
b. Auditing Standards Board
c. Internal Auditing
d. Auditor independence

47. _____ means the giving out of information, either voluntarily or to be in compliance with legal regulations or workplace rules.

- In Computer security, full _____ means disclosing full information about vulnerabilities.
- In computing, _____ widget
- Journalism, full _____ refers to disclosing the interests of the writer which may bear on the subject being written about, for example, if the writer has worked with an interview subject in the past.

- In law:
  - The law of England and Wales, _____ refers to a process that may form part of legal proceedings, whereby parties inform to other parties the existence of any relevant documents that are, or have been, in their control. This compares with the process known as discovery in the course of legal proceedings in the United States.
  - In U.S. civil procedure (litigation rules for civil cases), _____ is a stage prior to trial. In civil cases, each party must disclose to the opposing party the following: names of witnesses which it may use to support its side, copies of documents (or mere description of these documents) in its control which it may use to support its side, computation of damages claimed, and certain insurance information. _____ is related to, but technically prior to, the discovery stage.
  - In Company law (known as 'corporate law' in the United States), _____ refers to giving out information about public or limited companies or their officers, which might be kept secret if the company was a private company or a partnership.

- In real property transactions, _____ refers to providing to a buyer information known to the seller or broker/agent concerning the condition or other aspects of real property that would affect the property's value or desirability. These rules regarding what information must be disclosed, and whether the information must be disclosed even if a buyer does not ask, vary from one jurisdiction to the next.

a. Trailing
b. Tax harmonisation
c. Disclosure
d. Controlled Foreign Corporations

Chapter 4. Legal Liability of CPAs

1. In financial accounting, a _____ is defined as an obligation of an entity arising from past transactions or events, the settlement of which may result in the transfer or use of assets, provision of services or other yielding of economic benefits in the future.
   a. Corporate governance
   b. Vested
   c. Liability
   d. False Claims Act

2. In accounting/accountancy, _____ are journal entries usually made at the end of an accounting period to allocate income and expenditure to the period in which they actually occurred. The revenue recognition principle is the basis of making _____ that pertain to unearned and accrued revenues under accrual-basis accounting. They are sometimes called Balance Day adjustments because they are made on balance day.
   a. Earnings before interest, taxes, depreciation and amortization
   b. Accrued expense
   c. Accrual
   d. Adjusting entries

3. _____ is a legal concept in the common law legal systems usually used to achieve compensation for injuries (not accidents.) _____ is a type of tort or delict (also known as a civil wrong.)
   a. Robinson-Patman Act
   b. Hospital Survey and Construction Act
   c. Negligence
   d. Letter of credit

4. A _____ is a fungible, negotiable instrument representing financial value. they are broadly categorized into debt securities (such as banknotes, bonds and debentures), and equity securities; e.g., common stocks. The company or other entity issuing the _____ is called the issuer.
   a. Security
   b. Tracking stock
   c. BMC Software, Inc.
   d. 3M Company

5. Congress enacted the _____, in the aftermath of the stock market crash of 1929 and during the ensuing Great Depression.
   a. Sustainability measurement
   b. Bookkeeping
   c. Securities Act of 1933
   d. Monte Carlo methods

6. _____, in law and economics, is a form of risk management primarily used to hedge against the risk of a contingent loss. _____ is defined as the equitable transfer of the risk of a loss, from one entity to another, in exchange for a premium, and can be thought of as a guaranteed small loss to prevent a large, possibly devastating loss. An insurer is a company selling the _____; an insured is the person or entity buying the _____.
   a. AIG
   b. ABC Television Network
   c. AMEX
   d. Insurance

7. The _____ of 1934 is a law governing the secondary trading of securities (stocks, bonds, and debentures) in the United States of America. The Act, 48 Stat. 881 (enacted June 6, 1934), codified at 15 U.S.C.
   a. 3M Company
   b. Securities Exchange Act
   c. BNSF Railway
   d. BMC Software, Inc.

8. The _____ is a law governing the secondary trading of securities (stocks, bonds, and debentures) in the United States of America. The Act, 48 Stat. 881 (enacted June 6, 1934), codified at 15 U.S.C.
   a. 3M Company
   b. BNSF Railway
   c. Securities Exchange Act of 1934
   d. BMC Software, Inc.

34 *Chapter 4. Legal Liability of CPAs*

9. The _____ (sometimes called 'Peekaboo') is a private-sector, non-profit corporation created by the Sarbanes-Oxley Act, a 2002 United States federal law, to oversee the auditors of public companies. Its stated purpose is to 'protect the interests of investors and further the public interest in the preparation of informative, fair, and independent audit reports'. Although a private entity, the _____ has many government-like regulatory functions, making it in some ways similar to the private Self Regulatory Organizations (SROs) that regulate stock markets and other aspects of the financial markets in the United States.

   a. 3M Company
   b. Financial Crimes Enforcement Network
   c. Pension Benefit Guaranty Corporation
   d. Public Company Accounting Oversight Board

10. The U.S. _____ is an independent agency of the United States government which holds primary responsibility for enforcing the federal securities laws and regulating the securities industry, the nation's stock and options exchanges, and other electronic securities markets. The SEC was created by section 4 of the Securities Exchange Act of 1934 (now codified as 15 U.S.C. ÂÂ§ 78d and commonly referred to as the 1934 Act.)

   a. BNSF Railway
   b. 3M Company
   c. BMC Software, Inc.
   d. Securities and Exchange Commission

11. _____ LLP, based in Chicago, was once one of the 'Big Five' accounting firms among PricewaterhouseCoopers, Deloitte Touche Tohmatsu, Ernst ' Young and KPMG, providing auditing, tax, and consulting services to large corporations. In 2002, the firm voluntarily surrendered its licenses to practice as Certified Public Accountants in the United States after being found guilty of criminal charges relating to the firm's handling of the auditing of Enron, the energy corporation, resulting in the loss of 85,000 jobs. Although the verdict was subsequently overturned by the Supreme Court of the United States, it has not returned as a viable business.

   a. ABC Television Network
   b. AMEX
   c. AIG
   d. Arthur Andersen

12. In mathematics _____s are numbers or other things that get multiplied. In particular, see:

   - Factorization, the decomposition of an object into a product of other objects
   - Integer factorization, the process of breaking down a composite number into smaller non-trivial divisors
   - A coefficient
   - A divisor of a particular number, or of an element of a monoid
   - A von Neumann algebra with a trivial center

In statistics

   - _____ analysis is the study of how _____s or certain variables affect variables.

In technology:

   - Human _____s, a profession that focuses on how people interact with products, tools, or procedures
   - 'Functionality, Application domain, Conditions, Technology, Objects and Responsibility;', In object-oriented programming

Chapter 4. Legal Liability of CPAs

In computer science and information technology:

- Authentication _____, a piece of information used to verify a person's identity for security purposes
- _____, a Unix command for numbers factorization
- _____ (programming language), an experimental Forth-like programming language

In television:

- The O'Reilly _____, an American talk show hosted by Bill O'Reilly on Fox News.
- The Krypton _____, a British game show hosted by Gordon Burns, formally on ITV. Also had an American version.

a. Merck ' Co., Inc.
b. Valuation
c. Factor
d. The Goodyear Tire ' Rubber Company

13. The general definition of an _____ is an evaluation of a person, organization, system, process, project or product. _____s are performed to ascertain the validity and reliability of information; also to provide an assessment of a system's internal control. The goal of an _____ is to express an opinion on the person/organization/system (etc) in question, under evaluation based on work done on a test basis.
    a. Audit regime
    b. Assurance service
    c. Audit
    d. Institute of Chartered Accountants of India

14. _____ is a term used for a number of concepts involving either the performance of an investigation of a business or person, or the performance of an act with a certain standard of care. It can be a legal obligation, but the term will more commonly apply to voluntary investigations. A common example of _____ in various industries is the process through which a potential acquirer evaluates a target company or its assets for acquisition.
    a. Burden of proof
    b. Negligence
    c. Tax patent
    d. Due diligence

15. The term _____ usually refers to a company that is permitted to offer its registered securities (stock, bonds, etc.) for sale to the general public, typically through a stock exchange, or occasionally a company whose stock is traded over the counter (OTC) via market makers who use non-exchange quotation services.

The term '_____' may also refer to a company owned by the government.

    a. Professional association
    b. Public Company
    c. MicroStrategy
    d. Governmental Accounting Standards Board

16. _____ are formal records of a business' financial activities.

In British English, including United Kingdom company law, _____ are often referred to as accounts, although the term _____ is also used, particularly by accountants.

_____ provide an overview of a business' financial condition in both short and long term.

a. Notes to the financial statements
b. Statement of retained earnings
c. Financial statements
d. 3M Company

17. An _____ defines the legal relationship (or engagement) between a professional firm (e.g., law, investment banking, consulting, advisory or accountancy firm) and its client(s.) This letter states the terms and conditions of the engagement, principally addressing the scope of the engagement and the terms of compensation for the firm.

Most _____s follow a standard format.

a. Internal control
b. Audit risk
c. Audit evidence
d. Engagement letter

18. _____ are ten auditing standards, developed by the AICPA, consisting of general standards, standards of field work, and standards of reporting, along with interpretations. They were developed by the AICPA in 1947 and have undergone minor changes since then.

The _____ are as follows:

1. The auditor must have adequate technical training and proficiency to perform the audit
2. The auditor must maintain independence in mental attitude in all matters related to the audit.
3. The auditor must use due professional care during the performance of the audit and the preparation of the report.

1. The auditor must adequately plan the work and must properly supervise any assistants.
2. The auditor must obtain a sufficient understanding of the entity and its environment, including its internal control, to assess the risk of material misstatement of the financial statements whether due to error or fraud, and to design the nature, timing, and extent of further audit procedures.
3. The auditor must obtain sufficient appropriate audit evidence by performing audit procedures to afford a reasonable basis for an opinion regarding the financial statements under audit.

Chapter 4. Legal Liability of CPAs

The new standards are in effect for audits of financial statements for periods beginning on or after December 15, 2006.

1. The auditor must state in the auditor's report whether the financial statements are in accordance with generally accepted accounting principles (GAAP.)
2. The auditor must identify in the auditor's report those circumstances in which such principles have not been consistently observed in the current period in relation to the preceding period.
3. When the auditor determines that informative disclosures are not reasonably adequate, the auditor must so state in the auditor's report.
4. The auditor must either express an opinion regarding the financial statements, taken as a whole the auditor should state the reasons therefore in the auditor's report. In all cases where the auditor's name is associated with the financial statements, the auditor should clearly indicate the character of the auditor's work, if any, and the degree of responsibility the auditor is taking, in the auditor's report.

a. Generally accepted auditing standards
b. Joint audit
c. Negative assurance
d. Continuous auditing

19. _____, commonly abbreviated as SAS, provide guidance to external auditors on generally accepted auditing standards in regards to auditing an entity and issuing a report. They are usually issued by the certified public accountant authoritative body in the region where the standards apply, such as the American Institute of Certified Public Accountants in the United States.

- _____
- _____ (Taiwan)

a. Financial Instruments and Exchange Law
b. RSM International
c. GASB 45
d. Statements on Auditing Standards

20. A _____ is a type of debt Like all debt instruments, a _____ entails the redistribution of financial assets over time, between the lender and the borrower.
a. Lender
b. Loan to value
c. Debenture
d. Loan

Chapter 5. Audit Evidence and Documentation

1. The general definition of an _____ is an evaluation of a person, organization, system, process, project or product. _____s are performed to ascertain the validity and reliability of information; also to provide an assessment of a system's internal control. The goal of an _____ is to express an opinion on the person/organization/system (etc) in question, under evaluation based on work done on a test basis.
   a. Assurance service
   b. Audit regime
   c. Institute of Chartered Accountants of India
   d. Audit

2. _____ is evidence obtained during a financial audit and recorded in the audit working papers.

   - In the audit engagement acceptance or reappointment stage, _____ is the information that the auditor is to consider for the appointment. For examples, change in the entity control environment, inherent risk and nature of the entity business, and scope of audit work.

   - In the audit planning stage, _____ is the information that the auditor is to consider for the most effective and efficient audit approach. For examples, reliability of internal control procedures, and analytical review systems.

   - In the control testing stage, _____ is the information that the auditor is to consider for the mix of audit test of control and audit substantive tests.

   - In the substantive testing stage, _____ is the information that the auditor is to make sure the appropriation of financial statement assertions. For examples, existence, rights and obligations, occurrence, completeness, valuation, measurement, presentation and disclosure of a particular transaction or account balance.

   a. ITGCs
   b. Audit
   c. Institute of Chartered Accountants of India
   d. Audit evidence

3. In economics, the _____, (or _____) measures the payments that flow between any individual country and all other countries. It is used to summarize all international economic transactions for that country during a specific time period, usually a year. The _____ is determined by the country's exports and imports of goods, services, and financial capital, as well as financial transfers.
   a. Stock split
   b. Moving average
   c. Yield to maturity
   d. Balance of payments

4. _____ is a term that is commonly used in relation to the audit of the financial statements of an entity. (.
   a. Audit risk
   b. Auditor independence
   c. Engagement Letter
   d. Audit working paper

5. In finance, _____ is the process of estimating the potential market value of a financial asset or liability. They can be done on assets (for example, investments in marketable securities such as stocks, options, business enterprises, or intangible assets such as patents and trademarks) or on liabilities (e.g., Bonds issued by a company.) A _____ is required in many contexts including investment analysis, capital budgeting, merger and acquisition transactions, financial reporting, taxable events to determine the proper tax liability, and in litigation.
   a. Daybook
   b. Vyborg Appeal
   c. Disclosure
   d. Valuation

Chapter 5. Audit Evidence and Documentation

6. _____ means the giving out of information, either voluntarily or to be in compliance with legal regulations or workplace rules.

- In Computer security, full _____ means disclosing full information about vulnerabilities.
- In computing, _____ widget
- Journalism, full _____ refers to disclosing the interests of the writer which may bear on the subject being written about, for example, if the writer has worked with an interview subject in the past.

- In law:
    - The law of England and Wales, _____ refers to a process that may form part of legal proceedings, whereby parties inform to other parties the existence of any relevant documents that are, or have been, in their control. This compares with the process known as discovery in the course of legal proceedings in the United States.
    - In U.S. civil procedure (litigation rules for civil cases), _____ is a stage prior to trial. In civil cases, each party must disclose to the opposing party the following: names of witnesses which it may use to support its side, copies of documents (or mere description of these documents) in its control which it may use to support its side, computation of damages claimed, and certain insurance information. _____ is related to, but technically prior to, the discovery stage.
    - In Company law (known as 'corporate law' in the United States), _____ refers to giving out information about public or limited companies or their officers, which might be kept secret if the company was a private company or a partnership.

- In real property transactions, _____ refers to providing to a buyer information known to the seller or broker/agent concerning the condition or other aspects of real property that would affect the property's value or desirability. These rules regarding what information must be disclosed, and whether the information must be disclosed even if a buyer does not ask, vary from one jurisdiction to the next.

a. Trailing
c. Controlled Foreign Corporations
b. Disclosure
d. Tax harmonisation

7. An _____ is a term used in behavioral economics to describe those types of behaviors that impose costs on a person in the long-run that are not taken into account when making decisions in the present. Classical Economics discourages government from creating legislation that targets internalities, because it is assumed that the consumer takes these personal costs into account when paying for the good that causes the _____. For example, cigarettes should be taxed because of the negative consumption externalities that they impose, such as second-hand smoke, not because the smoker harms him or herself by smoking.

a. Inventory turnover ratio
c. Operating budget
b. Internality
d. Authorised capital

8. In accounting and organizational theory, _____ is defined as a process effected by an organization's structure, work and authority flows, people and management information systems, designed to help the organization accomplish specific goals or objectives. It is a means by which an organization's resources are directed, monitored, and measured. It plays an important role in preventing and detecting fraud and protecting the organization's resources, both physical (e.g., machinery and property) and intangible (e.g., reputation or intellectual property such as trademarks.)

a. Audit risk
b. Audit committee
c. Auditor independence
d. Internal control

9. _____ is a concept that denotes the precise probability of specific eventualities. Technically, the notion of _____ is independent from the notion of value and, as such, eventualities may have both beneficial and adverse consequences. However, in general usage the convention is to focus only on potential negative impact to some characteristic of value that may arise from a future event.
a. Discount factor
b. Risk adjusted return on capital
c. Discounting
d. Risk

10. _____ are professional standards for the performance of financial audit of financial information. These standards are issued by International Federation of Accountants through the International Auditing and Assurance Standards Board.

- ISA 200 Objective and General Principles Governing an Audit of Financial Statements
- ISA 210 Terms of Audit Engagements
- ISA 220 Quality Control for Audits of Historical Financial Information
- ISA 230 Documentation
- ISA 240 The Auditor's Responsibility to Consider Fraud in an Audit of Financial Statements
- ISA 250 Consideration of Laws and Regulations in an Audit of Financial Statements
- ISA 260 Communications of Audit Matters with Those Charged with Governance

- ISA 300 Planning and Audit of Financial Statements
- ISA 310 Knowledge of the Business
- ISA 315 Understanding the Entity and its Environment and Assessing the Risks of Material Misstatement
- ISA 320 Audit Materiality
- ISA 330 The Auditor's Procedures in Response to Assessed Risks

- ISA 400 Risk Assessments and Internal Control
- ISA 401 Auditing in a Computer Information Systems Environment
- ISA 402 Audit Considerations Relating to Entities Using Service Organisations

- ISA 500 Audit Evidence
- ISA 501 Audit Evidence - Additional Considerations for Specific Items
- ISA 505 External Confirmations
- ISA 510 Initial Engagements - Opening Balances
- ISA 520 Analytical Procedures
- ISA 530 Audit Sampling and Other Means of Testing
- ISA 540 Audit of Accounting Estimates
- ISA 545 Auditing Fair Value Measurements and Disclosures
- ISA 550 Related Parties
- ISA 560 Subsequent Events
- ISA 570 Going Concern
- ISA 580 Management Representations

- ISA 600 Using the Work of Another Auditor
- ISA 610 Considering the Work of Internal Auditing
- ISA 620 Using the Work of an Expert

- ISA 700 The Auditor's Report on Financial Statements
- ISA 710 Comparatives
- ISA 720 Other Information in Documents Containing Audited Financial Statements

- ISA 800 The Auditor's Report on Special Purpose Audit Engagements
- ISA 810 The Examination of Prospective Financial Information

a. Event data
b. International Standards on Auditing
c. Attestation Standards
d. Auditor independence

11. _____, in auditing, is the risk that a company's internal controls are insufficient to mitigate or detect errors or fraud.
a. 3M Company
b. BMC Software, Inc.
c. BNSF Railway
d. Control risk

12. _____ is the calculated approximation of a result which is usable even if input data may be incomplete or uncertain.

In statistics, see _____ theory, estimator.

In mathematics, approximation or _____ typically means finding upper or lower bounds of a quantity that cannot readily be computed precisely and is also an educated guess.

a. ABC Television Network
b. AIG
c. AMEX
d. Estimation

13. _____, in auditing, is the risk that the account or section being audited is materially misstated without considering internal controls due to error; _____ does not include an assessment of the risk of material misstatement due to fraud. The assessment of _____ depends on the professional judgement of the auditor, and it is done after assessing the business environment of the entity being audited.

_____ is typically assessed using a scale, with assessments being either low, medium, or high.

a. AMEX
b. AIG
c. ABC Television Network
d. Inherent risk

14. _____, in auditing, is the risk that the auditing procedures used will not find a material misstatement in the financial statements of the company being audited. .
a. BNSF Railway
b. BMC Software, Inc.
c. 3M Company
d. Detection risk

15. An _____ invented by esteemed professor Karen Osterheld is the system of records a business keeps to maintain its accounting system. This includes the purchase, sales, and other financial processes of the business. The purpose of an _____ is to accumulate data and provide decision makers (investors, creditors, and managers) with information to make decision While this was previously a paper-based process, most modern businesses now use accounting software such as UBS, MYOB etc.
a. AMEX
b. AIG
c. Accounting information system
d. ABC Television Network

16. An account statement or a _____ is a summary of all financial transactions occurring over a given period of time on a deposit account, a credit card, or any other type of account offered by a financial institution.

Chapter 5. Audit Evidence and Documentation

_____s are typically printed on one or several pieces of paper and either mailed directly to the account holder's address, or kept at the financial institution's local branch for pick-up. Certain ATMs offer the possibility to print, at any time, a condensed version of a _____.

a. 3M Company
b. BNSF Railway
c. BMC Software, Inc.
d. Bank statement

17. _____ refers to the structured transmission of data between organizations by electronic means. It is used to transfer electronic documents from one computer system to another (ie) from one trading partner to another trading partner. It is more than mere E-mail; for instance, organizations might replace bills of lading and even checks with appropriate _____ messages.

a. AIG
b. ABC Television Network
c. Electronic data interchange
d. Electronic commerce

18. _____ is a file or account that contains money that a person or company owes to suppliers, but has not paid yet (a form of debt.) When you receive an invoice you add it to the file, and then you remove it when you pay. Thus, the A/P is a form of credit that suppliers offer to their purchasers by allowing them to pay for a product or service after it has already been received.

a. Accounts payable
b. Earnings before interest, taxes, depreciation and amortization
c. Accrual
d. Accounts receivable

19. A _____ is a type of debt Like all debt instruments, a _____ entails the redistribution of financial assets over time, between the lender and the borrower.

a. Lender
b. Debenture
c. Loan
d. Loan to value

20. _____ is a letter issued by an auditor's client to the auditor in writing as one of audit evidences. The date of the document must not be later than the date of audit work completion. It is used to let the client's management declare in writing that the financial statements and other presentations to the auditor are sufficient and appropriate and without omission of material facts to the financial statements, to the best of the management's knowledge.

a. Joint audit
b. Statements on Auditing Standards
c. Management assertions
d. Management Representation

21. _____ is one of financial audit skill which help an auditor understand the client's business and changes in the business, to identify potential risk areas and to plan other audit procedures.

_____ include comparison of financial information (data in financial statement) with

1. prior periods
2. budgets
3. forecasts
4. similar industries and so on.

44 *Chapter 5. Audit Evidence and Documentation*

It also includes consideration of predictable relationships, such as:

1. gross profit to sales,
2. payroll costs to employees,
3. financial information and non-financial information, for examples the CEO's reports and the industry news.

possible sources of information about the client include:

1. interim financial information
2. Budgets
3. Management accounts
4. Non-Financial information
5. Bank and cash records
6. VAT returns
7. Board minutes
8. Discussion or correspondance with the client at they year-end

a. Assurance service

b. International Federation of Audit Bureaux of Circulations

c. External auditor

d. Analytical procedures

22. In economics, business, retail, and accounting, a _____ is the value of money that has been used up to produce something, and hence is not available for use anymore. In economics, a _____ is an alternative that is given up as a result of a decision. In business, the _____ may be one of acquisition, in which case the amount of money expended to acquire it is counted as _____.
    a. Prime cost
    b. Cost
    c. Cost of quality
    d. Cost allocation

23. In financial accounting, _____ or cost of sales includes the direct costs attributable to the production of the goods sold by a company. This amount includes the materials cost used in creating the goods along with the direct labor costs used to produce the good. It excludes indirect expenses such as distribution costs and sales force costs.
    a. Cost of goods sold
    b. Reorder point
    c. FIFO and LIFO accounting
    d. 3M Company

24. _____ is a business, economics or investment term that refers to an asset's ability to be easily converted through an act of buying or selling without causing a significant movement in the price and with minimum loss of value. Money, or cash on hand, is the most liquid asset. An act of exchange of a less liquid asset with a more liquid asset is called liquidation.
    a. Financial instruments
    b. Transfer agent
    c. Market liquidity
    d. Spot rate

25. In statistics, _____ refers to techniques for the modeling and analysis of numerical data consisting of values of a dependent variable and of one or more independent variables The dependent variable in the regression equation is modeled as a function of the independent variables, corresponding parameters, and an error term. The error term is treated as a random variable.

a. 3M Company
b. Regression analysis
c. Trend analysis
d. Multicollinearity

26. The term '_____' refers to the concept of collecting information and attempting to spot a pattern in the information. In some fields of study, the term '_____' has more formally-defined meanings.

In project management _____ is a mathematical technique that uses historical results to predict future outcome.

a. Regression analysis
b. 3M Company
c. Multicollinearity
d. Trend analysis

27. Book Value = Original Cost - _____

Book value at the end of year becomes book value at the beginning of next year. The asset is depreciated until the book value equals scrap value.

If the vehicle were to be sold and the sales price exceeded the depreciated value (net book value) then the excess would be considered a gain and subject to depreciation recapture.

a. Accumulated depreciation
b. AIG
c. ABC Television Network
d. AMEX

28. _____ is a term used in accounting, economics and finance to spread the cost of an asset over the span of several years.

In simple words we can say that _____ is the reduction in the value of an asset due to usage, passage of time, wear and tear, technological outdating or obsolescence, depletion, inadequacy, rot, rust, decay or other such factors.

In accounting, _____ is a term used to describe any method of attributing the historical or purchase cost of an asset across its useful life, roughly corresponding to normal wear and tear.

a. Net profit
b. Current asset
c. General ledger
d. Depreciation

29. _____ is that which is owed; usually referencing assets owed, but the term can also cover moral obligations and other interactions not requiring money. In the case of assets, _____ is a means of using future purchasing power in the present before a summation has been earned. Some companies and corporations use _____ as a part of their overall corporate finance strategy.

a. Debenture
b. Debt
c. Lender
d. Loan

46   *Chapter 5. Audit Evidence and Documentation*

30. In business and accounting, _____ are everything of value that is owned by a person or company. It is a claim on the property your income of a borrower. The balance sheet of a firm records the monetary value of the _____ owned by the firm.

    a. Earnings before interest, taxes, depreciation and amortization   b. Accounts receivable

    c. Accrual basis accounting   d. Assets

31. _____ is that part of statistical practice concerned with the selection of individual observations intended to yield some knowledge about a population of concern, especially for the purposes of statistical inference. Each observation measures one or more properties (weight, location, etc.) of an observable entity enumerated to distinguish objects or individuals.

    a. Arthur Betz Laffer   b. Alan Greenspan

    c. Abby Joseph Cohen   d. Sampling

32. _____, also called fair price (in a commonplace conflation of the two distinct concepts), is a concept used in finance and economics, defined as a rational and unbiased estimate of the potential market price of a good, service, or asset, taking into account such objective factors as:

- acquisition/production/distribution costs, replacement costs, or costs of close substitutes
- actual utility at a given level of development of social productive capability
- supply vs. demand

and subjective factors such as

- risk characteristics
- cost of capital
- individually perceived utility

In accounting, _____ is used as an estimate of the market value of an asset (or liability) for which a market price cannot be determined (usually because there is no established market for the asset.) Under GAAP (FAS 157), _____ is the amount at which the asset could be bought or sold in a current transaction between willing parties, or transferred to an equivalent party, other than in a liquidation sale. This is used for assets whose carrying value is based on mark-to-market valuations; for assets carried at historical cost, the _____ of the asset is not used. One example of where _____ is an issue is a College kitchen with a cost of $2 million which was built 5 years ago.

    a. BMC Software, Inc.   b. BNSF Railway

    c. 3M Company   d. Fair Value

33. _____ is a term in both law and accounting that is based on the economics term of 'market value.' It is also a common basis for assessing damages to be awarded for the loss of or damage to the property, generally in a claim under tort or a contract of insurance.

A _____ is often an estimate of what a willing buyer would pay to a willing seller, both in a free market, for an asset or any piece of property. If such a transaction actually occurs, then the actual transaction price is usually the _____.

Chapter 5. Audit Evidence and Documentation 47

a. Fair market value
c. Disposal tax effect
b. Shares authorized
d. Cash and cash equivalents

34. _____, in law and economics, is a form of risk management primarily used to hedge against the risk of a contingent loss. _____ is defined as the equitable transfer of the risk of a loss, from one entity to another, in exchange for a premium, and can be thought of as a guaranteed small loss to prevent a large, possibly devastating loss. An insurer is a company selling the _____; an insured is the person or entity buying the _____.

a. Insurance
c. ABC Television Network
b. AMEX
d. AIG

35. A _____ is any one of a variety of different systems, institutions, procedures, social relations and infrastructures whereby persons trade, and goods and services are exchanged, forming part of the economy. It is an arrangement that allows buyers and sellers to exchange things. _____s vary in size, range, geographic scale, location, types and variety of human communities, as well as the types of goods and services traded.

a. Market Failure
c. Recession
b. Perfect competition
d. Market

36. _____ is the price at which an asset would trade in a competitive Walrasian auction setting. _____ is often used interchangeably with open _____, fair value or fair _____, although these terms have distinct definitions in different standards, and may differ in some circumstances.

International Valuation Standards defines _____ as 'the estimated amount for which a property should exchange on the date of valuation between a willing buyer and a willing seller in an arme;s-length transaction after proper marketing wherein the parties had each acted knowledgeably, prudently, and without compulsion.'

_____ is a concept distinct from market price, which is e;the price at which one can transacte;, while _____ is e;the true underlying valuee; according to theoretical standards.

a. Market value
c. Sinking fund
b. Segregated portfolio company
d. Debtor

37. _____, commonly abbreviated as SAS, provide guidance to external auditors on generally accepted auditing standards in regards to auditing an entity and issuing a report. They are usually issued by the certified public accountant authoritative body in the region where the standards apply, such as the American Institute of Certified Public Accountants in the United States.

- _____
- _____ (Taiwan)

a. RSM International
c. GASB 45
b. Financial Instruments and Exchange Law
d. Statements on Auditing Standards

38. _____ is the state or fact of exclusive rights and control over property, which may be an object, land/real estate or intellectual property. An _____ right is also referred to as title.

_____ is the key building block in the development of the capitalist socio-economic system.

a. Administrative proceeding
b. Ownership
c. ABC Television Network
d. Encumbrance

39. The _____ of 2002 (Pub.L. 107-204, 116 Stat. 745, enacted July 30, 2002), also known as the Public Company Accounting Reform and Investor Protection Act of 2002, is a United States federal law enacted on July 30, 2002 in response to a number of major corporate and accounting scandals including those affecting Enron, Tyco International, Adelphia, Peregrine Systems and WorldCom. The legislation establishes new or enhanced standards for all U.S. public company boards, management, and public accounting firms. It does not apply to privately held companies.

a. FCPA
b. Fair Labor Standards Act
c. Lease
d. Sarbanes-Oxley Act

40. _____s are the documents which keeping all audit evidences obtained during financial statements auditing. _____ is to be able to support the audit works done in order, sufficient and assurance audit evidences have been obtained and reasonable assurance audit conclusion can be made in due course.

_____s are the property of the auditor.

a. Event data
b. Internal Auditing
c. Auditor independence
d. Audit working paper

41. In financial accounting, a _____ is defined as an obligation of an entity arising from past transactions or events, the settlement of which may result in the transfer or use of assets, provision of services or other yielding of economic benefits in the future.

a. Vested
b. Corporate governance
c. Liability
d. False Claims Act

42. _____, Quarterly Report Pursuant to Section 13 or 15(d) of the Securities Exchange Act of 1934, is an SEC filing that must be filed quarterly with the US Securities and Exchange Commission. It contains similar information to the annual form 10-K, however the information is generally less detailed, and the financial statements are generally unaudited. Information for the final quarter of a firm's fiscal year is included in the 10-K, so only three 10-Q filings are made each year.

a. Form 20-F
b. 3M Company
c. Form 8-K
d. Form 10-Q

43. In accounting, the _____ is a worksheet listing the balance at a certain date, of each ledger account in two columns, namely debit and credit. Under the double-entry system, in any transaction the total of any debits must equal the total of any credits, so in a _____ the total of the debit side should always be equal to the total of the credit side. The _____ thus serves as a tool to detect errors, which can result in the totals not being equal.

a. Bottom line
b. Trial balance
c. Current asset
d. Depreciation

Chapter 5. Audit Evidence and Documentation

44. A _____ has several related meanings:

- a daily record of events or business; a private _____ is usually referred to as a diary.
- a newspaper or other periodical, in the literal sense of one published each day;
- many publications issued at stated intervals, such as magazines, or scholarly academic _____s, or the record of the transactions of a society, are often called _____s. Although _____ is sometimes used, erroneously, as a synonym for 'magazine,' in academic use, a _____ refers to a serious, scholarly publication, most often peer-reviewed. A non-scholarly magazine written for an educated audience about an industry or an area of professional activity is usually called a professional magazine.

The word 'journalist' for one whose business is writing for the public press has been in use since the end of the 17th century.

Open access _____s are scholarly _____s that are available to the reader without financial or other barrier other than access to the internet itself. Some are subsidized, and some require payment on behalf of the author. Subsidized _____s are financed by an academic institution or a government information center.

a. 3M Company
b. Journal
c. BMC Software, Inc.
d. BNSF Railway

45. In engineering and manufacturing, _____ and quality engineering are used in developing systems to ensure products or services are designed and produced to meet or exceed customer requirements. Refer to the definition by Merriam-Webster for further information . These systems are often developed in conjunction with other business and engineering disciplines using a cross-functional approach.

a. BMC Software, Inc.
b. 3M Company
c. BNSF Railway
d. Quality control

Chapter 6. Planning the Audit; Linking Audit Procedures to Risk

1. The general definition of an _____ is an evaluation of a person, organization, system, process, project or product. _____s are performed to ascertain the validity and reliability of information; also to provide an assessment of a system's internal control. The goal of an _____ is to express an opinion on the person/organization/system (etc) in question, under evaluation based on work done on a test basis.
    a. Audit
    b. Institute of Chartered Accountants of India
    c. Audit regime
    d. Assurance service

2. _____ is a concept that denotes the precise probability of specific eventualities. Technically, the notion of _____ is independent from the notion of value and, as such, eventualities may have both beneficial and adverse consequences. However, in general usage the convention is to focus only on potential negative impact to some characteristic of value that may arise from a future event.
    a. Risk
    b. Risk adjusted return on capital
    c. Discounting
    d. Discount factor

3. NYSE Amex Equities, formerly known as the _____ is an _____ situated in New York. AMEX was a mutual organization, owned by its members. Until 1953 it was known as the New York Curb Exchange.
    a. AMEX
    b. AIG
    c. ABC Television Network
    d. American Stock Exchange

4. In a publicly-held company, an _____ is an operating committee of the Board of Directors, typically charged with oversight of financial reporting and disclosure. Committee members are drawn from members of the Company's board of directors, with a Chairperson selected from among the members. An _____ of a publicly-traded company in the United States is composed of independent and outside directors referred to as non-executive directors, at least one of which is typically a financial expert.
    a. External auditor
    b. Audit working paper
    c. Event data
    d. Audit committee

5. _____ is a legally declared inability or impairment of ability of an individual or organization to pay its creditors. Creditors may file a _____ petition against a debtor ('involuntary _____') in an effort to recoup a portion of what they are owed or initiate a restructuring. In the majority of cases, however, _____ is initiated by the debtor (a 'voluntary _____' that is filed by the bankrupt individual or organization.)
    a. BMC Software, Inc.
    b. Bankruptcy
    c. Bankruptcy protection
    d. 3M Company

6. The _____ (acronym of National Association of Securities Dealers Automated Quotations) is an American stock exchange. It is the largest electronic screen-based equity securities trading market in the United States. With approximately 3,800 companies, it has more trading volume per hour than any other stock exchange in the world.
    a. Sustainability measurement
    b. Sale of goods
    c. Variance
    d. NASDAQ

7. _____ is an equity (stock) exchange located at 11 Wall Street in lower Manhattan, New York, USA.) It is the largest stock exchange in the world by dollar value of its listed companies' securities. As of October 2008, the combined capitalization of all domestic _____ listed companies was US$10.1 trillion.
    a. BMC Software, Inc.
    b. 3M Company
    c. BNSF Railway
    d. New York Stock Exchange

Chapter 6. Planning the Audit; Linking Audit Procedures to Risk

8. A _____, (formerly a securities exchange) is a corporation or mutual organization which provides 'trading' facilities for stock brokers and traders, to trade stocks and other securities. _____s also provide facilities for the issue and redemption of securities as well as other financial instruments and capital events including the payment of income and dividends. The securities traded on a _____ include: shares issued by companies, unit trusts, derivatives, pooled investment products and bonds.
   a. Stock Exchange
   b. BMC Software, Inc.
   c. 3M Company
   d. BNSF Railway

9. _____ is a report required to be filed by public companies with the United States Securities and Exchange Commission pursuant to the Securities Exchange Act of 1934, as amended. After a significant event like bankruptcy or departure of a CEO, a public company generally must file a Current Report on _____ within four business days to provide an update to previously filed quartely reports on Form 10-Q and/or Annual Reports on Form 10-K. _____ is a very broad form used to notify investors of any unscheduled material event that is important to shareholders or the SEC.
   a. Form 10-Q
   b. Form 20-F
   c. 3M Company
   d. Form 8-K

10. The U.S. _____ is an independent agency of the United States government which holds primary responsibility for enforcing the federal securities laws and regulating the securities industry, the nation's stock and options exchanges, and other electronic securities markets. The SEC was created by section 4 of the Securities Exchange Act of 1934 (now codified as 15 U.S.C. §§ 78d and commonly referred to as the 1934 Act.)
    a. 3M Company
    b. BMC Software, Inc.
    c. BNSF Railway
    d. Securities and Exchange Commission

11. The _____ of 2002 (Pub.L. 107-204, 116 Stat. 745, enacted July 30, 2002), also known as the Public Company Accounting Reform and Investor Protection Act of 2002, is a United States federal law enacted on July 30, 2002 in response to a number of major corporate and accounting scandals including those affecting Enron, Tyco International, Adelphia, Peregrine Systems and WorldCom. The legislation establishes new or enhanced standards for all U.S. public company boards, management, and public accounting firms. It does not apply to privately held companies.
    a. Lease
    b. FCPA
    c. Sarbanes-Oxley Act
    d. Fair Labor Standards Act

12. _____ is one of financial audit skill which help an auditor understand the client's business and changes in the business, to identify potential risk areas and to plan other audit procedures.

_____ include comparison of financial information (data in financial statement) with

1. prior periods
2. budgets
3. forecasts
4. similar industries and so on.

It also includes consideration of predictable relationships, such as:

1. gross profit to sales,
2. payroll costs to employees,
3. financial information and non-financial information, for examples the CEO's reports and the industry news.

possible sources of information about the client include:

1. interim financial information
2. Budgets
3. Management accounts
4. Non-Financial information
5. Bank and cash records
6. VAT returns
7. Board minutes
8. Discussion or correspondance with the client at they year-end

a. International Federation of Audit Bureaux of Circulations
b. External auditor
c. Assurance service
d. Analytical procedures

13. _____ are formal records of a business' financial activities.

In British English, including United Kingdom company law, _____ are often referred to as accounts, although the term _____ is also used, particularly by accountants.

_____ provide an overview of a business' financial condition in both short and long term.

a. 3M Company
b. Statement of retained earnings
c. Notes to the financial statements
d. Financial statements

14. A _____ is a type of debt Like all debt instruments, a _____ entails the redistribution of financial assets over time, between the lender and the borrower.
a. Loan to value
b. Debenture
c. Lender
d. Loan

15. An _____ defines the legal relationship (or engagement) between a professional firm (e.g., law, investment banking, consulting, advisory or accountancy firm) and its client(s.) This letter states the terms and conditions of the engagement, principally addressing the scope of the engagement and the terms of compensation for the firm.

Most _____s follow a standard format.

Chapter 6. Planning the Audit; Linking Audit Procedures to Risk

a. Audit evidence
b. Audit risk
c. Engagement letter
d. Internal control

16. _____, in auditing, is the risk that the account or section being audited is materially misstated without considering internal controls due to error; _____ does not include an assessment of the risk of material misstatement due to fraud. The assessment of _____ depends on the professional judgement of the auditor, and it is done after assessing the business environment of the entity being audited.

_____ is typically assessed using a scale, with assessments being either low, medium, or high.

a. AIG
b. ABC Television Network
c. AMEX
d. Inherent risk

17. In mathematics _____s are numbers or other things that get multiplied. In particular, see:

- Factorization, the decomposition of an object into a product of other objects
- Integer factorization, the process of breaking down a composite number into smaller non-trivial divisors
- A coefficient
- A divisor of a particular number, or of an element of a monoid
- A von Neumann algebra with a trivial center

In statistics

- _____ analysis is the study of how _____s or certain variables affect variables.

In technology:

- Human _____s, a profession that focuses on how people interact with products, tools, or procedures
- 'Functionality, Application domain, Conditions, Technology, Objects and Responsibility;', In object-oriented programming

In computer science and information technology:

- Authentication _____, a piece of information used to verify a person's identity for security purposes
- _____, a Unix command for numbers factorization
- _____ (programming language), an experimental Forth-like programming language

In television:

- The O'Reilly _____, an American talk show hosted by Bill O'Reilly on Fox News.
- The Krypton _____, a British game show hosted by Gordon Burns, formally on ITV. Also had an American version.

a. Merck ' Co., Inc.
c. Valuation

b. The Goodyear Tire ' Rubber Company
d. Factor

18. The _____ is a performance management tool which began as a concept for measuring whether the smaller-scale operational activities of a company are aligned with its larger-scale objectives in terms of vision and strategy.

By focusing not only on financial outcomes but also on the operational, marketing and developmental inputs to these, the _____ helps provide a more comprehensive view of a business, which in turn helps organizations act in their best long-term interests. This tool is also being used to address business response to climate change and greenhouse gas emissions.

a. Balanced scorecard
c. Best practice

b. Management by objectives
d. Trustee

19. _____ is the process whereby an organization establishes the parameters within which programs, investments, and acquisitions are reaching the desired results. Performance Reference Model of the Federal Enterprise Architecture, 2005.

This process of measuring performance often requires the use of statistical evidence to determine progress toward specific defined organizational objectives.

There are many types of measurements.

a. Management by exception
c. Performance measurement

b. Trustee
d. Management by objectives

20. _____ is a file or account that contains money that a person or company owes to suppliers, but has not paid yet (a form of debt.) When you receive an invoice you add it to the file, and then you remove it when you pay. Thus, the A/P is a form of credit that suppliers offer to their purchasers by allowing them to pay for a product or service after it has already been received.

a. Earnings before interest, taxes, depreciation and amortization
c. Accounts payable

b. Accounts receivable
d. Accrual

21. An _____ is a term used in behavioral economics to describe those types of behaviors that impose costs on a person in the long-run that are not taken into account when making decisions in the present. Classical Economics discourages government from creating legislation that targets internalities, because it is assumed that the consumer takes these personal costs into account when paying for the good that causes the _____. For example, cigarettes should be taxed because of the negative consumption externalities that they impose, such as second-hand smoke, not because the smoker harms him or herself by smoking.

a. Authorised capital
c. Operating budget

b. Internality
d. Inventory turnover ratio

Chapter 6. Planning the Audit; Linking Audit Procedures to Risk

22. In accounting and organizational theory, _____ is defined as a process effected by an organization's structure, work and authority flows, people and management information systems, designed to help the organization accomplish specific goals or objectives. It is a means by which an organization's resources are directed, monitored, and measured. It plays an important role in preventing and detecting fraud and protecting the organization's resources, both physical (e.g., machinery and property) and intangible (e.g., reputation or intellectual property such as trademarks.)

a. Internal control
c. Audit risk
b. Auditor independence
d. Audit committee

23. _____ means the giving out of information, either voluntarily or to be in compliance with legal regulations or workplace rules.

- In Computer security, full _____ means disclosing full information about vulnerabilities.
- In computing, _____ widget
- Journalism, full _____ refers to disclosing the interests of the writer which may bear on the subject being written about, for example, if the writer has worked with an interview subject in the past.

- In law:
    - The law of England and Wales, _____ refers to a process that may form part of legal proceedings, whereby parties inform to other parties the existence of any relevant documents that are, or have been, in their control. This compares with the process known as discovery in the course of legal proceedings in the United States.
    - In U.S. civil procedure (litigation rules for civil cases), _____ is a stage prior to trial. In civil cases, each party must disclose to the opposing party the following: names of witnesses which it may use to support its side, copies of documents (or mere description of these documents) in its control which it may use to support its side, computation of damages claimed, and certain insurance information. _____ is related to, but technically prior to, the discovery stage.
    - In Company law (known as 'corporate law' in the United States), _____ refers to giving out information about public or limited companies or their officers, which might be kept secret if the company was a private company or a partnership.

- In real property transactions, _____ refers to providing to a buyer information known to the seller or broker/agent concerning the condition or other aspects of real property that would affect the property's value or desirability. These rules regarding what information must be disclosed, and whether the information must be disclosed even if a buyer does not ask, vary from one jurisdiction to the next.

a. Trailing
c. Controlled Foreign Corporations
b. Disclosure
d. Tax harmonisation

24. _____, the Electronic Data-Gathering, Analysis, and Retrieval system, performs automated collection, validation, indexing, acceptance, and forwarding of submissions by companies and others who are required by law to file forms with the U.S. Securities and Exchange Commission (the 'SEC'.) The database is freely available to the public via Web or FTP, typically posting in excess of 3,000 filings per day.

Not all SEC filings by public companies are available on _____.

a. EDGAR
b. AMEX
c. AIG
d. ABC Television Network

25. _____ is the realization of an application idea, model, design, specification, standard, algorithm an _____ is a realization of a technical specification or algorithm as a program, software component, or other computer system. Many _____s may exist for a given specification or standard.
   a. AIG
   b. AMEX
   c. ABC Television Network
   d. Implementation

26. In business and accounting, _____ are everything of value that is owned by a person or company. It is a claim on the property your income of a borrower. The balance sheet of a firm records the monetary value of the _____ owned by the firm.
   a. Accounts receivable
   b. Earnings before interest, taxes, depreciation and amortization
   c. Accrual basis accounting
   d. Assets

27. _____ is that part of statistical practice concerned with the selection of individual observations intended to yield some knowledge about a population of concern, especially for the purposes of statistical inference. Each observation measures one or more properties (weight, location, etc.) of an observable entity enumerated to distinguish objects or individuals.
   a. Abby Joseph Cohen
   b. Sampling
   c. Arthur Betz Laffer
   d. Alan Greenspan

28. _____ is the calculated approximation of a result which is usable even if input data may be incomplete or uncertain.

In statistics, see _____ theory, estimator.

In mathematics, approximation or _____ typically means finding upper or lower bounds of a quantity that cannot readily be computed precisely and is also an educated guess.

   a. Estimation
   b. AIG
   c. ABC Television Network
   d. AMEX

29. _____ is systematic determination of merit, worth, and significance of something or someone using criteria against a set of standards. _____ often is used to characterize and appraise subjects of interest in a wide range of human enterprises, including the arts, criminal justice, foundations and non-profit organizations, government, health care, and other human services.

Depending on the topic of interest, there are professional groups which look to the quality and rigor of the _____ process.

   a. Evaluation
   b. ABC Television Network
   c. AMEX
   d. AIG

30. _____ is a term that is commonly used in relation to the audit of the financial statements of an entity. (.

Chapter 6. Planning the Audit; Linking Audit Procedures to Risk

a. Audit working paper
b. Engagement Letter
c. Audit risk
d. Auditor independence

31. In finance, _____ is the process of estimating the potential market value of a financial asset or liability. They can be done on assets (for example, investments in marketable securities such as stocks, options, business enterprises, or intangible assets such as patents and trademarks) or on liabilities (e.g., Bonds issued by a company.) A _____ is required in many contexts including investment analysis, capital budgeting, merger and acquisition transactions, financial reporting, taxable events to determine the proper tax liability, and in litigation.
   a. Disclosure
   b. Valuation
   c. Daybook
   d. Vyborg Appeal

32. In accounting/accountancy, _____ are journal entries usually made at the end of an accounting period to allocate income and expenditure to the period in which they actually occurred. The revenue recognition principle is the basis of making _____ that pertain to unearned and accrued revenues under accrual-basis accounting. They are sometimes called Balance Day adjustments because they are made on balance day.
   a. Accrued expense
   b. Accrual
   c. Earnings before interest, taxes, depreciation and amortization
   d. Adjusting entries

33. In economics and sociology, an _____ is any factor (financial or non-financial) that enables or motivates a particular course of action, or counts as a reason for preferring one choice to the alternatives. It is an expectation that encourages people to behave in a certain way. Since human beings are purposeful creatures, the study of _____ structures is central to the study of all economic activity (both in terms of individual decision-making and in terms of co-operation and competition within a larger institutional structure.)
   a. ABC Television Network
   b. Incentive
   c. AMEX
   d. AIG

34. Internal auditing is a profession and activity involved in helping organisations achieve their stated objectives. It does this by utilizing a systematic methodology for analyzing business processes, procedures and activities with the goal of highlighting organizational problems and recommending solutions. Professionals called _____ are employed by organizations to perform the internal auditing activity.
   a. Auditor independence
   b. Internal Auditing
   c. Auditing Standards Board
   d. Internal auditors

35. _____ is that which is owed; usually referencing assets owed, but the term can also cover moral obligations and other interactions not requiring money. In the case of assets, _____ is a means of using future purchasing power in the present before a summation has been earned. Some companies and corporations use _____ as a part of their overall corporate finance strategy.
   a. Debenture
   b. Lender
   c. Debt
   d. Loan

58 Chapter 6. Planning the Audit; Linking Audit Procedures to Risk

36. A _____ has several related meanings:

   - a daily record of events or business; a private _____ is usually referred to as a diary.
   - a newspaper or other periodical, in the literal sense of one published each day;
   - many publications issued at stated intervals, such as magazines, or scholarly academic _____s, or the record of the transactions of a society, are often called _____s. Although _____ is sometimes used, erroneously, as a synonym for 'magazine,' in academic use, a _____ refers to a serious, scholarly publication, most often peer-reviewed. A non-scholarly magazine written for an educated audience about an industry or an area of professional activity is usually called a professional magazine.

The word 'journalist' for one whose business is writing for the public press has been in use since the end of the 17th century.

Open access _____s are scholarly _____s that are available to the reader without financial or other barrier other than access to the internet itself. Some are subsidized, and some require payment on behalf of the author. Subsidized _____s are financed by an academic institution or a government information center.

   a. BNSF Railway
   c. 3M Company
   b. BMC Software, Inc.
   d. Journal

37. _____ is evidence obtained during a financial audit and recorded in the audit working papers.

   - In the audit engagement acceptance or reappointment stage, _____ is the information that the auditor is to consider for the appointment. For examples, change in the entity control environment, inherent risk and nature of the entity business, and scope of audit work.

   - In the audit planning stage, _____ is the information that the auditor is to consider for the most effective and efficient audit approach. For examples, reliability of internal control procedures, and analytical review systems.

   - In the control testing stage, _____ is the information that the auditor is to consider for the mix of audit test of control and audit substantive tests.

   - In the substantive testing stage, _____ is the information that the auditor is to make sure the appropriation of financial statement assertions. For examples, existence, rights and obligations, occurrence, completeness, valuation, measurement, presentation and disclosure of a particular transaction or account balance.

   a. Institute of Chartered Accountants of India
   c. ITGCs
   b. Audit
   d. Audit evidence

38. Project _____: The project _____ is a prediction of the costs associated with a particular company project. These costs include labor, materials, and other related expenses. The project _____ is often broken down into specific tasks, with task _____s assigned to each.
   a. 3M Company
   c. BNSF Railway
   b. Budget
   d. BMC Software, Inc.

Chapter 6. Planning the Audit; Linking Audit Procedures to Risk

39. _____, in auditing, is the risk that a company's internal controls are insufficient to mitigate or detect errors or fraud.
   a. BMC Software, Inc.
   b. 3M Company
   c. BNSF Railway
   d. Control risk

40. _____ is a step in a risk management process. _____ is the determination of quantitative or qualitative value of risk related to a concrete situation and a recognized threat (also called hazard.) Quantitative _____ requires calculations of two components of risk: R, the magnitude of the potential loss L, and the probability p that the loss will occur.
   a. BNSF Railway
   b. BMC Software, Inc.
   c. 3M Company
   d. Risk assessment

41. _____ or audit log is a chronological sequence of audit records, each of which contains evidence directly pertaining to and resulting from the execution of a business process or system function.

Audit records typically result from activities such as transactions or communications by individual people, systems, accounts or other entities.

Webopedia defines an _____ as 'a record showing who has accessed a computer system and what operations he or she has performed during a given period of time.' ()

In telecommunication, the term means a record of both completed and attempted accesses and service, or data forming a logical path linking a sequence of events, used to trace the transactions that have affected the contents of a record.

   a. AIG
   b. ABC Television Network
   c. AMEX
   d. Audit trail

42. _____ is an organization's process of defining its strategy and making decisions on allocating its resources to pursue this strategy, including its capital and people. Various business analysis techniques can be used in _____, including SWOT analysis (Strengths, Weaknesses, Opportunities, and Threats) and PEST analysis (Political, Economic, Social, and Technological analysis) or STEER analysis involving Socio-cultural, Technological, Economic, Ecological, and Regulatory factors and EPISTEL (Environment, Political, Informatic, Social, Technological, Economic and Legal)

_____ is the formal consideration of an organization's future course. All _____ deals with at least one of three key questions:

1. 'What do we do?'
2. 'For whom do we do it?'
3. 'How do we excel?'

In business _____, the third question is better phrased 'How can we beat or avoid competition?'. (Bradford and Duncan, page 1.)

Chapter 6. Planning the Audit; Linking Audit Procedures to Risk

    a. 3M Company
    c. BMC Software, Inc.
    b. Strategic planning
    d. BNSF Railway

43. An _____ is the buying of one company by another. An _____ may be friendly or hostile. In the former case, the companies cooperate in negotiations; in the latter case, the takeover target is unwilling to be bought or the target's board has no prior knowledge of the offer. _____ usually refers to a purchase of a smaller firm by a larger one. Sometimes, however, a smaller firm will acquire management control of a larger or longer established company and keep its name for the combined entity. This is known as a reverse takeover.
    a. AIG
    c. ABC Television Network
    b. AMEX
    d. Acquisition

44. In a company, _____ is the sum of all financial records of salaries, wages, bonuses and deductions.

A paycheck, is traditionally a paper document issued by an employer to pay an employee for services rendered. While most commonly used in the United States, recently the physical paycheck has been increasingly replaced by electronic direct deposit to bank accounts.

    a. Tax expense
    c. Payroll
    b. Total Expense Ratio
    d. 3M Company

45. In financial accounting, a _____ or statement of financial position is a summary of a person's or organization's balances. Assets, liabilities and ownership equity are listed as of a specific date, such as the end of its financial year. A _____ is often described as a snapshot of a company's financial condition.
    a. Financial statements
    c. Balance sheet
    b. Statement of retained earnings
    d. 3M Company

46. _____ is a company's financial statement that indicates how the revenue is transformed into the net income The purpose of the _____ is to show managers and investors whether the company made or lost money during the period being reported.

The important thing to remember about an _____ is that it represents a period of time.

    a. ABC Television Network
    c. AMEX
    b. AIG
    d. Income statement

47. In economics, the _____, (or _____) measures the payments that flow between any individual country and all other countries. It is used to summarize all international economic transactions for that country during a specific time period, usually a year. The _____ is determined by the country's exports and imports of goods, services, and financial capital, as well as financial transfers.
    a. Balance of payments
    c. Yield to maturity
    b. Moving average
    d. Stock split

48. _____ is a process where a business physically counts its entire inventory. A _____ may be mandated by financial accounting rules or the tax regulations to place an accurate value on the inventory, or the business may need to count inventory so component parts or raw materials can be restocked. Businesses may use several different tactics to minimize the disruption caused by _____.

a. 3M Company	b. BNSF Railway
c. Physical inventory	d. BMC Software, Inc.

49. _____ is a term in both law and accounting that is based on the economics term of 'market value.' It is also a common basis for assessing damages to be awarded for the loss of or damage to the property, generally in a claim under tort or a contract of insurance.

A _____ is often an estimate of what a willing buyer would pay to a willing seller, both in a free market, for an asset or any piece of property. If such a transaction actually occurs, then the actual transaction price is usually the _____.

a. Cash and cash equivalents	b. Disposal tax effect
c. Shares authorized	d. Fair market value

50. _____, also called fair price (in a commonplace conflation of the two distinct concepts), is a concept used in finance and economics, defined as a rational and unbiased estimate of the potential market price of a good, service, or asset, taking into account such objective factors as:

- acquisition/production/distribution costs, replacement costs, or costs of close substitutes
- actual utility at a given level of development of social productive capability
- supply vs. demand

and subjective factors such as

- risk characteristics
- cost of capital
- individually perceived utility

In accounting, _____ is used as an estimate of the market value of an asset (or liability) for which a market price cannot be determined (usually because there is no established market for the asset.) Under GAAP (FAS 157), _____ is the amount at which the asset could be bought or sold in a current transaction between willing parties, or transferred to an equivalent party, other than in a liquidation sale. This is used for assets whose carrying value is based on mark-to-market valuations; for assets carried at historical cost, the _____ of the asset is not used. One example of where _____ is an issue is a College kitchen with a cost of $2 million which was built 5 years ago.

a. 3M Company	b. BMC Software, Inc.
c. BNSF Railway	d. Fair value

51. A _____ is any one of a variety of different systems, institutions, procedures, social relations and infrastructures whereby persons trade, and goods and services are exchanged, forming part of the economy. It is an arrangement that allows buyers and sellers to exchange things. _____s vary in size, range, geographic scale, location, types and variety of human communities, as well as the types of goods and services traded.

Chapter 6. Planning the Audit; Linking Audit Procedures to Risk

a. Market Failure
c. Recession
b. Perfect competition
d. Market

52. _____ is the price at which an asset would trade in a competitive Walrasian auction setting. _____ is often used interchangeably with open _____, fair value or fair _____, although these terms have distinct definitions in different standards, and may differ in some circumstances.

International Valuation Standards defines _____ as 'the estimated amount for which a property should exchange on the date of valuation between a willing buyer and a willing seller in an arme;s-length transaction after proper marketing wherein the parties had each acted knowledgeably, prudently, and without compulsion.'

_____ is a concept distinct from market price, which is e;the price at which one can transacte;, while _____ is e;the true underlying valuee; according to theoretical standards.

a. Segregated portfolio company
c. Market value
b. Sinking fund
d. Debtor

53. _____ is one of a series of accounting transactions dealing with the billing of customers who owe money to a person, company or organization for goods and services that have been provided to the customer. In most business entities this is typically done by generating an invoice and mailing or electronically delivering it to the customer, who in turn must pay it within an established timeframe called credit or payment terms.

An example of a common payment term is Net 30, meaning payment is due in the amount of the invoice 30 days from the date of invoice.

a. Accrued revenue
c. Accrual
b. Accounts receivable
d. Adjusting entries

54. The _____ of 1977 (15 U.S.C. ÂÂ§ÅÂ§ 78dd-1, et seq.) is a United States federal law known primarily for two of its main provisions, one that addresses accounting transparency requirements under the Securities Exchange Act of 1934 and another concerning bribery of foreign officials.

a. Pre-emption right
c. Foreign Corrupt Practices Act
b. Lease
d. Competition law

55. A _____ is a common type of chart, that represents an algorithm or process, showing the steps as boxes of various kinds, and their order by connecting these with arrows. _____s are used in analyzing, designing, documenting or managing a process or program in various fields.

The first structured method for documenting process flow, the 'flow process chart', was introduced by Frank Gilbreth to members of ASME in 1921 as the presentation e;Process Charts--First Steps in Finding the One Best Waye;.

a. 3M Company
c. BNSF Railway
b. Flowchart
d. BMC Software, Inc.

Chapter 6. Planning the Audit; Linking Audit Procedures to Risk

56. An _____ is a practitioner of accountancy, which is the measurement, disclosure or provision of assurance about financial information that helps managers, investors, tax authorities and other decision makers make resource allocation decisions.

The word '_____' is derived from the French 'Compter' which took its origin from the Latin 'Computare'. The word was formerly written in English as 'Accomptant', but in process of time the word, which was always pronounced by dropping the 'p', became gradually changed both in pronunciation and in orthography to its present form.

a. AIG
b. ABC Television Network
c. AMEX
d. Accountant

57. The _____ is the national, professional association of CPAs in the United States, with more than 330,000 members, including CPAs in business and industry, public practice, government, and education; student affiliates; and international associates. It sets ethical standards for the profession and U.S. auditing standards for audits of private companies; federal, state and local governments; and non-profit organizations.

Approximately 40% of its members are engaged in the practice of public accounting, in areas such as auditing, accounting, taxation, general business consulting, business valuation, personal financial planning and business technology.

a. Other postemployment benefits
b. ABC Television Network
c. AIG
d. American Institute of Certified Public Accountants

58. _____ is the statutory title of qualified accountants in the United States who have passed the Uniform _____ Examination and have met additional state education and experience requirements for certification as a _____. Individuals who have passed the Exam but have not either accomplished the required on-the-job experience or have previously met it but in the meantime have lapsed their continuing professional education are, in many states, permitted the designation '_____ Inactive' or an equivalent phrase. In most U.S. states, only _____s who are licensed are able to provide to the public attestation (including auditing) opinions on financial statements.

a. Certified Public Accountant
b. Chartered Certified Accountant
c. Chartered Accountant
d. Certified General Accountant

59. Established in 1941, The _____ is internationally recognized as a trustworthy guidance-setting body. Serving members in 165 countries, The IIA is the internal audit profession's global voice, chief advocate, recognized authority, acknowledged leader, and principal educator, with global headquarters in Altamonte Springs, Fla., United States.

The stated mission of The _____ is to provide dynamic leadership for the global profession of internal auditing.

a. Event data
b. Audit regime
c. Auditor independence
d. Institute of Internal Auditors

60. _____ is the world's largest professional services firm. It was formed in 1998 from a merger between Price Waterhouse and Coopers ' Lybrand, both formed in London.

Chapter 6. Planning the Audit; Linking Audit Procedures to Risk

_____ earned aggregated worldwide revenues of $28 billion for fiscal 2008, and employed over 146,000 people in 150 countries.

a. Total-factor productivity
b. Daybook
c. Serial bonds
d. PricewaterhouseCoopers

61. The term _____ usually refers to a company that is permitted to offer its registered securities (stock, bonds, etc.) for sale to the general public, typically through a stock exchange, or occasionally a company whose stock is traded over the counter (OTC) via market makers who use non-exchange quotation services.

The term '_____' may also refer to a company owned by the government.

a. Professional association
b. Public Company
c. MicroStrategy
d. Governmental Accounting Standards Board

62. The _____ (sometimes called 'Peekaboo') is a private-sector, non-profit corporation created by the Sarbanes-Oxley Act, a 2002 United States federal law, to oversee the auditors of public companies. Its stated purpose is to 'protect the interests of investors and further the public interest in the preparation of informative, fair, and independent audit reports'. Although a private entity, the _____ has many government-like regulatory functions, making it in some ways similar to the private Self Regulatory Organizations (SROs) that regulate stock markets and other aspects of the financial markets in the United States.

a. Pension Benefit Guaranty Corporation
b. Financial Crimes Enforcement Network
c. 3M Company
d. Public Company Accounting Oversight Board

63. A _____ is a fungible, negotiable instrument representing financial value. they are broadly categorized into debt securities (such as banknotes, bonds and debentures), and equity securities; e.g., common stocks. The company or other entity issuing the _____ is called the issuer.

a. BMC Software, Inc.
b. 3M Company
c. Tracking stock
d. Security

Chapter 7. Internal Control

1. An _____ is a term used in behavioral economics to describe those types of behaviors that impose costs on a person in the long-run that are not taken into account when making decisions in the present. Classical Economics discourages government from creating legislation that targets internalities, because it is assumed that the consumer takes these personal costs into account when paying for the good that causes the _____. For example, cigarettes should be taxed because of the negative consumption externalities that they impose, such as second-hand smoke, not because the smoker harms him or herself by smoking.

   a. Internality
   b. Authorised capital
   c. Inventory turnover ratio
   d. Operating budget

2. In accounting and organizational theory, _____ is defined as a process effected by an organization's structure, work and authority flows, people and management information systems, designed to help the organization accomplish specific goals or objectives. It is a means by which an organization's resources are directed, monitored, and measured. It plays an important role in preventing and detecting fraud and protecting the organization's resources, both physical (e.g., machinery and property) and intangible (e.g., reputation or intellectual property such as trademarks.)

   a. Audit risk
   b. Auditor independence
   c. Internal control
   d. Audit committee

3. An _____ is a practitioner of accountancy, which is the measurement, disclosure or provision of assurance about financial information that helps managers, investors, tax authorities and other decision makers make resource allocation decisions.

   The word '_____' is derived from the French 'Compter' which took its origin from the Latin 'Computare'. The word was formerly written in English as 'Accomptant', but in process of time the word, which was always pronounced by dropping the 'p', became gradually changed both in pronunciation and in orthography to its present form.

   a. AIG
   b. AMEX
   c. ABC Television Network
   d. Accountant

4. The _____ is the national, professional association of CPAs in the United States, with more than 330,000 members, including CPAs in business and industry, public practice, government, and education; student affiliates; and international associates. It sets ethical standards for the profession and U.S. auditing standards for audits of private companies; federal, state and local governments; and non-profit organizations.

   Approximately 40% of its members are engaged in the practice of public accounting, in areas such as auditing, accounting, taxation, general business consulting, business valuation, personal financial planning and business technology.

   a. ABC Television Network
   b. Other postemployment benefits
   c. AIG
   d. American Institute of Certified Public Accountants

5. The general definition of an _____ is an evaluation of a person, organization, system, process, project or product. _____s are performed to ascertain the validity and reliability of information; also to provide an assessment of a system's internal control. The goal of an _____ is to express an opinion on the person/organization/system (etc) in question, under evaluation based on work done on a test basis.

a. Audit
b. Assurance service
c. Institute of Chartered Accountants of India
d. Audit regime

6. _____ is the statutory title of qualified accountants in the United States who have passed the Uniform _____ Examination and have met additional state education and experience requirements for certification as a _____. Individuals who have passed the Exam but have not either accomplished the required on-the-job experience or have previously met it but in the meantime have lapsed their continuing professional education are, in many states, permitted the designation '_____ Inactive' or an equivalent phrase. In most U.S. states, only _____s who are licensed are able to provide to the public attestation (including auditing) opinions on financial statements.

a. Chartered Accountant
b. Certified General Accountant
c. Chartered Certified Accountant
d. Certified Public Accountant

7. The _____ of 1977 (15 U.S.C. §§ 78dd-1, et seq.) is a United States federal law known primarily for two of its main provisions, one that addresses accounting transparency requirements under the Securities Exchange Act of 1934 and another concerning bribery of foreign officials.

a. Competition law
b. Lease
c. Pre-emption right
d. Foreign Corrupt Practices Act

8. Established in 1941, The _____ is internationally recognized as a trustworthy guidance-setting body. Serving members in 165 countries, The IIA is the internal audit profession's global voice, chief advocate, recognized authority, acknowledged leader, and principal educator, with global headquarters in Altamonte Springs, Fla., United States.

The stated mission of The _____ is to provide dynamic leadership for the global profession of internal auditing.

a. Auditor independence
b. Institute of Internal Auditors
c. Event data
d. Audit regime

9. Internal auditing is a profession and activity involved in helping organisations achieve their stated objectives. It does this by utilizing a systematic methodology for analyzing business processes, procedures and activities with the goal of highlighting organizational problems and recommending solutions. Professionals called _____ are employed by organizations to perform the internal auditing activity.

a. Auditing Standards Board
b. Internal Auditing
c. Internal auditors
d. Auditor independence

10. In accounting, _____ or carrying value is the value of an asset according to its balance sheet account balance. For assets, the value is based on the original cost of the asset less any depreciation, amortization or impairment costs made against the asset. Traditionally, a company's _____ is its total assets minus intangible assets and liabilities.

a. Matching principle
b. Book value
c. Generally accepted accounting principles
d. Depreciation

11. In a financial audit, _____ or financial statement assertions is the set of information that the preparer of financial statements (management) is providing to another party. Financial statements represent a very complex and interrelated set of assertions. At the most aggregate level, the financial statements include broad assertions such as 'total liabilities as at 31 December are $50 million', 'total revenue for the year is $9 million' and 'net income for the year is $3 million'.

Chapter 7. Internal Control

a. Mainframe audit
b. Lead Auditor
c. Sales Tax Audit
d. Management assertions

12. _____ is a concept that denotes the precise probability of specific eventualities. Technically, the notion of _____ is independent from the notion of value and, as such, eventualities may have both beneficial and adverse consequences. However, in general usage the convention is to focus only on potential negative impact to some characteristic of value that may arise from a future event.

a. Discounting
b. Risk adjusted return on capital
c. Discount factor
d. Risk

13. _____, Quarterly Report Pursuant to Section 13 or 15(d) of the Securities Exchange Act of 1934, is an SEC filing that must be filed quarterly with the US Securities and Exchange Commission. It contains similar information to the annual form 10-K, however the information is generally less detailed, and the financial statements are generally unaudited. Information for the final quarter of a firm's fiscal year is included in the 10-K, so only three 10-Q filings are made each year.

a. Form 20-F
b. Form 8-K
c. 3M Company
d. Form 10-Q

14. In probability theory and statistics, the _____ (or expectation value or mean and for continuous random variables with a density function it is the probability density -weighted integral of the possible values.

The term '_____' can be misleading.

a. AIG
b. AMEX
c. Expected value
d. ABC Television Network

15. In a publicly-held company, an _____ is an operating committee of the Board of Directors, typically charged with oversight of financial reporting and disclosure. Committee members are drawn from members of the Company's board of directors, with a Chairperson selected from among the members. An _____ of a publicly-traded company in the United States is composed of independent and outside directors referred to as non-executive directors, at least one of which is typically a financial expert.

a. External auditor
b. Audit working paper
c. Event data
d. Audit committee

16. A _____ is a body of elected or appointed members who jointly oversee the activities of a company or organization. The body sometimes has a different name, such as board of trustees, board of governors, board of managers, or executive board. It is often simply referred to as 'the board.'

A board's activities are determined by the powers, duties, and responsibilities delegated to it or conferred on it by an authority outside itself.

a. Consumer protection laws
b. Chief Financial Officers Act of 1990
c. Hospital Survey and Construction Act
d. Board of directors

17. Employment is a contract between two parties, one being the employer and the other being the _____. An _____ may be defined as: 'A person in the service of another under any contract of hire, express or implied, oral or written, where the employer has the power or right to control and direct the _____ in the material details of how the work is to be performed.' Black's Law Dictionary page 471 (5th ed. 1979.)

   a. Employee
   b. AIG
   c. AMEX
   d. ABC Television Network

18. The _____ of 2002 (Pub.L. 107-204, 116 Stat. 745, enacted July 30, 2002), also known as the Public Company Accounting Reform and Investor Protection Act of 2002, is a United States federal law enacted on July 30, 2002 in response to a number of major corporate and accounting scandals including those affecting Enron, Tyco International, Adelphia, Peregrine Systems and WorldCom. The legislation establishes new or enhanced standards for all U.S. public company boards, management, and public accounting firms. It does not apply to privately held companies.

   a. Fair Labor Standards Act
   b. Lease
   c. FCPA
   d. Sarbanes-Oxley Act

19. _____ is a file or account that contains money that a person or company owes to suppliers, but has not paid yet (a form of debt.) When you receive an invoice you add it to the file, and then you remove it when you pay. Thus, the A/P is a form of credit that suppliers offer to their purchasers by allowing them to pay for a product or service after it has already been received.

   a. Accounts payable
   b. Earnings before interest, taxes, depreciation and amortization
   c. Accrual
   d. Accounts receivable

20. _____ also called 'Internal _____'. It is a term of financial audit, internal audit and Enterprise Risk Management. It means the overall attitude, awareness and actions of directors and management (i.e. 'those charged with governance') regarding the internal control system and its importance to the entity.

   a. Mainframe audit
   b. SOFT audit
   c. Control environment
   d. Negative assurance

21. In business and accounting, _____ are everything of value that is owned by a person or company. It is a claim on the property your income of a borrower. The balance sheet of a firm records the monetary value of the _____ owned by the firm.

   a. Earnings before interest, taxes, depreciation and amortization
   b. Accounts receivable
   c. Accrual basis accounting
   d. Assets

22. An _____ is a mostly hierarchical concept of subordination of entities that collaborate and contribute to serve one common aim.

Organizations are a variant of clustered entities. The structure of an organization is usually set up in many a styles, dependent on their objectives and ambience.

   a. AMEX
   b. ABC Television Network
   c. AIG
   d. Organizational structure

Chapter 7. Internal Control

23. A _____ is the person responsible for running the treasury of an organization. In A new way to pay the National Debt (1786), James Gillray caricatured Queen Charlotte and George III awash with treasury funds to cover royal debts, with Pitt handing them another moneybag.

The Treasury of a country is the department responsible for the country's economy, finance and revenue. The _____ is generally the head of the Treasury, although, in some countries (such as the U.S. or the UK) the _____ reports to a Secretary of the Treasury, or Chancellor of the Exchequer.

a. Treasurer
c. BNSF Railway
b. 3M Company
d. BMC Software, Inc.

24. _____ is an organization's process of defining its strategy and making decisions on allocating its resources to pursue this strategy, including its capital and people. Various business analysis techniques can be used in _____, including SWOT analysis (Strengths, Weaknesses, Opportunities, and Threats) and PEST analysis (Political, Economic, Social, and Technological analysis) or STEER analysis involving Socio-cultural, Technological, Economic, Ecological, and Regulatory factors and EPISTEL (Environment, Political, Informatic, Social, Technological, Economic and Legal)

_____ is the formal consideration of an organization's future course. All _____ deals with at least one of three key questions:

1. 'What do we do?'
2. 'For whom do we do it?'
3. 'How do we excel?'

In business _____, the third question is better phrased 'How can we beat or avoid competition?'. (Bradford and Duncan, page 1.)

a. BNSF Railway
c. 3M Company
b. Strategic planning
d. BMC Software, Inc.

25. _____ is a step in a risk management process. _____ is the determination of quantitative or qualitative value of risk related to a concrete situation and a recognized threat (also called hazard.) Quantitative _____ requires calculations of two components of risk: R, the magnitude of the potential loss L, and the probability p that the loss will occur.

a. Risk assessment
c. 3M Company
b. BMC Software, Inc.
d. BNSF Railway

26. In finance, a _____ is a debt security, in which the authorized issuer owes the holders a debt and, depending on the terms of the _____, is obliged to pay interest (the coupon) and/or to repay the principal at a later date, termed maturity. It is a formal contract to repay borrowed money with interest at fixed intervals.

Thus a _____ is like a loan: the issuer is the borrower, the _____ holder is the lender, and the coupon is the interest.

a. Coupon rate
b. Zero-coupon bond
c. Revenue bonds
d. Bond

27. _____ is an increasingly broadening term with which an organization knowledge and experience, Employee Relations and resource planning at various levels. The field draws upon concepts developed in Industrial/Organizational Psychology and System Theory. _____ has at least two related interpretations depending on context.

a. 3M Company
b. BMC Software, Inc.
c. Human resources
d. Separation of duties

28. _____ is a list of the accounts including a unique number of each allowing to locate it in each ledger. The list is typically arranged in the order of the customary appearance of accounts in the financial statements. A _____ can track a specific financial information.

a. General journal
b. Journal entry
c. General ledger
d. Chart of accounts

29. _____ is the process whereby an organization establishes the parameters within which programs, investments, and acquisitions are reaching the desired results. Performance Reference Model of the Federal Enterprise Architecture, 2005.

This process of measuring performance often requires the use of statistical evidence to determine progress toward specific defined organizational objectives.

There are many types of measurements.

a. Performance measurement
b. Management by exception
c. Management by objectives
d. Trustee

30. _____ is the term used to refer to the standard framework of guidelines for financial accounting used in any given jurisdiction. _____ includes the standards, conventions, and rules accountants follow in recording and summarizing transactions, and in the preparation of financial statements.

Financial accounting information must be assembled and reported objectively.

a. Generally accepted accounting principles
b. General ledger
c. Current asset
d. Long-term liabilities

31. _____ is the concept of having more than one person required to complete a task. It is alternatively called segregation of duties or, in the political realm, separation of powers.

_____ is one of the key concepts of internal control and is the most difficult and sometimes the most costly one to achieve. The term _____ is already well-known in financial accounting systems. Companies in all sizes understand not to combine roles such as receiving checks (payment on account) and approving write-offs, depositing cash and reconciling bank statements, approving time cards and have custody of pay checks, etc.

Chapter 7. Internal Control

a. Separation of duties
b. Salary
c. BMC Software, Inc.
d. 3M Company

32. _____ in business includes the methods and processes used by organizations to manage risks and seize opportunities related to the achievement of their objectives. _____ provides a framework for risk management, which typically involves identifying particular events or circumstances relevant to the organization's objectives (risks and opportunities), assessing them in terms of likelihood and magnitude of impact, determining a response strategy, and monitoring progress. By identifying and proactively addressing risks and opportunities, business enterprises protect and create value for their stakeholders, including owners, employees, customers, regulators, and society overall.
a. AMEX
b. Enterprise risk management
c. AIG
d. ABC Television Network

33. _____ is systematic determination of merit, worth, and significance of something or someone using criteria against a set of standards. _____ often is used to characterize and appraise subjects of interest in a wide range of human enterprises, including the arts, criminal justice, foundations and non-profit organizations, government, health care, and other human services.

Depending on the topic of interest, there are professional groups which look to the quality and rigor of the _____ process.

a. AIG
b. Evaluation
c. ABC Television Network
d. AMEX

34. _____ is activity directed towards the assessing, mitigating (to an acceptable level) and monitoring of risks. In some cases the acceptable risk may be near zero. Risks can come from accidents, natural causes and disasters as well as deliberate attacks from an adversary.
a. Kanban
b. Risk management
c. Trademark
d. FIFO

35. _____, in auditing, is the risk that a company's internal controls are insufficient to mitigate or detect errors or fraud.
a. BNSF Railway
b. BMC Software, Inc.
c. 3M Company
d. Control risk

36. _____ is the realization of an application idea, model, design, specification, standard, algorithm an _____ is a realization of a technical specification or algorithm as a program, software component, or other computer system. Many _____s may exist for a given specification or standard.
a. Implementation
b. ABC Television Network
c. AMEX
d. AIG

37. _____, in auditing, is the risk that the account or section being audited is materially misstated without considering internal controls due to error; _____ does not include an assessment of the risk of material misstatement due to fraud. The assessment of _____ depends on the professional judgement of the auditor, and it is done after assessing the business environment of the entity being audited.

_____ is typically assessed using a scale, with assessments being either low, medium, or high.

a. ABC Television Network
b. Inherent risk
c. AMEX
d. AIG

38. An _____ is the buying of one company by another. An _____ may be friendly or hostile. In the former case, the companies cooperate in negotiations; in the latter case, the takeover target is unwilling to be bought or the target's board has no prior knowledge of the offer. _____ usually refers to a purchase of a smaller firm by a larger one. Sometimes, however, a smaller firm will acquire management control of a larger or longer established company and keep its name for the combined entity. This is known as a reverse takeover.

a. AIG
b. Acquisition
c. ABC Television Network
d. AMEX

39. In a company, _____ is the sum of all financial records of salaries, wages, bonuses and deductions.

A paycheck, is traditionally a paper document issued by an employer to pay an employee for services rendered. While most commonly used in the United States, recently the physical paycheck has been increasingly replaced by electronic direct deposit to bank accounts.

a. Tax expense
b. 3M Company
c. Payroll
d. Total Expense Ratio

40. A _____ is a common type of chart, that represents an algorithm or process, showing the steps as boxes of various kinds, and their order by connecting these with arrows. _____s are used in analyzing, designing, documenting or managing a process or program in various fields.

The first structured method for documenting process flow, the 'flow process chart', was introduced by Frank Gilbreth to members of ASME in 1921 as the presentation e;Process Charts--First Steps in Finding the One Best Waye;.

a. BMC Software, Inc.
b. Flowchart
c. 3M Company
d. BNSF Railway

41. _____ is one of financial audit skill which help an auditor understand the client's business and changes in the business, to identify potential risk areas and to plan other audit procedures.

_____ include comparison of financial information (data in financial statement) with

1. prior periods
2. budgets
3. forecasts
4. similar industries and so on.

It also includes consideration of predictable relationships, such as:

1. gross profit to sales,
2. payroll costs to employees,
3. financial information and non-financial information, for examples the CEO's reports and the industry news.

possible sources of information about the client include:

1. interim financial information
2. Budgets
3. Management accounts
4. Non-Financial information
5. Bank and cash records
6. VAT returns
7. Board minutes
8. Discussion or correspondance with the client at they year-end

a. Assurance service
c. International Federation of Audit Bureaux of Circulations
b. External auditor
d. Analytical procedures

42. _____ are formal records of a business' financial activities.

In British English, including United Kingdom company law, _____ are often referred to as accounts, although the term _____ is also used, particularly by accountants.

_____ provide an overview of a business' financial condition in both short and long term.

a. Statement of retained earnings
c. 3M Company
b. Notes to the financial statements
d. Financial Statements

43. A _____ is an annual report required by the U.S. Securities and Exchange Commission (SEC), that gives a comprehensive summary of a public company's performance. Although similarly named, the annual report on _____ is distinct from the often glossy 'annual report to shareholders', which a company must send to its shareholders when it holds an annual meeting to elect directors (though some companies combine the annual report and the 10-K into one document.) The 10-K includes information such as company history, organizational structure, executive compensation, equity, subsidiaries, and audited financial statements, among other information.
   a. 3M Company
   c. Form 10-Q
   b. Form 8-K
   d. Form 10-K

44. The U.S. _____ is an independent agency of the United States government which holds primary responsibility for enforcing the federal securities laws and regulating the securities industry, the nation's stock and options exchanges, and other electronic securities markets. The SEC was created by section 4 of the Securities Exchange Act of 1934 (now codified as 15 U.S.C. ÂÂ§ 78d and commonly referred to as the 1934 Act.)

   a. 3M Company
   c. Securities and Exchange Commission
   b. BNSF Railway
   d. BMC Software, Inc.

45. The term _____ usually refers to a company that is permitted to offer its registered securities (stock, bonds, etc.) for sale to the general public, typically through a stock exchange, or occasionally a company whose stock is traded over the counter (OTC) via market makers who use non-exchange quotation services.

The term '_____' may also refer to a company owned by the government.

   a. Professional association
   c. MicroStrategy
   b. Public company
   d. Governmental Accounting Standards Board

46. _____, commonly abbreviated as SAS, provide guidance to external auditors on generally accepted auditing standards in regards to auditing an entity and issuing a report. They are usually issued by the certified public accountant authoritative body in the region where the standards apply, such as the American Institute of Certified Public Accountants in the United States.

- _____
- _____ (Taiwan)

   a. GASB 45
   c. Financial Instruments and Exchange Law
   b. RSM International
   d. Statements on Auditing Standards

47. Accounting _____ define the basic standards for representing attestation engagements. Attestation is defined as an engagement in which a practitioner is hired to issue written communication that expresses a conclusion about the reliability of written assertions prepared by a separate party. The American Institute of Certified Public Accountants identified a number of different engagements that fall under the scope of _____, including: examining financial forecasts and projections, examining pro forma financial statements, evaluating internal control, assessing compliance with rules, regulations, and contractual obligations, as well as evaluating management discussions and analysis of financial results.

   a. Audit working paper
   c. Institute of Chartered Accountants of India
   b. Attestation standards
   d. Audit management

Chapter 8. Consideration of Internal Control in an Information Technology Environment 75

1. _____ is a company-wide computer software system used to manage and coordinate all the resources, information, and functions of a business from shared data stores.

An _____ system has a service-oriented architecture with modular hardware and software units or 'services' that communicate on a local area network. The modular design allows a business to add or reconfigure modules (perhaps from different vendors) while preserving data integrity in one shared database that may be centralized or distributed.

a. AIG
b. AMEX
c. ABC Television Network
d. Enterprise resource planning

2. _____, commonly known as e-commerce or eCommerce, consists of the buying and selling of products or services over electronic systems such as the Internet and other computer networks. The amount of trade conducted electronically has grown extraordinarily since the spread of the Internet. A wide variety of commerce is conducted in this way, spurring and drawing on innovations in electronic funds transfer, supply chain management, Internet marketing, online transaction processing, electronic data interchange (EDI), inventory management systems, and automated data collection systems.

a. ABC Television Network
b. Electronic commerce
c. AIG
d. Electronic data interchange

3. The general definition of an _____ is an evaluation of a person, organization, system, process, project or product. _____s are performed to ascertain the validity and reliability of information; also to provide an assessment of a system's internal control. The goal of an _____ is to express an opinion on the person/organization/system (etc) in question, under evaluation based on work done on a test basis.

a. Institute of Chartered Accountants of India
b. Audit regime
c. Assurance service
d. Audit

4. _____ is that part of statistical practice concerned with the selection of individual observations intended to yield some knowledge about a population of concern, especially for the purposes of statistical inference. Each observation measures one or more properties (weight, location, etc.) of an observable entity enumerated to distinguish objects or individuals.

a. Abby Joseph Cohen
b. Arthur Betz Laffer
c. Alan Greenspan
d. Sampling

5. A _____ is a fungible, negotiable instrument representing financial value. they are broadly categorized into debt securities (such as banknotes, bonds and debentures), and equity securities; e.g., common stocks. The company or other entity issuing the _____ is called the issuer.

a. BMC Software, Inc.
b. 3M Company
c. Tracking stock
d. Security

6. _____ is a repository of an organization's electronically stored data. _____s are designed to facilitate reporting and analysis.

This definition of the _____ focuses on data storage.

Chapter 8. Consideration of Internal Control in an Information Technology Environment

a. Data warehouse
b. BMC Software, Inc.
c. 3M Company
d. BNSF Railway

7. A _____ is a commercial building for storage of goods. _____s are used by manufacturers, importers, exporters, wholesalers, transport businesses, customs, etc. They are usually large plain buildings in industrial areas of cities and towns.
a. 3M Company
b. BMC Software, Inc.
c. BNSF Railway
d. Warehouse

8. _____ or audit log is a chronological sequence of audit records, each of which contains evidence directly pertaining to and resulting from the execution of a business process or system function.

Audit records typically result from activities such as transactions or communications by individual people, systems, accounts or other entities.

Webopedia defines an _____ as 'a record showing who has accessed a computer system and what operations he or she has performed during a given period of time.' ()

In telecommunication, the term means a record of both completed and attempted accesses and service, or data forming a logical path linking a sequence of events, used to trace the transactions that have affected the contents of a record.

a. Audit trail
b. AMEX
c. ABC Television Network
d. AIG

9. _____ refers to the structured transmission of data between organizations by electronic means. It is used to transfer electronic documents from one computer system to another (ie) from one trading partner to another trading partner. It is more than mere E-mail; for instance, organizations might replace bills of lading and even checks with appropriate _____ messages.
a. ABC Television Network
b. Electronic data interchange
c. AIG
d. Electronic commerce

10. An _____ invented by esteemed professor Karen Osterheld is the system of records a business keeps to maintain its accounting system. This includes the purchase, sales, and other financial processes of the business. The purpose of an _____ is to accumulate data and provide decision makers (investors, creditors, and managers) with information to make decision While this was previously a paper-based process, most modern businesses now use accounting software such as UBS, MYOB etc.
a. AIG
b. AMEX
c. ABC Television Network
d. Accounting information system

11. An _____ is a mostly hierarchical concept of subordination of entities that collaborate and contribute to serve one common aim.

Organizations are a variant of clustered entities. The structure of an organization is usually set up in many a styles, dependent on their objectives and ambience.

Chapter 8. Consideration of Internal Control in an Information Technology Environment 77

a. ABC Television Network
b. AIG
c. AMEX
d. Organizational structure

12. _____ is evidence obtained during a financial audit and recorded in the audit working papers.

- In the audit engagement acceptance or reappointment stage, _____ is the information that the auditor is to consider for the appointment. For examples, change in the entity control environment, inherent risk and nature of the entity business, and scope of audit work.

- In the audit planning stage, _____ is the information that the auditor is to consider for the most effective and efficient audit approach. For examples, reliability of internal control procedures, and analytical review systems.

- In the control testing stage, _____ is the information that the auditor is to consider for the mix of audit test of control and audit substantive tests.

- In the substantive testing stage, _____ is the information that the auditor is to make sure the appropriation of financial statement assertions. For examples, existence, rights and obligations, occurrence, completeness, valuation, measurement, presentation and disclosure of a particular transaction or account balance.

a. Audit evidence
b. Institute of Chartered Accountants of India
c. Audit
d. ITGCs

13. An _____ is a term used in behavioral economics to describe those types of behaviors that impose costs on a person in the long-run that are not taken into account when making decisions in the present. Classical Economics discourages government from creating legislation that targets internalities, because it is assumed that the consumer takes these personal costs into account when paying for the good that causes the _____. For example, cigarettes should be taxed because of the negative consumption externalities that they impose, such as second-hand smoke, not because the smoker harms him or herself by smoking.
a. Operating budget
b. Authorised capital
c. Inventory turnover ratio
d. Internality

14. In accounting and organizational theory, _____ is defined as a process effected by an organization's structure, work and authority flows, people and management information systems, designed to help the organization accomplish specific goals or objectives. It is a means by which an organization's resources are directed, monitored, and measured. It plays an important role in preventing and detecting fraud and protecting the organization's resources, both physical (e.g., machinery and property) and intangible (e.g., reputation or intellectual property such as trademarks.)
a. Auditor independence
b. Audit committee
c. Audit risk
d. Internal control

15. _____ is a profession and activity involved in helping organisations achieve their stated objectives. It does this by using a systematic methodology for analyzing business processes, procedures and activities with the goal of highlighting organizational problems and recommending solutions. Professionals called internal auditors are employed by organizations to perform the _____ activity.
a. Information audit
b. Assurance service
c. ITGCs
d. Internal auditing

78 *Chapter 8. Consideration of Internal Control in an Information Technology Environment*

16. In mathematics _____s are numbers or other things that get multiplied. In particular, see:

- Factorization, the decomposition of an object into a product of other objects
- Integer factorization, the process of breaking down a composite number into smaller non-trivial divisors
- A coefficient
- A divisor of a particular number, or of an element of a monoid
- A von Neumann algebra with a trivial center

In statistics

- _____ analysis is the study of how _____s or certain variables affect variables.

In technology:

- Human _____s, a profession that focuses on how people interact with products, tools, or procedures
- 'Functionality, Application domain, Conditions, Technology, Objects and Responsibility;', In object-oriented programming

In computer science and information technology:

- Authentication _____, a piece of information used to verify a person's identity for security purposes
- _____, a Unix command for numbers factorization
- _____ (programming language), an experimental Forth-like programming language

In television:

- The O'Reilly _____, an American talk show hosted by Bill O'Reilly on Fox News.
- The Krypton _____, a British game show hosted by Gordon Burns, formally on ITV. Also had an American version.

    a. Merck ' Co., Inc.
    c. The Goodyear Tire ' Rubber Company
    b. Valuation
    d. Factor

17. _____ is a concept that denotes the precise probability of specific eventualities. Technically, the notion of _____ is independent from the notion of value and, as such, eventualities may have both beneficial and adverse consequences. However, in general usage the convention is to focus only on potential negative impact to some characteristic of value that may arise from a future event.
    a. Risk adjusted return on capital
    c. Risk
    b. Discount factor
    d. Discounting

18. _____ is an agreement, usually secretive, which occurs between two or more persons to deceive, mislead, or defraud others of their legal rights, or to obtain an objective forbidden by law typically involving fraud or gaining an unfair advantage. It is an agreement among firms to divide the market, set prices kickbacks, or misrepresenting the independence of the relationship between the colluding parties.' All acts effected by _____ are considered void.

Chapter 8. Consideration of Internal Control in an Information Technology Environment 79

a. Limited partnership
c. Collusion
b. Debt
d. Bond market

19. In economics, _____ or _____ goods or real _____ refers to factors of production used to create goods or services that are not themselves significantly consumed (though they may depreciate) in the production process. _____ goods may be acquired with money or financial _____. In finance and accounting, _____ generally refers to financial wealth, especially that used to start or maintain a business.
   a. Vyborg Appeal
   c. Screening
   b. Capital
   d. Disclosure

20. _____s are cash, evidence of an ownership interest in an entity or deliver, cash or another _____.

   _____s can be categorized by form depending on whether they are cash instruments or derivative instruments:

   - Cash instruments are _____s whose value is determined directly by markets. They can be divided into securities, which are readily transferable, and other cash instruments such as loans and deposits, where both borrower and lender have to agree on a transfer.
   - Derivative instruments are _____s which derive their value from the value and characteristics of one or more underlying assets. They can be divided into exchange-traded derivatives and over-the-counter (OTC) derivatives.

Alternatively, _____s can be categorized by 'asset class' depending on whether they are equity based (reflecting ownership of the issuing entity) or debt based (reflecting a loan the investor has made to the issuing entity.) If it is debt, it can be further categorised into short term (less than one year) or long term.

Foreign Exchange instruments and transactions are neither debt nor equity based and belong in their own category.

   a. Mark-to-market
   c. Market price
   b. Financial instruments
   d. Financial instrument

21. _____ are cash, evidence of an ownership interest in an entity, or a contractual right to receive, or deliver, cash or another financial instrument.

   _____ can be categorized by form depending on whether they are cash instruments or derivative instruments:

   - Cash instruments are _____ whose value is determined directly by markets. They can be divided into securities, which are readily transferable, and other cash instruments such as loans and deposits, where both borrower and lender have to agree on a transfer.
   - Derivative instruments are _____ which derive their value from the value and characteristics of one or more underlying assets. They can be divided into exchange-traded derivatives and over-the-counter (OTC) derivatives.

Alternatively, _____ can be categorized by 'asset class' depending on whether they are equity based (reflecting ownership of the issuing entity) or debt based (reflecting a loan the investor has made to the issuing entity.) If it is debt, it can be further categorised into short term (less than one year) or long term.

Foreign Exchange instruments and transactions are neither debt nor equity based and belong in their own category.

a. Financial instruments
b. Spot rate
c. Market liquidity
d. Transfer agent

22. A _____ is a common type of chart, that represents an algorithm or process, showing the steps as boxes of various kinds, and their order by connecting these with arrows. _____s are used in analyzing, designing, documenting or managing a process or program in various fields.

The first structured method for documenting process flow, the 'flow process chart', was introduced by Frank Gilbreth to members of ASME in 1921 as the presentation e;Process Charts--First Steps in Finding the One Best Waye;.

a. 3M Company
b. BNSF Railway
c. BMC Software, Inc.
d. Flowchart

23. _____ is a file or account that contains money that a person or company owes to suppliers, but has not paid yet (a form of debt.) When you receive an invoice you add it to the file, and then you remove it when you pay. Thus, the A/P is a form of credit that suppliers offer to their purchasers by allowing them to pay for a product or service after it has already been received.

a. Earnings before interest, taxes, depreciation and amortization
b. Accrual
c. Accounts payable
d. Accounts receivable

24. _____, in auditing, is the risk that a company's internal controls are insufficient to mitigate or detect errors or fraud.
a. BMC Software, Inc.
b. BNSF Railway
c. 3M Company
d. Control risk

25. _____ is a term that is commonly used in relation to the audit of the financial statements of an entity. (.
a. Audit risk
b. Audit working paper
c. Auditor independence
d. Engagement Letter

26. _____, in auditing, is the risk that the auditing procedures used will not find a material misstatement in the financial statements of the company being audited. .
a. BNSF Railway
b. 3M Company
c. Detection risk
d. BMC Software, Inc.

Chapter 8. Consideration of Internal Control in an Information Technology Environment

27. _____ is subcontracting a process, such as product design or manufacturing, to a third-party company. The decision to outsource is often made in the interest of lowering cost or making better use of time and energy costs, redirecting or conserving energy directed at the competencies of a particular business, or to make more efficient use of land, labor, capital, (information) technology and resources. _____ became part of the business lexicon during the 1980s.

a. US Airways, Inc.
b. Economic Growth and Tax Relief Reconciliation Act of 2001
c. USA Today
d. Outsourcing

28. _____ is a process where a business physically counts its entire inventory. A _____ may be mandated by financial accounting rules or the tax regulations to place an accurate value on the inventory, or the business may need to count inventory so component parts or raw materials can be restocked. Businesses may use several different tactics to minimize the disruption caused by _____.

a. BNSF Railway
b. 3M Company
c. Physical inventory
d. BMC Software, Inc.

29. In accounting, the _____ is a worksheet listing the balance at a certain date, of each ledger account in two columns, namely debit and credit. Under the double-entry system, in any transaction the total of any debits must equal the total of any credits, so in a _____ the total of the debit side should always be equal to the total of the credit side. The _____ thus serves as a tool to detect errors, which can result in the totals not being equal.

a. Depreciation
b. Trial balance
c. Current asset
d. Bottom line

30. _____ is that which is owed; usually referencing assets owed, but the term can also cover moral obligations and other interactions not requiring money. In the case of assets, _____ is a means of using future purchasing power in the present before a summation has been earned. Some companies and corporations use _____ as a part of their overall corporate finance strategy.

a. Lender
b. Debt
c. Debenture
d. Loan

31. A _____ is a type of debt Like all debt instruments, a _____ entails the redistribution of financial assets over time, between the lender and the borrower.

a. Loan to value
b. Debenture
c. Loan
d. Lender

Chapter 9. Audit Sampling

1. _____ is that part of statistical practice concerned with the selection of individual observations intended to yield some knowledge about a population of concern, especially for the purposes of statistical inference. Each observation measures one or more properties (weight, location, etc.) of an observable entity enumerated to distinguish objects or individuals.
   - a. Abby Joseph Cohen
   - b. Arthur Betz Laffer
   - c. Sampling
   - d. Alan Greenspan

2. An _____ is a practitioner of accountancy, which is the measurement, disclosure or provision of assurance about financial information that helps managers, investors, tax authorities and other decision makers make resource allocation decisions.

   The word '_____' is derived from the French 'Compter' which took its origin from the Latin 'Computare'. The word was formerly written in English as 'Accomptant', but in process of time the word, which was always pronounced by dropping the 'p', became gradually changed both in pronunciation and in orthography to its present form.

   - a. Accountant
   - b. AIG
   - c. AMEX
   - d. ABC Television Network

3. The _____ is the national, professional association of CPAs in the United States, with more than 330,000 members, including CPAs in business and industry, public practice, government, and education; student affiliates; and international associates. It sets ethical standards for the profession and U.S. auditing standards for audits of private companies; federal, state and local governments; and non-profit organizations.

   Approximately 40% of its members are engaged in the practice of public accounting, in areas such as auditing, accounting, taxation, general business consulting, business valuation, personal financial planning and business technology.

   - a. ABC Television Network
   - b. Other postemployment benefits
   - c. American Institute of Certified Public Accountants
   - d. AIG

4. _____ is the statutory title of qualified accountants in the United States who have passed the Uniform _____ Examination and have met additional state education and experience requirements for certification as a _____. Individuals who have passed the Exam but have not either accomplished the required on-the-job experience or have previously met it but in the meantime have lapsed their continuing professional education are, in many states, permitted the designation '_____ Inactive' or an equivalent phrase. In most U.S. states, only _____s who are licensed are able to provide to the public attestation (including auditing) opinions on financial statements.
   - a. Chartered Certified Accountant
   - b. Chartered Accountant
   - c. Certified General Accountant
   - d. Certified Public Accountant

5. _____ is a concept that denotes the precise probability of specific eventualities. Technically, the notion of _____ is independent from the notion of value and, as such, eventualities may have both beneficial and adverse consequences. However, in general usage the convention is to focus only on potential negative impact to some characteristic of value that may arise from a future event.
   - a. Risk adjusted return on capital
   - b. Discounting
   - c. Discount factor
   - d. Risk

Chapter 9. Audit Sampling

6. A _____ is a computer application that simulates a paper worksheet. It displays multiple cells that together make up a grid consisting of rows and columns, each cell containing either alphanumeric text or numeric values. A _____ cell may alternatively contain a formula that defines how the contents of that cell is to be calculated from the contents of any other cell (or combination of cells) each time any cell is updated.

    a. Linear regression
    c. Merck ' Co., Inc.
    b. Spreadsheet
    d. Mutual fund

7. The general definition of an _____ is an evaluation of a person, organization, system, process, project or product. _____s are performed to ascertain the validity and reliability of information; also to provide an assessment of a system's internal control. The goal of an _____ is to express an opinion on the person/organization/system (etc) in question, under evaluation based on work done on a test basis.

    a. Audit
    c. Institute of Chartered Accountants of India
    b. Assurance service
    d. Audit regime

8. A _____ is a bond which is worth a certain monetary value and which may only be spent for specific reasons or on specific goods. Examples include -- but are not limited to -- housing, travel and food _____s. The term _____ is also a synonym for receipt, and is often used to refer to receipts used as evidence of, for example, the declaration that a service has been performed or that an expenditure has been made.

    a. Source document
    c. 3M Company
    b. BMC Software, Inc.
    d. Voucher

9. _____ is the calculated approximation of a result which is usable even if input data may be incomplete or uncertain.

In statistics, see _____ theory, estimator.

In mathematics, approximation or _____ typically means finding upper or lower bounds of a quantity that cannot readily be computed precisely and is also an educated guess .

    a. AIG
    c. Estimation
    b. ABC Television Network
    d. AMEX

10. _____ is systematic determination of merit, worth, and significance of something or someone using criteria against a set of standards. _____ often is used to characterize and appraise subjects of interest in a wide range of human enterprises, including the arts, criminal justice, foundations and non-profit organizations, government, health care, and other human services.

Depending on the topic of interest, there are professional groups which look to the quality and rigor of the _____ process.

    a. AMEX
    c. AIG
    b. ABC Television Network
    d. Evaluation

11. _____, in auditing, is the risk that a company's internal controls are insufficient to mitigate or detect errors or fraud.

a. Control risk
c. BNSF Railway
b. 3M Company
d. BMC Software, Inc.

12. In probability theory and statistics, the _____ (or expectation value or mean and for continuous random variables with a density function it is the probability density -weighted integral of the possible values.

The term '_____' can be misleading.

a. AMEX
c. ABC Television Network
b. AIG
d. Expected value

13. In probability theory and statistics, _____ is a measure of the variability or dispersion of a population, a data set, or a probability distribution. A low _____ indicates that the data points tend to be very close to the same value (the mean), while high _____ indicates that the data are 'spread out' over a large range of values.

For example, the average height for adult men in the United States is about 70 inches, with a _____ of around 3 inches.

a. Standard deviation
c. Probability distribution
b. Variance
d. Moving average

14. In accounting, _____ or carrying value is the value of an asset according to its balance sheet account balance. For assets, the value is based on the original cost of the asset less any depreciation, amortization or impairment costs made against the asset. Traditionally, a company's _____ is its total assets minus intangible assets and liabilities.

a. Depreciation
c. Matching principle
b. Generally accepted accounting principles
d. Book value

15. In mathematics _____s are numbers or other things that get multiplied. In particular, see:

- Factorization, the decomposition of an object into a product of other objects
- Integer factorization, the process of breaking down a composite number into smaller non-trivial divisors
- A coefficient
- A divisor of a particular number, or of an element of a monoid
- A von Neumann algebra with a trivial center

In statistics

- _____ analysis is the study of how _____s or certain variables affect variables.

In technology:

- Human _____s, a profession that focuses on how people interact with products, tools, or procedures
- 'Functionality, Application domain, Conditions, Technology, Objects and Responsibility;', In object-oriented programming

Chapter 9. Audit Sampling

In computer science and information technology:

- Authentication _____, a piece of information used to verify a person's identity for security purposes
- _____, a Unix command for numbers factorization
- _____ (programming language), an experimental Forth-like programming language

In television:

- The O'Reilly _____, an American talk show hosted by Bill O'Reilly on Fox News.
- The Krypton _____, a British game show hosted by Gordon Burns, formally on ITV. Also had an American version.

a. Merck ' Co., Inc.
b. Factor
c. Valuation
d. The Goodyear Tire ' Rubber Company

16. _____ is a term that is commonly used in relation to the audit of the financial statements of an entity. (.
a. Auditor independence
b. Audit risk
c. Audit working paper
d. Engagement Letter

17. _____, in auditing, is the risk that the auditing procedures used will not find a material misstatement in the financial statements of the company being audited. .
a. BMC Software, Inc.
b. 3M Company
c. BNSF Railway
d. Detection risk

18. _____, in auditing, is the risk that the account or section being audited is materially misstated without considering internal controls due to error; _____ does not include an assessment of the risk of material misstatement due to fraud. The assessment of _____ depends on the professional judgement of the auditor, and it is done after assessing the business environment of the entity being audited.

_____ is typically assessed using a scale, with assessments being either low, medium, or high.

a. AMEX
b. AIG
c. Inherent risk
d. ABC Television Network

Chapter 10. Cash and Financial Investments

1. _____ are the most liquid assets found within the asset portion of a company's balance sheet. Cash equivalents are assets that are readily convertible into cash, such as money market holdings, short-term government bonds or Treasury bills, marketable securities and commercial paper. _____ are distinguished from other investments through their short-term existence; they mature within 3 months whereas short-term investments are 12 months or less, and long-term investments are any investments that mature in excess of 12 months.

   a. Debtor
   b. Cash and cash equivalents
   c. Par value
   d. Payback period

2. _____, in auditing, is the risk that the account or section being audited is materially misstated without considering internal controls due to error; _____ does not include an assessment of the risk of material misstatement due to fraud. The assessment of _____ depends on the professional judgement of the auditor, and it is done after assessing the business environment of the entity being audited.

   _____ is typically assessed using a scale, with assessments being either low, medium, or high.

   a. ABC Television Network
   b. AMEX
   c. AIG
   d. Inherent risk

3. An _____ is a term used in behavioral economics to describe those types of behaviors that impose costs on a person in the long-run that are not taken into account when making decisions in the present. Classical Economics discourages government from creating legislation that targets internalities, because it is assumed that the consumer takes these personal costs into account when paying for the good that causes the _____. For example, cigarettes should be taxed because of the negative consumption externalities that they impose, such as second-hand smoke, not because the smoker harms him or herself by smoking.

   a. Operating budget
   b. Authorised capital
   c. Inventory turnover ratio
   d. Internality

4. In accounting and organizational theory, _____ is defined as a process effected by an organization's structure, work and authority flows, people and management information systems, designed to help the organization accomplish specific goals or objectives. It is a means by which an organization's resources are directed, monitored, and measured. It plays an important role in preventing and detecting fraud and protecting the organization's resources, both physical (e.g., machinery and property) and intangible (e.g., reputation or intellectual property such as trademarks.)

   a. Audit risk
   b. Auditor independence
   c. Audit committee
   d. Internal control

5. _____ is a method of evaluating an asset's worth when held in inventory, in the field of accounting. _____ is part of the Generally Accepted Accounting Principles that apply to valuing inventory, so as to not overstate or understate the value of inventory goods. Net realisable value is generally equal to the selling price of the inventory goods less the selling costs (completion and disposal).

   a. 3M Company
   b. Revenue recognition
   c. Net realizable value
   d. BMC Software, Inc.

6. In finance, _____ is the process of estimating the potential market value of a financial asset or liability. They can be done on assets (for example, investments in marketable securities such as stocks, options, business enterprises, or intangible assets such as patents and trademarks) or on liabilities (e.g., Bonds issued by a company.) A _____ is required in many contexts including investment analysis, capital budgeting, merger and acquisition transactions, financial reporting, taxable events to determine the proper tax liability, and in litigation.

Chapter 10. Cash and Financial Investments

a. Valuation
c. Daybook
b. Vyborg Appeal
d. Disclosure

7. _____ is a file or account that contains money that a person or company owes to suppliers, but has not paid yet (a form of debt.) When you receive an invoice you add it to the file, and then you remove it when you pay. Thus, the A/P is a form of credit that suppliers offer to their purchasers by allowing them to pay for a product or service after it has already been received.

a. Accounts receivable
b. Earnings before interest, taxes, depreciation and amortization
c. Accrual
d. Accounts payable

8. The general definition of an _____ is an evaluation of a person, organization, system, process, project or product. _____s are performed to ascertain the validity and reliability of information; also to provide an assessment of a system's internal control. The goal of an _____ is to express an opinion on the person/organization/system (etc) in question, under evaluation based on work done on a test basis.

a. Audit
b. Institute of Chartered Accountants of India
c. Audit regime
d. Assurance service

9. _____, in auditing, is the risk that a company's internal controls are insufficient to mitigate or detect errors or fraud.

a. 3M Company
b. Control risk
c. BNSF Railway
d. BMC Software, Inc.

10. _____ means the giving out of information, either voluntarily or to be in compliance with legal regulations or workplace rules.

- In Computer security, full _____ means disclosing full information about vulnerabilities.
- In computing, _____ widget
- Journalism, full _____ refers to disclosing the interests of the writer which may bear on the subject being written about, for example, if the writer has worked with an interview subject in the past.

- In law:
    - The law of England and Wales, _____ refers to a process that may form part of legal proceedings, whereby parties inform to other parties the existence of any relevant documents that are, or have been, in their control. This compares with the process known as discovery in the course of legal proceedings in the United States.
    - In U.S. civil procedure (litigation rules for civil cases), _____ is a stage prior to trial. In civil cases, each party must disclose to the opposing party the following: names of witnesses which it may use to support its side, copies of documents (or mere description of these documents) in its control which it may use to support its side, computation of damages claimed, and certain insurance information. _____ is related to, but technically prior to, the discovery stage.
    - In Company law (known as 'corporate law' in the United States), _____ refers to giving out information about public or limited companies or their officers, which might be kept secret if the company was a private company or a partnership.

- In real property transactions, _____ refers to providing to a buyer information known to the seller or broker/agent concerning the condition or other aspects of real property that would affect the property's value or desirability. These rules regarding what information must be disclosed, and whether the information must be disclosed even if a buyer does not ask, vary from one jurisdiction to the next.

a. Controlled Foreign Corporations
b. Trailing
c. Disclosure
d. Tax harmonisation

11. _____ is a concept that denotes the precise probability of specific eventualities. Technically, the notion of _____ is independent from the notion of value and, as such, eventualities may have both beneficial and adverse consequences. However, in general usage the convention is to focus only on potential negative impact to some characteristic of value that may arise from a future event.

a. Discount factor
b. Risk adjusted return on capital
c. Discounting
d. Risk

12. _____ is the concept of having more than one person required to complete a task. It is alternatively called segregation of duties or, in the political realm, separation of powers.

_____ is one of the key concepts of internal control and is the most difficult and sometimes the most costly one to achieve. The term _____ is already well-known in financial accounting systems. Companies in all sizes understand not to combine roles such as receiving checks (payment on account) and approving write-offs, depositing cash and reconciling bank statements, approving time cards and have custody of pay checks, etc.

a. Salary
b. Separation of duties
c. BMC Software, Inc.
d. 3M Company

13. _____ is an organization's process of defining its strategy and making decisions on allocating its resources to pursue this strategy, including its capital and people. Various business analysis techniques can be used in _____, including SWOT analysis (Strengths, Weaknesses, Opportunities, and Threats) and PEST analysis (Political, Economic, Social, and Technological analysis) or STEER analysis involving Socio-cultural, Technological, Economic, Ecological, and Regulatory factors and EPISTEL (Environment, Political, Informatic, Social, Technological, Economic and Legal)

_____ is the formal consideration of an organization's future course. All _____ deals with at least one of three key questions:

1. 'What do we do?'
2. 'For whom do we do it?'
3. 'How do we excel?'

In business _____, the third question is better phrased 'How can we beat or avoid competition?'. (Bradford and Duncan, page 1.)

a. 3M Company
b. BMC Software, Inc.
c. Strategic planning
d. BNSF Railway

14. A _____ is the pinnacle activity involved in selling products or services in return for money or other compensation. It is an act of completion of a commercial activity.

A _____ is completed by the seller, the owner of the goods.

a. Maturity
b. Sale
c. Tertiary sector of economy
d. High yield stock

15. A _____, also client, buyer or purchaser is the buyer or user of the paid products of an individual or organization, mostly called the supplier or seller. This is typically through purchasing or renting goods or services.
a. BNSF Railway
b. BMC Software, Inc.
c. 3M Company
d. Customer

16. _____ refers to the structured transmission of data between organizations by electronic means. It is used to transfer electronic documents from one computer system to another (ie) from one trading partner to another trading partner. It is more than mere E-mail; for instance, organizations might replace bills of lading and even checks with appropriate _____ messages.
a. Electronic commerce
b. ABC Television Network
c. AIG
d. Electronic data interchange

17. _____ refers to the computer-based systems used to perform financial transactions electronically.

The term is used for a number of different concepts:

- Cardholder-initiated transactions, where a cardholder makes use of a payment card
- Direct deposit payroll payments for a business to its employees, possibly via a payroll services company
- Direct debit payments from customer to business, where the transaction is initiated by the business with customer permission
- Electronic bill payment in online banking, which may be delivered by _____ or paper check
- Transactions involving stored value of electronic money, possibly in a private currency
- Wire transfer via an international banking network (generally carries a higher fee)
- Electronic Benefit Transfer

electronic funds transferPOS (short for _____ at Point of Sale) is an Australian and New Zealand electronic processing system for credit cards, debit cards and charge cards.

European banks and card companies also sometimes reference 'electronic funds transferPOS' as the system used for processing card transactions through terminals on points of sale, though the system is not the trademarked Australian/New Zealand variant.

Credit cards

_____ may be initiated by a cardholder when a payment card such as a credit card or debit card is used.

a. Electronic funds transfer
b. AMEX
c. ABC Television Network
d. AIG

18. A _____ is a deposit account held at a bank or other financial institution, for the purpose of securely and quickly providing frequent access to funds on demand, through a variety of different channels. Because money is available on demand these accounts are also referred to as demand accounts or demand deposit accounts.

They are meant neither for the purpose of earning interest nor for the purpose of savings, but for convenience of the business or personal client; hence they tend not to bear interest.

a. Transactional account
b. Reserve requirement
c. Prime rate
d. Variable rate mortgage

19. A _____ is a bond which is worth a certain monetary value and which may only be spent for specific reasons or on specific goods. Examples include -- but are not limited to -- housing, travel and food _____s. The term _____ is also a synonym for receipt, and is often used to refer to receipts used as evidence of, for example, the declaration that a service has been performed or that an expenditure has been made.

a. Voucher
b. 3M Company
c. Source document
d. BMC Software, Inc.

20. An account statement or a _____ is a summary of all financial transactions occurring over a given period of time on a deposit account, a credit card, or any other type of account offered by a financial institution.

Chapter 10. Cash and Financial Investments

_____s are typically printed on one or several pieces of paper and either mailed directly to the account holder's address, or kept at the financial institution's local branch for pick-up. Certain ATMs offer the possibility to print, at any time, a condensed version of a _____.

a. BMC Software, Inc.
b. Bank statement
c. BNSF Railway
d. 3M Company

21. _____ is often a small amount of discretionary funds in the form of cash used for expenditures where it is not sensible to make the disbursement by check, because of the inconvenience and costs of writing, signing and then cashing the check.

The most common way of accounting expenditures is to use the imprest system. The initial fund would be created by issuing a check for the desired amount.

a. Petty cash
b. Remittance advice
c. Fixed asset
d. Minority interest

22. _____ refers to a business or organization attempting to acquire goods or services to accomplish the goals of the enterprise. Though there are several organizations that attempt to set standards in the _____ process, processes can vary greatly between organizations. Typically the word e;_____e; is not used interchangeably with the word e;procuremente;, since procurement typically includes Expediting, Supplier Quality, and Traffic and Logistics (T'L) in addition to _____.

a. Consignor
b. Supply chain
c. Free port
d. Purchasing

23. A _____ is a common type of chart, that represents an algorithm or process, showing the steps as boxes of various kinds, and their order by connecting these with arrows. _____s are used in analyzing, designing, documenting or managing a process or program in various fields.

The first structured method for documenting process flow, the 'flow process chart', was introduced by Frank Gilbreth to members of ASME in 1921 as the presentation e;Process Charts--First Steps in Finding the One Best Waye;.

a. BMC Software, Inc.
b. 3M Company
c. BNSF Railway
d. Flowchart

24. The _____ of 1977 (15 U.S.C. ÂÂ§ÂÂ§ 78dd-1, et seq.) is a United States federal law known primarily for two of its main provisions, one that addresses accounting transparency requirements under the Securities Exchange Act of 1934 and another concerning bribery of foreign officials.

a. Lease
b. Pre-emption right
c. Foreign Corrupt Practices Act
d. Competition law

25. _____ is the realization of an application idea, model, design, specification, standard, algorithm an _____ is a realization of a technical specification or algorithm as a program, software component, or other computer system. Many _____s may exist for a given specification or standard.

a. AIG
b. AMEX
c. ABC Television Network
d. Implementation

26. The U.S. _____ is an independent agency of the United States government which holds primary responsibility for enforcing the federal securities laws and regulating the securities industry, the nation's stock and options exchanges, and other electronic securities markets. The SEC was created by section 4 of the Securities Exchange Act of 1934 (now codified as 15 U.S.C. ÂÂ§ 78d and commonly referred to as the 1934 Act.)
a. Securities and Exchange Commission
b. BNSF Railway
c. 3M Company
d. BMC Software, Inc.

27. In the global money market, _____ is an unsecured promissory note with a fixed maturity of one to 270 days. _____ is a money-market security issued (sold) by large banks and corporations to get money to meet short term debt obligations (for example, payroll), and is only backed by an issuing bank or corporation's promise to pay the face amount on the maturity date specified on the note. Since it is not backed by collateral, only firms with excellent credit ratings from a recognized rating agency will be able to sell their _____ at a reasonable price.
a. Flow-through entity
b. Gross profit margin
c. Controlling interest
d. Commercial paper

28. A _____ is the transfer of an interest in property (or the equivalent in law - a charge) to a lender as a security for a debt - usually a loan of money. While a _____ in itself is not a debt, it is the lender's security for a debt. It is a transfer of an interest in land (or the equivalent) from the owner to the _____ lender, on the condition that this interest will be returned to the owner when the terms of the _____ have been satisfied or performed.
a. 3M Company
b. BNSF Railway
c. Mortgage
d. BMC Software, Inc.

29. _____, in law and economics, is a form of risk management primarily used to hedge against the risk of a contingent loss. _____ is defined as the equitable transfer of the risk of a loss, from one entity to another, in exchange for a premium, and can be thought of as a guaranteed small loss to prevent a large, possibly devastating loss. An insurer is a company selling the _____; an insured is the person or entity buying the _____.
a. AMEX
b. AIG
c. ABC Television Network
d. Insurance

30. A _____ is the transfer of wealth from one party (such as a person or company) to another. A _____ is usually made in exchange for the provision of goods, services or both, or to fulfill a legal obligation.

The simplest and oldest form of _____ is barter, the exchange of one good or service for another.

a. Payee
b. 3M Company
c. BMC Software, Inc.
d. Payment

31. A _____ is a fungible, negotiable instrument representing financial value. they are broadly categorized into debt securities (such as banknotes, bonds and debentures), and equity securities; e.g., common stocks. The company or other entity issuing the _____ is called the issuer.
a. Tracking stock
b. 3M Company
c. BMC Software, Inc.
d. Security

Chapter 10. Cash and Financial Investments

32. _____ are payments made by a corporation to its shareholder members. It is the portion of corporate profits paid out to stockholders. When a corporation earns a profit or surplus, that money can be put to two uses: it can either be re-invested in the business (called retained earnings), or it can be paid to the shareholders as a dividend.

   a. Dividend yield
   b. Dividend payout ratio
   c. Dividends
   d. Dividend stripping

33. Book Value = Original Cost - _____

Book value at the end of year becomes book value at the beginning of next year. The asset is depreciated until the book value equals scrap value.

If the vehicle were to be sold and the sales price exceeded the depreciated value (net book value) then the excess would be considered a gain and subject to depreciation recapture.

   a. AIG
   b. AMEX
   c. ABC Television Network
   d. Accumulated depreciation

34. _____ is a term used in accounting, economics and finance to spread the cost of an asset over the span of several years.

In simple words we can say that _____ is the reduction in the value of an asset due to usage, passage of time, wear and tear, technological outdating or obsolescence, depletion, inadequacy, rot, rust, decay or other such factors.

In accounting, _____ is a term used to describe any method of attributing the historical or purchase cost of an asset across its useful life, roughly corresponding to normal wear and tear.

   a. Net profit
   b. General ledger
   c. Current asset
   d. Depreciation

35. _____s are cash, evidence of an ownership interest in an entity or deliver, cash or another _____.

_____s can be categorized by form depending on whether they are cash instruments or derivative instruments:

- Cash instruments are _____s whose value is determined directly by markets. They can be divided into securities, which are readily transferable, and other cash instruments such as loans and deposits, where both borrower and lender have to agree on a transfer.
- Derivative instruments are _____s which derive their value from the value and characteristics of one or more underlying assets. They can be divided into exchange-traded derivatives and over-the-counter (OTC) derivatives.

Alternatively, _____s can be categorized by 'asset class' depending on whether they are equity based (reflecting ownership of the issuing entity) or debt based (reflecting a loan the investor has made to the issuing entity.) If it is debt, it can be further categorised into short term (less than one year) or long term.

Chapter 10. Cash and Financial Investments

Foreign Exchange instruments and transactions are neither debt nor equity based and belong in their own category.

a. Market price
b. Financial instruments
c. Mark-to-market
d. Financial instrument

36. _____ are cash, evidence of an ownership interest in an entity, or a contractual right to receive, or deliver, cash or another financial instrument.

_____ can be categorized by form depending on whether they are cash instruments or derivative instruments:

- Cash instruments are _____ whose value is determined directly by markets. They can be divided into securities, which are readily transferable, and other cash instruments such as loans and deposits, where both borrower and lender have to agree on a transfer.
- Derivative instruments are _____ which derive their value from the value and characteristics of one or more underlying assets. They can be divided into exchange-traded derivatives and over-the-counter (OTC) derivatives.

Alternatively, _____ can be categorized by 'asset class' depending on whether they are equity based (reflecting ownership of the issuing entity) or debt based (reflecting a loan the investor has made to the issuing entity.) If it is debt, it can be further categorised into short term (less than one year) or long term.

Foreign Exchange instruments and transactions are neither debt nor equity based and belong in their own category.

a. Spot rate
b. Transfer agent
c. Financial instruments
d. Market liquidity

37. _____ is a form of corporation equity ownership represented in the securities. It is a stock whose dividends are based on market fluctuations. It is dangerous in comparison to preferred shares and some other investment options, in that in the event of bankruptcy, _____ investors receive their funds after preferred stock holders, bondholders, creditors, etc. On the other hand, common shares on average perform better than preferred shares or bonds over time.

a. Growth investing
b. Stock split
c. 3M Company
d. Common stock

38. _____ is that which is owed; usually referencing assets owed, but the term can also cover moral obligations and other interactions not requiring money. In the case of assets, _____ is a means of using future purchasing power in the present before a summation has been earned. Some companies and corporations use _____ as a part of their overall corporate finance strategy.

a. Debenture
b. Loan
c. Lender
d. Debt

Chapter 10. Cash and Financial Investments

39. _____ in accounting is the process of treating equity investments, usually 20-50%, in associate companies. The investor keeps such equities as an asset. Proportional share of associate company's net income increases the investment, and proportional payment of dividends decreases it.
   a. AIG
   b. Equity method
   c. Out-of-pocket
   d. ABC Television Network

40. _____ is that part of statistical practice concerned with the selection of individual observations intended to yield some knowledge about a population of concern, especially for the purposes of statistical inference. Each observation measures one or more properties (weight, location, etc.) of an observable entity enumerated to distinguish objects or individuals.
   a. Alan Greenspan
   b. Abby Joseph Cohen
   c. Arthur Betz Laffer
   d. Sampling

Chapter 11. Accounts Receivable, Notes Receivable, and Revenue

1. _____ is one of a series of accounting transactions dealing with the billing of customers who owe money to a person, company or organization for goods and services that have been provided to the customer. In most business entities this is typically done by generating an invoice and mailing or electronically delivering it to the customer, who in turn must pay it within an established timeframe called credit or payment terms.

An example of a common payment term is Net 30, meaning payment is due in the amount of the invoice 30 days from the date of invoice.

   a. Accrued revenue
   b. Adjusting entries
   c. Accrual
   d. Accounts receivable

2. The _____ of 1977 (15 U.S.C. §§ 78dd-1, et seq.) is a United States federal law known primarily for two of its main provisions, one that addresses accounting transparency requirements under the Securities Exchange Act of 1934 and another concerning bribery of foreign officials.
   a. Lease
   b. Competition law
   c. Pre-emption right
   d. Foreign Corrupt Practices Act

3. _____, in auditing, is the risk that the account or section being audited is materially misstated without considering internal controls due to error; _____ does not include an assessment of the risk of material misstatement due to fraud. The assessment of _____ depends on the professional judgement of the auditor, and it is done after assessing the business environment of the entity being audited.

_____ is typically assessed using a scale, with assessments being either low, medium, or high.

   a. AMEX
   b. AIG
   c. ABC Television Network
   d. Inherent risk

4. _____ represents claims for which formal instruments of credit are issued as evidence of debt, such as a promissory note. The credit instrument normally requires the debtor to pay interest and extends for time periods of 60-90 days or longer.
   a. Restricted stock
   b. Notes receivable
   c. Moving average
   d. Public offering

5. In finance, _____ is the process of estimating the potential market value of a financial asset or liability. They can be done on assets (for example, investments in marketable securities such as stocks, options, business enterprises, or intangible assets such as patents and trademarks) or on liabilities (e.g., Bonds issued by a company.) A _____ is required in many contexts including investment analysis, capital budgeting, merger and acquisition transactions, financial reporting, taxable events to determine the proper tax liability, and in litigation.
   a. Vyborg Appeal
   b. Daybook
   c. Valuation
   d. Disclosure

6. _____ is a file or account that contains money that a person or company owes to suppliers, but has not paid yet (a form of debt.) When you receive an invoice you add it to the file, and then you remove it when you pay. Thus, the A/P is a form of credit that suppliers offer to their purchasers by allowing them to pay for a product or service after it has already been received.

Chapter 11. Accounts Receivable, Notes Receivable, and Revenue 97

a. Earnings before interest, taxes, depreciation and amortization

b. Accounts receivable

c. Accrual

d. Accounts payable

7. _____ means the giving out of information, either voluntarily or to be in compliance with legal regulations or workplace rules.

- In Computer security, full _____ means disclosing full information about vulnerabilities.
- In computing, _____ widget
- Journalism, full _____ refers to disclosing the interests of the writer which may bear on the subject being written about, for example, if the writer has worked with an interview subject in the past.

- In law:
    - The law of England and Wales, _____ refers to a process that may form part of legal proceedings, whereby parties inform to other parties the existence of any relevant documents that are, or have been, in their control. This compares with the process known as discovery in the course of legal proceedings in the United States.
    - In U.S. civil procedure (litigation rules for civil cases), _____ is a stage prior to trial. In civil cases, each party must disclose to the opposing party the following: names of witnesses which it may use to support its side, copies of documents (or mere description of these documents) in its control which it may use to support its side, computation of damages claimed, and certain insurance information. _____ is related to, but technically prior to, the discovery stage.
    - In Company law (known as 'corporate law' in the United States), _____ refers to giving out information about public or limited companies or their officers, which might be kept secret if the company was a private company or a partnership.

- In real property transactions, _____ refers to providing to a buyer information known to the seller or broker/agent concerning the condition or other aspects of real property that would affect the property's value or desirability. These rules regarding what information must be disclosed, and whether the information must be disclosed even if a buyer does not ask, vary from one jurisdiction to the next.

a. Trailing

b. Controlled Foreign Corporations

c. Disclosure

d. Tax harmonisation

8. An _____ is a term used in behavioral economics to describe those types of behaviors that impose costs on a person in the long-run that are not taken into account when making decisions in the present. Classical Economics discourages government from creating legislation that targets internalities, because it is assumed that the consumer takes these personal costs into account when paying for the good that causes the _____. For example, cigarettes should be taxed because of the negative consumption externalities that they impose, such as second-hand smoke, not because the smoker harms him or herself by smoking.

a. Operating budget

b. Authorised capital

c. Inventory turnover ratio

d. Internality

9. In accounting and organizational theory, _____ is defined as a process effected by an organization's structure, work and authority flows, people and management information systems, designed to help the organization accomplish specific goals or objectives. It is a means by which an organization's resources are directed, monitored, and measured. It plays an important role in preventing and detecting fraud and protecting the organization's resources, both physical (e.g., machinery and property) and intangible (e.g., reputation or intellectual property such as trademarks.)
   a. Audit risk
   b. Auditor independence
   c. Audit committee
   d. Internal control

10. _____ is a concept that denotes the precise probability of specific eventualities. Technically, the notion of _____ is independent from the notion of value and, as such, eventualities may have both beneficial and adverse consequences. However, in general usage the convention is to focus only on potential negative impact to some characteristic of value that may arise from a future event.
    a. Discounting
    b. Risk
    c. Discount factor
    d. Risk adjusted return on capital

11. The general definition of an _____ is an evaluation of a person, organization, system, process, project or product. _____s are performed to ascertain the validity and reliability of information; also to provide an assessment of a system's internal control. The goal of an _____ is to express an opinion on the person/organization/system (etc) in question, under evaluation based on work done on a test basis.
    a. Assurance service
    b. Institute of Chartered Accountants of India
    c. Audit regime
    d. Audit

12. In a publicly-held company, an _____ is an operating committee of the Board of Directors, typically charged with oversight of financial reporting and disclosure. Committee members are drawn from members of the Company's board of directors, with a Chairperson selected from among the members. An _____ of a publicly-traded company in the United States is composed of independent and outside directors referred to as non-executive directors, at least one of which is typically a financial expert.
    a. External auditor
    b. Event data
    c. Audit working paper
    d. Audit committee

13. _____ also called 'Internal _____'. It is a term of financial audit, internal audit and Enterprise Risk Management. It means the overall attitude, awareness and actions of directors and management (i.e. 'those charged with governance') regarding the internal control system and its importance to the entity.
    a. Control environment
    b. Negative assurance
    c. Mainframe audit
    d. SOFT audit

14. _____ is an increasingly broadening term with which an organization knowledge and experience, Employee Relations and resource planning at various levels. The field draws upon concepts developed in Industrial/Organizational Psychology and System Theory. _____ has at least two related interpretations depending on context.
    a. Separation of duties
    b. BMC Software, Inc.
    c. 3M Company
    d. Human resources

15. _____ is a step in a risk management process. _____ is the determination of quantitative or qualitative value of risk related to a concrete situation and a recognized threat (also called hazard.) Quantitative _____ requires calculations of two components of risk: R, the magnitude of the potential loss L, and the probability p that the loss will occur.

Chapter 11. Accounts Receivable, Notes Receivable, and Revenue

a. 3M Company
b. Risk assessment
c. BNSF Railway
d. BMC Software, Inc.

16. A _____, also client, buyer or purchaser is the buyer or user of the paid products of an individual or organization, mostly called the supplier or seller. This is typically through purchasing or renting goods or services.

a. BNSF Railway
b. BMC Software, Inc.
c. 3M Company
d. Customer

17. A _____ is a commercial document issued by a buyer to a seller, indicating types, quantities, and agreed prices for products or services the seller will provide to the buyer. Sending a _____ to a supplier constitutes a legal offer to buy products or services. Acceptance of a _____ by a seller usually forms a once-off contract between the buyer and seller, so no contract exists until the _____ is accepted.

a. Purchase order
b. BMC Software, Inc.
c. Voucher
d. 3M Company

18. A _____ is the pinnacle activity involved in selling products or services in return for money or other compensation. It is an act of completion of a commercial activity.

A _____ is completed by the seller, the owner of the goods.

a. Tertiary sector of economy
b. Maturity
c. High yield stock
d. Sale

19. An _____ or bill is a commercial document issued by a seller to the buyer, indicating the products, quantities, and agreed prices for products or services the seller has provided the buyer. An _____ indicates the buyer must pay the seller, according to the payment terms.

In the rental industry, an _____ must include a specific reference to the duration of the time being billed, so rather than quantity, price and discount the invoicing amount is based on quantity, price, discount and duration.

a. AIG
b. ABC Television Network
c. AMEX
d. Invoice

20. In accounting, the _____ is a worksheet listing the balance at a certain date, of each ledger account in two columns, namely debit and credit. Under the double-entry system, in any transaction the total of any debits must equal the total of any credits, so in a _____ the total of the debit side should always be equal to the total of the credit side. The _____ thus serves as a tool to detect errors, which can result in the totals not being equal.

a. Current asset
b. Trial balance
c. Depreciation
d. Bottom line

Chapter 11. Accounts Receivable, Notes Receivable, and Revenue

21. A _____ has several related meanings:

- a daily record of events or business; a private _____ is usually referred to as a diary.
- a newspaper or other periodical, in the literal sense of one published each day;
- many publications issued at stated intervals, such as magazines, or scholarly academic _____s, or the record of the transactions of a society, are often called _____s. Although _____ is sometimes used, erroneously, as a synonym for 'magazine,' in academic use, a _____ refers to a serious, scholarly publication, most often peer-reviewed. A non-scholarly magazine written for an educated audience about an industry or an area of professional activity is usually called a professional magazine.

The word 'journalist' for one whose business is writing for the public press has been in use since the end of the 17th century.

Open access _____s are scholarly _____s that are available to the reader without financial or other barrier other than access to the internet itself. Some are subsidized, and some require payment on behalf of the author. Subsidized _____s are financed by an academic institution or a government information center.

a. BNSF Railway
b. Journal
c. 3M Company
d. BMC Software, Inc.

22. _____ is the concept of having more than one person required to complete a task. It is alternatively called segregation of duties or, in the political realm, separation of powers.

_____ is one of the key concepts of internal control and is the most difficult and sometimes the most costly one to achieve. The term _____ is already well-known in financial accounting systems. Companies in all sizes understand not to combine roles such as receiving checks (payment on account) and approving write-offs, depositing cash and reconciling bank statements, approving time cards and have custody of pay checks, etc.

a. BMC Software, Inc.
b. Separation of duties
c. 3M Company
d. Salary

23. _____, in auditing, is the risk that a company's internal controls are insufficient to mitigate or detect errors or fraud.

a. 3M Company
b. BNSF Railway
c. BMC Software, Inc.
d. Control risk

24. A _____ is a common type of chart, that represents an algorithm or process, showing the steps as boxes of various kinds, and their order by connecting these with arrows. _____s are used in analyzing, designing, documenting or managing a process or program in various fields.

The first structured method for documenting process flow, the 'flow process chart', was introduced by Frank Gilbreth to members of ASME in 1921 as the presentation e;Process Charts--First Steps in Finding the One Best Waye;.

Chapter 11. Accounts Receivable, Notes Receivable, and Revenue

a. Flowchart
c. 3M Company
b. BMC Software, Inc.
d. BNSF Railway

25. A _____ is the transfer of an interest in property (or the equivalent in law - a charge) to a lender as a security for a debt - usually a loan of money. While a _____ in itself is not a debt, it is the lender's security for a debt. It is a transfer of an interest in land (or the equivalent) from the owner to the _____ lender, on the condition that this interest will be returned to the owner when the terms of the _____ have been satisfied or performed.
 a. 3M Company
 c. BNSF Railway
 b. BMC Software, Inc.
 d. Mortgage

26. A _____ is a type of debt Like all debt instruments, a _____ entails the redistribution of financial assets over time, between the lender and the borrower.
 a. Loan to value
 c. Loan
 b. Debenture
 d. Lender

27. _____ is the realization of an application idea, model, design, specification, standard, algorithm an _____ is a realization of a technical specification or algorithm as a program, software component, or other computer system. Many _____s may exist for a given specification or standard.
 a. AIG
 c. ABC Television Network
 b. Implementation
 d. AMEX

28. _____ principle is a cornerstone of accrual accounting together with matching principle. They both determine the accounting period, in which revenues and expenses are recognized. According to the principle, revenues are recognized when they are (1) realized or realizable, and are (2) earned (usually when goods are transferred or services rendered), no matter when cash is received.
 a. 3M Company
 c. Revenue recognition
 b. Net realizable value
 d. BMC Software, Inc.

29. Discounting is a financial mechanism in which a debtor obtains the right to delay payments to a creditor, for a defined period of time, in exchange for a charge or fee. Essentially, the party that owes money in the present purchases the right to delay the payment until some future date. The _____, or charge, is simply the difference between the original amount owed in the present and the amount that has to be paid in the future to settle the debt.
 a. Discount factor
 c. Discount
 b. Risk aversion
 d. Discounting

30. _____ is one of the four Ps of the marketing mix. The other three aspects are product, promotion, and place. It is also a key variable in microeconomic price allocation theory.
 a. Cost-plus pricing
 c. Target costing
 b. Pricing
 d. Price

31. _____, in accrual accounting, (e.g. advance payment received from a client) is, according to revenue recognition, revenue not earned until the delivery of goods or services, which until then, is still owed to the payer, hence remaining a liability.

_____, sometimes referred to as deferred revenue or unearned revenue, shares characteristics with accrued expense with the difference that a liability to be covered latter is cash received FROM a counterpart, while goods or services are to be delivered in a latter period, when such income item is earned, the related revenue item is recognized, and the same amount is deducted from deferred revenues.

a. Treasury stock
b. Matching principle
c. Gross sales
d. Deferred income

32. The _____ is the national, professional association of CPAs in the United States, with more than 330,000 members, including CPAs in business and industry, public practice, government, and education; student affiliates; and international associates. It sets ethical standards for the profession and U.S. auditing standards for audits of private companies; federal, state and local governments; and non-profit organizations.

Approximately 40% of its members are engaged in the practice of public accounting, in areas such as auditing, accounting, taxation, general business consulting, business valuation, personal financial planning and business technology.

a. ABC Television Network
b. AIG
c. Other postemployment benefits
d. American Institute of Certified Public Accountants

33. Book Value = Original Cost - _____

Book value at the end of year becomes book value at the beginning of next year. The asset is depreciated until the book value equals scrap value.

If the vehicle were to be sold and the sales price exceeded the depreciated value (net book value) then the excess would be considered a gain and subject to depreciation recapture.

a. ABC Television Network
b. AMEX
c. Accumulated depreciation
d. AIG

34. _____ is a term used in accounting, economics and finance to spread the cost of an asset over the span of several years.

In simple words we can say that _____ is the reduction in the value of an asset due to usage, passage of time, wear and tear, technological outdating or obsolescence, depletion, inadequacy, rot, rust, decay or other such factors.

In accounting, _____ is a term used to describe any method of attributing the historical or purchase cost of an asset across its useful life, roughly corresponding to normal wear and tear.

a. Net profit
b. General ledger
c. Current asset
d. Depreciation

Chapter 11. Accounts Receivable, Notes Receivable, and Revenue

35. In economics, _____ or _____ goods or real _____ refers to factors of production used to create goods or services that are not themselves significantly consumed (though they may depreciate) in the production process. _____ goods may be acquired with money or financial _____. In finance and accounting, _____ generally refers to financial wealth, especially that used to start or maintain a business.
    a. Screening
    b. Vyborg Appeal
    c. Disclosure
    d. Capital

36. _____ is that part of statistical practice concerned with the selection of individual observations intended to yield some knowledge about a population of concern, especially for the purposes of statistical inference. Each observation measures one or more properties (weight, location, etc.) of an observable entity enumerated to distinguish objects or individuals.
    a. Abby Joseph Cohen
    b. Alan Greenspan
    c. Sampling
    d. Arthur Betz Laffer

37. _____ is the business practice where a company or a a sales force within a company, inflates its sales figures by forcing more products through a distribution channel than the channel is capable of selling to the world at large. Also known as 'trade loading', this can be the result of a company attempting to inflate its sales figures. Alternatively, it can be a consequence of a poorly managed sales force attempting to meet short term objectives and quotas in a way that is detrimental to the company in the long term.
    a. Price variance
    b. Channel stuffing
    c. Consolidated financial statements
    d. Refunding

38. _____ is that which is owed; usually referencing assets owed, but the term can also cover moral obligations and other interactions not requiring money. In the case of assets, _____ is a means of using future purchasing power in the present before a summation has been earned. Some companies and corporations use _____ as a part of their overall corporate finance strategy.
    a. Debenture
    b. Loan
    c. Lender
    d. Debt

39. _____ is a term that is commonly used in relation to the audit of the financial statements of an entity. (.
    a. Audit working paper
    b. Engagement Letter
    c. Audit Risk
    d. Auditor independence

40. _____ is a fee paid on borrowed assets. It is the price paid for the use of borrowed money , or, money earned by deposited funds .Assets that are sometimes lent with _____ include money, shares, consumer goods through hire purchase, major assets such as aircraft, and even entire factories in finance lease arrangements. The _____ is calculated upon the value of the assets in the same manner as upon money.
    a. ABC Television Network
    b. Insolvency
    c. Interest
    d. AIG

Chapter 11. Accounts Receivable, Notes Receivable, and Revenue

41. _____ is evidence obtained during a financial audit and recorded in the audit working papers.

- In the audit engagement acceptance or reappointment stage, _____ is the information that the auditor is to consider for the appointment. For examples, change in the entity control environment, inherent risk and nature of the entity business, and scope of audit work.

- In the audit planning stage, _____ is the information that the auditor is to consider for the most effective and efficient audit approach. For examples, reliability of internal control procedures, and analytical review systems.

- In the control testing stage, _____ is the information that the auditor is to consider for the mix of audit test of control and audit substantive tests.

- In the substantive testing stage, _____ is the information that the auditor is to make sure the appropriation of financial statement assertions. For examples, existence, rights and obligations, occurrence, completeness, valuation, measurement, presentation and disclosure of a particular transaction or account balance.

a. Institute of Chartered Accountants of India
b. Audit
c. ITGCs
d. Audit evidence

42. In economic models, the _____ time frame assumes no fixed factors of production. Firms can enter or leave the marketplace, and the cost (and availability) of land, labor, raw materials, and capital goods can be assumed to vary. In contrast, in the short-run time frame, certain factors are assumed to be fixed, because there is not sufficient time for them to change.

a. Short-run
b. BMC Software, Inc.
c. 3M Company
d. Long-run

43. _____ is systematic determination of merit, worth, and significance of something or someone using criteria against a set of standards. _____ often is used to characterize and appraise subjects of interest in a wide range of human enterprises, including the arts, criminal justice, foundations and non-profit organizations, government, health care, and other human services.

Depending on the topic of interest, there are professional groups which look to the quality and rigor of the _____ process.

a. AIG
b. Evaluation
c. AMEX
d. ABC Television Network

44. _____ is the risk of loss due to a debtor's non-payment of a loan or other line of credit (either the principal or interest (coupon) or both)

Most lenders employ their own models (credit scorecards) to rank potential and existing customers according to risk, and then apply appropriate strategies. With products such as unsecured personal loans or mortgages, lenders charge a higher price for higher risk customers and vice versa. With revolving products such as credit cards and overdrafts, risk is controlled through the setting of credit limits.

a. Currency risk	b. 3M Company
c. Market risk	d. Credit Risk

45. _____s are cash, evidence of an ownership interest in an entity or deliver, cash or another _____.

_____s can be categorized by form depending on whether they are cash instruments or derivative instruments:

- Cash instruments are _____s whose value is determined directly by markets. They can be divided into securities, which are readily transferable, and other cash instruments such as loans and deposits, where both borrower and lender have to agree on a transfer.
- Derivative instruments are _____s which derive their value from the value and characteristics of one or more underlying assets. They can be divided into exchange-traded derivatives and over-the-counter (OTC) derivatives.

Alternatively, _____s can be categorized by 'asset class' depending on whether they are equity based (reflecting ownership of the issuing entity) or debt based (reflecting a loan the investor has made to the issuing entity.) If it is debt, it can be further categorised into short term (less than one year) or long term.

Foreign Exchange instruments and transactions are neither debt nor equity based and belong in their own category.

a. Financial Instrument	b. Financial instruments
c. Mark-to-market	d. Market price

46. _____ are cash, evidence of an ownership interest in an entity, or a contractual right to receive, or deliver, cash or another financial instrument.

_____ can be categorized by form depending on whether they are cash instruments or derivative instruments:

- Cash instruments are _____ whose value is determined directly by markets. They can be divided into securities, which are readily transferable, and other cash instruments such as loans and deposits, where both borrower and lender have to agree on a transfer.
- Derivative instruments are _____ which derive their value from the value and characteristics of one or more underlying assets. They can be divided into exchange-traded derivatives and over-the-counter (OTC) derivatives.

Alternatively, _____ can be categorized by 'asset class' depending on whether they are equity based (reflecting ownership of the issuing entity) or debt based (reflecting a loan the investor has made to the issuing entity.) If it is debt, it can be further categorised into short term (less than one year) or long term.

Foreign Exchange instruments and transactions are neither debt nor equity based and belong in their own category.

a. Market liquidity
c. Spot rate
b. Transfer agent
d. Financial Instruments

47. An _____ is the buying of one company by another. An _____ may be friendly or hostile. In the former case, the companies cooperate in negotiations; in the latter case, the takeover target is unwilling to be bought or the target's board has no prior knowledge of the offer. _____ usually refers to a purchase of a smaller firm by a larger one. Sometimes, however, a smaller firm will acquire management control of a larger or longer established company and keep its name for the combined entity. This is known as a reverse takeover.
   a. AMEX
   c. ABC Television Network
   b. AIG
   d. Acquisition

48. An _____, or organogram(me)) is a diagram that shows the structure of an organization and the relationships and relative ranks of its parts and positions/jobs. The term is also used for similar diagrams, for example ones showing the different elements of a field of knowledge or a group of languages. The French Encyclopédie had one of the first _____s of knowledge in general.
   a. Organizational chart
   c. ABC Television Network
   b. AIG
   d. AMEX

Chapter 12. Inventories and Cost of Goods Sold

1. The _____ of 1977 (15 U.S.C. §§ 78dd-1, et seq.) is a United States federal law known primarily for two of its main provisions, one that addresses accounting transparency requirements under the Securities Exchange Act of 1934 and another concerning bribery of foreign officials.
   a. Competition law
   b. Pre-emption right
   c. Lease
   d. Foreign Corrupt Practices Act

2. A _____ is an annual report required by the U.S. Securities and Exchange Commission (SEC), that gives a comprehensive summary of a public company's performance. Although similarly named, the annual report on _____ is distinct from the often glossy 'annual report to shareholders', which a company must send to its shareholders when it holds an annual meeting to elect directors (though some companies combine the annual report and the 10-K into one document.) The 10-K includes information such as company history, organizational structure, executive compensation, equity, subsidiaries, and audited financial statements, among other information.
   a. Form 10-K
   b. 3M Company
   c. Form 10-Q
   d. Form 8-K

3. _____, in auditing, is the risk that the account or section being audited is materially misstated without considering internal controls due to error; _____ does not include an assessment of the risk of material misstatement due to fraud. The assessment of _____ depends on the professional judgement of the auditor, and it is done after assessing the business environment of the entity being audited.

   _____ is typically assessed using a scale, with assessments being either low, medium, or high.

   a. Inherent risk
   b. ABC Television Network
   c. AMEX
   d. AIG

4. _____ in economics and business is the result of an exchange and from that trade we assign a numerical monetary value to a good, service or asset. If Alice trades Bob 4 apples for an orange, the _____ of an orange is 4 apples. Inversely, the _____ of an apple is 1/4 oranges.
   a. Discounts and allowances
   b. Price
   c. Transactional Net Margin Method
   d. Price discrimination

5. The U.S. _____ is an independent agency of the United States government which holds primary responsibility for enforcing the federal securities laws and regulating the securities industry, the nation's stock and options exchanges, and other electronic securities markets. The SEC was created by section 4 of the Securities Exchange Act of 1934 (now codified as 15 U.S.C. § 78d and commonly referred to as the 1934 Act.)
   a. 3M Company
   b. Securities and Exchange Commission
   c. BNSF Railway
   d. BMC Software, Inc.

6. In finance, _____ is the process of estimating the potential market value of a financial asset or liability. They can be done on assets (for example, investments in marketable securities such as stocks, options, business enterprises, or intangible assets such as patents and trademarks) or on liabilities (e.g., Bonds issued by a company.) A _____ is required in many contexts including investment analysis, capital budgeting, merger and acquisition transactions, financial reporting, taxable events to determine the proper tax liability, and in litigation.
   a. Valuation
   b. Disclosure
   c. Daybook
   d. Vyborg Appeal

Chapter 12. Inventories and Cost of Goods Sold

7. _____ is a file or account that contains money that a person or company owes to suppliers, but has not paid yet (a form of debt.) When you receive an invoice you add it to the file, and then you remove it when you pay. Thus, the A/P is a form of credit that suppliers offer to their purchasers by allowing them to pay for a product or service after it has already been received.

   a. Accrual

   b. Earnings before interest, taxes, depreciation and amortization

   c. Accounts payable

   d. Accounts receivable

8. _____ means the giving out of information, either voluntarily or to be in compliance with legal regulations or workplace rules.

   - In Computer security, full _____ means disclosing full information about vulnerabilities.
   - In computing, _____ widget
   - Journalism, full _____ refers to disclosing the interests of the writer which may bear on the subject being written about, for example, if the writer has worked with an interview subject in the past.

   - In law:
     - The law of England and Wales, _____ refers to a process that may form part of legal proceedings, whereby parties inform to other parties the existence of any relevant documents that are, or have been, in their control. This compares with the process known as discovery in the course of legal proceedings in the United States.
     - In U.S. civil procedure (litigation rules for civil cases), _____ is a stage prior to trial. In civil cases, each party must disclose to the opposing party the following: names of witnesses which it may use to support its side, copies of documents (or mere description of these documents) in its control which it may use to support its side, computation of damages claimed, and certain insurance information. _____ is related to, but technically prior to, the discovery stage.
     - In Company law (known as 'corporate law' in the United States), _____ refers to giving out information about public or limited companies or their officers, which might be kept secret if the company was a private company or a partnership.

   - In real property transactions, _____ refers to providing to a buyer information known to the seller or broker/agent concerning the condition or other aspects of real property that would affect the property's value or desirability. These rules regarding what information must be disclosed, and whether the information must be disclosed even if a buyer does not ask, vary from one jurisdiction to the next.

   a. Tax harmonisation

   b. Trailing

   c. Controlled Foreign Corporations

   d. Disclosure

9. An _____ is a term used in behavioral economics to describe those types of behaviors that impose costs on a person in the long-run that are not taken into account when making decisions in the present. Classical Economics discourages government from creating legislation that targets internalities, because it is assumed that the consumer takes these personal costs into account when paying for the good that causes the _____. For example, cigarettes should be taxed because of the negative consumption externalities that they impose, such as second-hand smoke, not because the smoker harms him or herself by smoking.

a. Internality
b. Operating budget
c. Inventory turnover ratio
d. Authorised capital

10. In accounting and organizational theory, _____ is defined as a process effected by an organization's structure, work and authority flows, people and management information systems, designed to help the organization accomplish specific goals or objectives. It is a means by which an organization's resources are directed, monitored, and measured. It plays an important role in preventing and detecting fraud and protecting the organization's resources, both physical (e.g., machinery and property) and intangible (e.g., reputation or intellectual property such as trademarks.)
a. Audit committee
b. Internal control
c. Audit risk
d. Auditor independence

11. _____ is a concept that denotes the precise probability of specific eventualities. Technically, the notion of _____ is independent from the notion of value and, as such, eventualities may have both beneficial and adverse consequences. However, in general usage the convention is to focus only on potential negative impact to some characteristic of value that may arise from a future event.
a. Risk adjusted return on capital
b. Discount factor
c. Discounting
d. Risk

12. _____ is an equity (stock) exchange located at 11 Wall Street in lower Manhattan, New York, USA.) It is the largest stock exchange in the world by dollar value of its listed companies' securities. As of October 2008, the combined capitalization of all domestic _____ listed companies was US$10.1 trillion.
a. 3M Company
b. BMC Software, Inc.
c. New York Stock Exchange
d. BNSF Railway

13. An _____ is a mostly hierarchical concept of subordination of entities that collaborate and contribute to serve one common aim.

Organizations are a variant of clustered entities. The structure of an organization is usually set up in many a styles, dependent on their objectives and ambience.

a. AIG
b. ABC Television Network
c. Organizational structure
d. AMEX

14. A _____, (formerly a securities exchange) is a corporation or mutual organization which provides 'trading' facilities for stock brokers and traders, to trade stocks and other securities. _____s also provide facilities for the issue and redemption of securities as well as other financial instruments and capital events including the payment of income and dividends. The securities traded on a _____ include: shares issued by companies, unit trusts, derivatives, pooled investment products and bonds.
a. BMC Software, Inc.
b. 3M Company
c. Stock Exchange
d. BNSF Railway

15. The general definition of an _____ is an evaluation of a person, organization, system, process, project or product. _____s are performed to ascertain the validity and reliability of information; also to provide an assessment of a system's internal control. The goal of an _____ is to express an opinion on the person/organization/system (etc) in question, under evaluation based on work done on a test basis.

Chapter 12. Inventories and Cost of Goods Sold

a. Audit regime
c. Assurance service
b. Institute of Chartered Accountants of India
d. Audit

16. In a publicly-held company, an _____ is an operating committee of the Board of Directors, typically charged with oversight of financial reporting and disclosure. Committee members are drawn from members of the Company's board of directors, with a Chairperson selected from among the members. An _____ of a publicly-traded company in the United States is composed of independent and outside directors referred to as non-executive directors, at least one of which is typically a financial expert.
   a. Audit working paper
   c. Audit committee
   b. External auditor
   d. Event data

17. _____ also called 'Internal _____'. It is a term of financial audit, internal audit and Enterprise Risk Management. It means the overall attitude, awareness and actions of directors and management (i.e. 'those charged with governance') regarding the internal control system and its importance to the entity.
   a. SOFT audit
   c. Mainframe audit
   b. Negative assurance
   d. Control environment

18. A _____ is a commercial document issued by a buyer to a seller, indicating types, quantities, and agreed prices for products or services the seller will provide to the buyer. Sending a _____ to a supplier constitutes a legal offer to buy products or services. Acceptance of a _____ by a seller usually forms a once-off contract between the buyer and seller, so no contract exists until the _____ is accepted.
   a. Purchase order
   c. BMC Software, Inc.
   b. Voucher
   d. 3M Company

19. As part of an organization's internal financial controls, the accounting department may institute a _____ process to help manage requests for purchases. Requests for the creation of purchase of goods and services are documented and routed for approval within the organization and then delivered to the accounting group.

Typically an accounting staff member is assigned responsibility for purchase order management, referred to commonly as the PO (purchase order) Coordinator.

   a. BMC Software, Inc.
   c. 3M Company
   b. BNSF Railway
   d. Purchase requisition

20. _____ refers to a business or organization attempting to acquire goods or services to accomplish the goals of the enterprise. Though there are several organizations that attempt to set standards in the _____ process, processes can vary greatly between organizations. Typically the word e;_____e; is not used interchangeably with the word e;procuremente;, since procurement typically includes Expediting, Supplier Quality, and Traffic and Logistics (T'L) in addition to _____.
   a. Free port
   c. Consignor
   b. Purchasing
   d. Supply chain

21. _____ is a step in a risk management process. _____ is the determination of quantitative or qualitative value of risk related to a concrete situation and a recognized threat (also called hazard.) Quantitative _____ requires calculations of two components of risk: R, the magnitude of the potential loss L, and the probability p that the loss will occur.

Chapter 12. Inventories and Cost of Goods Sold

a. Risk assessment
c. BMC Software, Inc.
b. BNSF Railway
d. 3M Company

22. A _____ is the pinnacle activity involved in selling products or services in return for money or other compensation. It is an act of completion of a commercial activity.

A _____ is completed by the seller, the owner of the goods.

a. Sale
c. Tertiary sector of economy
b. High yield stock
d. Maturity

23. In economics, business, retail, and accounting, a _____ is the value of money that has been used up to produce something, and hence is not available for use anymore. In economics, a _____ is an alternative that is given up as a result of a decision. In business, the _____ may be one of acquisition, in which case the amount of money expended to acquire it is counted as _____.

a. Cost
c. Prime cost
b. Cost allocation
d. Cost of quality

24. In management accounting, _____ establishes budget and actual cost of operations, processes, departments or product and the analysis of variances, profitability or social use of funds. Managers use _____ to support decision-making to cut a company's costs and improve profitability. As a form of management accounting, _____ need not follow standards such as GAAP, because its primary use is for internal managers, rather than outside users, and what to compute is instead decided pragmatically.

a. Cost-volume-profit analysis
c. Marginal cost
b. Prime cost
d. Cost accounting

25. _____ refers to the structured transmission of data between organizations by electronic means. It is used to transfer electronic documents from one computer system to another (ie) from one trading partner to another trading partner. It is more than mere E-mail; for instance, organizations might replace bills of lading and even checks with appropriate _____ messages.

a. Electronic data interchange
c. ABC Television Network
b. Electronic commerce
d. AIG

26. Just in Time could refer to the following:

- _____, an inventory strategy that reduces in-process inventory
- _____ compilation, a technique for improving the performance of bytecode-compiled programming systems

a. Help desk and incident reporting auditing
c. Fiscal
b. Comparable
d. Just-in-time

27. _____ is the concept of having more than one person required to complete a task. It is alternatively called segregation of duties or, in the political realm, separation of powers.

_____ is one of the key concepts of internal control and is the most difficult and sometimes the most costly one to achieve. The term _____ is already well-known in financial accounting systems. Companies in all sizes understand not to combine roles such as receiving checks (payment on account) and approving write-offs, depositing cash and reconciling bank statements, approving time cards and have custody of pay checks, etc.

a. 3M Company
c. BMC Software, Inc.
b. Salary
d. Separation of duties

28. _____ is the realization of an application idea, model, design, specification, standard, algorithm an _____ is a realization of a technical specification or algorithm as a program, software component, or other computer system. Many _____s may exist for a given specification or standard.

a. ABC Television Network
c. AMEX
b. AIG
d. Implementation

29. _____, in auditing, is the risk that a company's internal controls are insufficient to mitigate or detect errors or fraud.

a. BNSF Railway
c. 3M Company
b. BMC Software, Inc.
d. Control risk

30. In financial accounting, _____ or cost of sales includes the direct costs attributable to the production of the goods sold by a company. This amount includes the materials cost used in creating the goods along with the direct labor costs used to produce the good. It excludes indirect expenses such as distribution costs and sales force costs.

a. Reorder point
c. 3M Company
b. FIFO and LIFO accounting
d. Cost of goods sold

31. In business, _____, Overhead cost or _____ expense refers to an ongoing expense of operating a business. The term _____ is usually used to group expenses that are necessary to the continued functioning of the business, but do not directly generate profits.

_____ expenses are all costs on the income statement except for direct labor and direct materials.

a. AIG
c. Intangible assets
b. Overhead
d. ABC Television Network

32. _____ is a process where a business physically counts its entire inventory. A _____ may be mandated by financial accounting rules or the tax regulations to place an accurate value on the inventory, or the business may need to count inventory so component parts or raw materials can be restocked. Businesses may use several different tactics to minimize the disruption caused by _____.

a. BNSF Railway
c. 3M Company
b. Physical inventory
d. BMC Software, Inc.

33. An _____ or bill is a commercial document issued by a seller to the buyer, indicating the products, quantities, and agreed prices for products or services the seller has provided the buyer. An _____ indicates the buyer must pay the seller, according to the payment terms.

In the rental industry, an _____ must include a specific reference to the duration of the time being billed, so rather than quantity, price and discount the invoicing amount is based on quantity, price, discount and duration.

a. AIG
c. AMEX
b. ABC Television Network
d. Invoice

34. _____ is an acronym for First In, First Out, an abstraction in ways of organizing and manipulation of data relative to time and prioritization. This expression describes the principle of a queue processing technique or servicing conflicting demands by ordering process by first-come, first-served (FCFS) behaviour: what comes in first is handled first, what comes in next waits until the first is finished, etc.

Thus it is analogous to the behaviour of persons queueing (or 'standing in line', in common American parlance), where the persons leave the queue in the order they arrive, or waiting one's turn at a traffic control signal.

a. Trademark
c. Kanban
b. Risk management
d. FIFO

35. _____ methods are means of managing inventory and financial matters involving the money a company ties up within inventory of produced goods, raw materials, parts, components, or feed stocks. FIFO stands for first-in, first-out, meaning that the oldest inventory items are recorded as sold first. LIFO stands for last-in, first-out, meaning that the most recently purchased items are recorded as sold first.

a. 3M Company
c. Finished good
b. Reorder point
d. FIFO and LIFO accounting

36. Book Value = Original Cost - _____

Book value at the end of year becomes book value at the beginning of next year. The asset is depreciated until the book value equals scrap value.

If the vehicle were to be sold and the sales price exceeded the depreciated value (net book value) then the excess would be considered a gain and subject to depreciation recapture.

a. AMEX
c. ABC Television Network
b. AIG
d. Accumulated depreciation

37. Under the average-cost method, it is assumed that the cost of inventory is based on the _____ of the goods available for sale during the period. _____ is computed by dividing the total cost of goods available for sale by the total units available for sale. This gives a weighted-average unit cost that is applied to the units in the ending inventory.

a. Average cost
c. AIG
b. ABC Television Network
d. Ending inventory

38. Under the _____, it is assumed that the cost of inventory is based on the average cost of the goods available for sale during the period. Average cost is computed by dividing the total cost of goods available for sale by the total units available for sale. This gives a weighted-average unit cost that is applied to the units in the ending inventory.

Chapter 12. Inventories and Cost of Goods Sold

a. Average-cost method
b. ABC Television Network
c. AMEX
d. AIG

39. _____ is a term used in accounting, economics and finance to spread the cost of an asset over the span of several years.

In simple words we can say that _____ is the reduction in the value of an asset due to usage, passage of time, wear and tear, technological outdating or obsolescence, depletion, inadequacy, rot, rust, decay or other such factors.

In accounting, _____ is a term used to describe any method of attributing the historical or purchase cost of an asset across its useful life, roughly corresponding to normal wear and tear.

a. General ledger
b. Net profit
c. Current asset
d. Depreciation

40. Discounting is a financial mechanism in which a debtor obtains the right to delay payments to a creditor, for a defined period of time, in exchange for a charge or fee. Essentially, the party that owes money in the present purchases the right to delay the payment until some future date. The _____, or charge, is simply the difference between the original amount owed in the present and the amount that has to be paid in the future to settle the debt.

a. Discount factor
b. Discounting
c. Risk aversion
d. Discount

41. _____ is one of the four Ps of the marketing mix. The other three aspects are product, promotion, and place. It is also a key variable in microeconomic price allocation theory.

a. Target costing
b. Price
c. Pricing
d. Cost-plus pricing

42. In accounting, _____ or sales profit is the difference between revenue and the cost of making a product or providing a service, before deducting overhead, payroll, taxation, and interest payments. Note that this is different from operating profit (earnings before interest and taxes.)

Net sales are calculated:

Net sales = Sales - Sales returns and allowances.

a. Gross profit
b. Commercial paper
c. Capital structure
d. Participating preferred stock

43. _____ is a financial ratio used to assess the profitability of a firm's core activities, excluding fixed costs.

The general calculation is:

Chapter 12. Inventories and Cost of Goods Sold

The _____ is related to the net profit margin, which assesses the profitability of an organization after including fixed costs.

_____ indicates the relationship between net sales revenue and the cost of goods sold.

a. Gross income
b. Participating preferred stock
c. Commercial paper
d. Gross profit margin

44. The _____ is an equation that equals the cost of goods sold divided by the average inventory. Average inventory equals beginning inventory plus ending inventory divided by 2.

The formula for _____:

$$\text{Inventory Turnover} = \frac{\text{Cost of Goods Sold}}{\text{Average Inventory}}$$

The formula for average inventory:

$$\text{Average Inventory} = \frac{\text{Beginning inventory} + \text{Ending inventory}}{2}$$

A low turnover rate may point to overstocking, obsolescence, or deficiencies in the product line or marketing effort.

a. Earnings per share
b. Upside potential ratio
c. Enterprise Value/Sales
d. Inventory turnover

45. _____ is that which is owed; usually referencing assets owed, but the term can also cover moral obligations and other interactions not requiring money. In the case of assets, _____ is a means of using future purchasing power in the present before a summation has been earned. Some companies and corporations use _____ as a part of their overall corporate finance strategy.

a. Loan
b. Debenture
c. Lender
d. Debt

46. _____, net margin, net _____ or net profit ratio all refer to a measure of profitability. It is calculated by finding the net profit as a percentage of the revenue.

$$\text{Net profit margin} = \frac{\text{Net profit (after taxes)}}{\text{Revenue}} \times 100$$

The _____ is mostly used for internal comparison.

a. BNSF Railway
b. 3M Company
c. BMC Software, Inc.
d. Profit margin

Chapter 12. Inventories and Cost of Goods Sold

47. _____ Management is the succession of strategies used by management as a product goes through its _____. The conditions in which a product is sold changes over time and must be managed as it moves through its succession of stages.

The _____ goes through many phases, involves many professional disciplines, and requires many skills, tools and processes.

   a. Procurement
   c. Product life cycle
   b. Kaizen
   d. Safety stock

48. A _____ is a type of debt Like all debt instruments, a _____ entails the redistribution of financial assets over time, between the lender and the borrower.
   a. Debenture
   c. Loan to value
   b. Lender
   d. Loan

49. _____ is a term that is commonly used in relation to the audit of the financial statements of an entity. (.
   a. Audit risk
   c. Auditor independence
   b. Engagement Letter
   d. Audit working paper

Chapter 13. Property, Plant, and Equipment: Depreciation and Depletion

1. _____ is any physical or virtual entity that is owned by an individual or jointly by a group of individuals. An owner of _____ has the right to consume, sell, rent, mortgage, transfer and exchange his or her _____. Important widely-recognized types of _____ include real _____, personal _____ (other physical possessions), and intellectual _____ (rights over artistic creations, inventions, etc.), although the latter is not always as widely recognized or enforced.
   a. Primary authority
   b. Disclosure requirement
   c. Fiduciary
   d. Property

2. _____, also known as property, plant, and equipment (PP&E), is a term used in accountancy for assets and property which cannot easily be converted into cash. This can be compared with current assets such as cash or bank accounts, which are described as liquid assets. In most cases, only tangible assets are referred to as fixed.
   a. Minority interest
   b. Fixed asset
   c. Subledger
   d. Bankruptcy prediction

3. In business and accounting, _____ are everything of value that is owned by a person or company. It is a claim on the property your income of a borrower. The balance sheet of a firm records the monetary value of the _____ owned by the firm.
   a. Earnings before interest, taxes, depreciation and amortization
   b. Accrual basis accounting
   c. Assets
   d. Accounts receivable

4. The _____ of 1977 (15 U.S.C. §§ 78dd-1, et seq.) is a United States federal law known primarily for two of its main provisions, one that addresses accounting transparency requirements under the Securities Exchange Act of 1934 and another concerning bribery of foreign officials.
   a. Foreign Corrupt Practices Act
   b. Competition law
   c. Pre-emption right
   d. Lease

5. _____, in auditing, is the risk that the account or section being audited is materially misstated without considering internal controls due to error; _____ does not include an assessment of the risk of material misstatement due to fraud. The assessment of _____ depends on the professional judgement of the auditor, and it is done after assessing the business environment of the entity being audited.

   _____ is typically assessed using a scale, with assessments being either low, medium, or high.

   a. AIG
   b. ABC Television Network
   c. Inherent risk
   d. AMEX

6. _____ or land amelioration refers to investments making land more usable by humans. In terms of accounting, _____s refer to any variety of projects that increase the value of the property. Most are depreciable, but some _____s are not able to be depreciated because a useful life cannot be determined.
   a. Land improvement
   b. 3M Company
   c. BNSF Railway
   d. BMC Software, Inc.

7. In finance, _____ is the process of estimating the potential market value of a financial asset or liability. They can be done on assets (for example, investments in marketable securities such as stocks, options, business enterprises, or intangible assets such as patents and trademarks) or on liabilities (e.g., Bonds issued by a company.) A _____ is required in many contexts including investment analysis, capital budgeting, merger and acquisition transactions, financial reporting, taxable events to determine the proper tax liability, and in litigation.

a. Vyborg Appeal
b. Daybook
c. Disclosure
d. Valuation

8. _____ is a file or account that contains money that a person or company owes to suppliers, but has not paid yet (a form of debt.) When you receive an invoice you add it to the file, and then you remove it when you pay. Thus, the A/P is a form of credit that suppliers offer to their purchasers by allowing them to pay for a product or service after it has already been received.

a. Accounts receivable
b. Accounts payable
c. Earnings before interest, taxes, depreciation and amortization
d. Accrual

9. The general definition of an _____ is an evaluation of a person, organization, system, process, project or product. _____s are performed to ascertain the validity and reliability of information; also to provide an assessment of a system's internal control. The goal of an _____ is to express an opinion on the person/organization/system (etc) in question, under evaluation based on work done on a test basis.

a. Assurance service
b. Audit regime
c. Institute of Chartered Accountants of India
d. Audit

10. In accounting, a _____ is an asset on the balance sheet which is expected to be sold or otherwise used up in the near future, usually within one year, or one business cycle - whichever is longer. Typical _____s include cash, cash equivalents, accounts receivable, inventory, the portion of prepaid accounts which will be used within a year, and short-term investments.

On the balance sheet, assets will typically be classified into _____s and long-term assets.

a. Deferred
b. Pro forma
c. Current asset
d. General ledger

11. _____ is a term used in accounting, economics and finance to spread the cost of an asset over the span of several years.

In simple words we can say that _____ is the reduction in the value of an asset due to usage, passage of time, wear and tear, technological outdating or obsolescence, depletion, inadequacy, rot, rust, decay or other such factors.

In accounting, _____ is a term used to describe any method of attributing the historical or purchase cost of an asset across its useful life, roughly corresponding to normal wear and tear.

a. Current asset
b. Net profit
c. General ledger
d. Depreciation

Chapter 13. Property, Plant, and Equipment: Depreciation and Depletion

12. _____ means the giving out of information, either voluntarily or to be in compliance with legal regulations or workplace rules.

- In Computer security, full _____ means disclosing full information about vulnerabilities.
- In computing, _____ widget
- Journalism, full _____ refers to disclosing the interests of the writer which may bear on the subject being written about, for example, if the writer has worked with an interview subject in the past.

- In law:
    - The law of England and Wales, _____ refers to a process that may form part of legal proceedings, whereby parties inform to other parties the existence of any relevant documents that are, or have been, in their control. This compares with the process known as discovery in the course of legal proceedings in the United States.
    - In U.S. civil procedure (litigation rules for civil cases), _____ is a stage prior to trial. In civil cases, each party must disclose to the opposing party the following: names of witnesses which it may use to support its side, copies of documents (or mere description of these documents) in its control which it may use to support its side, computation of damages claimed, and certain insurance information. _____ is related to, but technically prior to, the discovery stage.
    - In Company law (known as 'corporate law' in the United States), _____ refers to giving out information about public or limited companies or their officers, which might be kept secret if the company was a private company or a partnership.

- In real property transactions, _____ refers to providing to a buyer information known to the seller or broker/agent concerning the condition or other aspects of real property that would affect the property's value or desirability. These rules regarding what information must be disclosed, and whether the information must be disclosed even if a buyer does not ask, vary from one jurisdiction to the next.

a. Controlled Foreign Corporations
b. Trailing
c. Tax harmonisation
d. Disclosure

13. An _____ is a term used in behavioral economics to describe those types of behaviors that impose costs on a person in the long-run that are not taken into account when making decisions in the present. Classical Economics discourages government from creating legislation that targets internalities, because it is assumed that the consumer takes these personal costs into account when paying for the good that causes the _____. For example, cigarettes should be taxed because of the negative consumption externalities that they impose, such as second-hand smoke, not because the smoker harms him or herself by smoking.

a. Internality
b. Inventory turnover ratio
c. Operating budget
d. Authorised capital

14. In accounting and organizational theory, _____ is defined as a process effected by an organization's structure, work and authority flows, people and management information systems, designed to help the organization accomplish specific goals or objectives. It is a means by which an organization's resources are directed, monitored, and measured. It plays an important role in preventing and detecting fraud and protecting the organization's resources, both physical (e.g., machinery and property) and intangible (e.g., reputation or intellectual property such as trademarks.)

a. Audit committee
c. Audit risk
b. Auditor independence
d. Internal control

15. _____ is a concept that denotes the precise probability of specific eventualities. Technically, the notion of _____ is independent from the notion of value and, as such, eventualities may have both beneficial and adverse consequences. However, in general usage the convention is to focus only on potential negative impact to some characteristic of value that may arise from a future event.
    a. Risk adjusted return on capital
    b. Discounting
    c. Discount factor
    d. Risk

16. In economics, _____ or _____ goods or real _____ refers to factors of production used to create goods or services that are not themselves significantly consumed (though they may depreciate) in the production process. _____ goods may be acquired with money or financial _____. In finance and accounting, _____ generally refers to financial wealth, especially that used to start or maintain a business.
    a. Disclosure
    b. Vyborg Appeal
    c. Screening
    d. Capital

17. A _____ is an expenditure creating future benefits. A _____ is incurred when a business spends money either to buy fixed assets or to add to the value of an existing fixed asset with a useful life that extends beyond the taxable year. Capex are used by a company to acquire or upgrade physical assets such as equipment, property, or industrial buildings.
    a. Cost of capital
    b. Capital expenditure
    c. BMC Software, Inc.
    d. 3M Company

18. _____ is a process where a business physically counts its entire inventory. A _____ may be mandated by financial accounting rules or the tax regulations to place an accurate value on the inventory, or the business may need to count inventory so component parts or raw materials can be restocked. Businesses may use several different tactics to minimize the disruption caused by _____.
    a. Physical inventory
    b. 3M Company
    c. BNSF Railway
    d. BMC Software, Inc.

19. An _____, operating expenditure, operational expense, operational expenditure or OPEX is an on-going cost for running a product, business, or system. Its counterpart, a capital expenditure (CAPEX), is the cost of developing or providing non-consumable parts for the product or system. For example, the purchase of a photocopier is the CAPEX, and the annual paper and toner cost is the OPEX.
    a. AIG
    b. ABC Television Network
    c. Operating expense
    d. AMEX

20. A _____, in business matters, is an entity that is controlled by a bigger and more powerful entity. The controlled entity is called a company, corporation, or limited liability company, and the controlling entity is called its parent (or the parent company.) The reason for this distinction is that a lone company cannot be a _____ of any organization; only an entity representing a legal fiction as a separate entity can be a _____.
    a. 3M Company
    b. Parent company
    c. Subsidiary
    d. BMC Software, Inc.

Chapter 13. Property, Plant, and Equipment: Depreciation and Depletion 121

21. The _____ is a subset of the general ledger used in accounting. The _____ shows detail for part of the accounting records such as property and equipment, prepaid expenses, etc. The detail would include such items as date the item was purchased or expense incurred, a description of the item, the original balance, and the net book value.
   a. Minority interest
   b. Credit memo
   c. Remittance advice
   d. Subledger

22. Project _____: The project _____ is a prediction of the costs associated with a particular company project. These costs include labor, materials, and other related expenses. The project _____ is often broken down into specific tasks, with task _____s assigned to each.
   a. BMC Software, Inc.
   b. 3M Company
   c. Budget
   d. BNSF Railway

23. Book Value = Original Cost - _____

Book value at the end of year becomes book value at the beginning of next year. The asset is depreciated until the book value equals scrap value.

If the vehicle were to be sold and the sales price exceeded the depreciated value (net book value) then the excess would be considered a gain and subject to depreciation recapture.

   a. ABC Television Network
   b. AIG
   c. Accumulated Depreciation
   d. AMEX

24. _____, in auditing, is the risk that a company's internal controls are insufficient to mitigate or detect errors or fraud.
   a. BNSF Railway
   b. 3M Company
   c. Control risk
   d. BMC Software, Inc.

25. _____ is the realization of an application idea, model, design, specification, standard, algorithm an _____ is a realization of a technical specification or algorithm as a program, software component, or other computer system. Many _____s may exist for a given specification or standard.
   a. AIG
   b. ABC Television Network
   c. AMEX
   d. Implementation

26. An _____ is the buying of one company by another. An _____ may be friendly or hostile. In the former case, the companies cooperate in negotiations; in the latter case, the takeover target is unwilling to be bought or the target's board has no prior knowledge of the offer. _____ usually refers to a purchase of a smaller firm by a larger one. Sometimes, however, a smaller firm will acquire management control of a larger or longer established company and keep its name for the combined entity. This is known as a reverse takeover.
   a. ABC Television Network
   b. Acquisition
   c. AMEX
   d. AIG

27. A maritime _____ is a _____ on a vessel, given to secure the claim of a creditor who provided maritime services to the vessel or who suffered an injury from the vessel's use. Maritime _____s are sometimes referred to as tacit hypothecation. Maritime _____s have little in common with other _____s under the laws of most jurisdictions.

a. Vested
b. Fiduciary
c. Recharacterisation
d. Lien

28. _____ is the state or fact of exclusive rights and control over property, which may be an object, land/real estate or intellectual property. An _____ right is also referred to as title.

_____ is the key building block in the development of the capitalist socio-economic system.

a. Administrative proceeding
b. ABC Television Network
c. Encumbrance
d. Ownership

29. In financial accounting, a _____ or statement of financial position is a summary of a person's or organization's balances. Assets, liabilities and ownership equity are listed as of a specific date, such as the end of its financial year. A _____ is often described as a snapshot of a company's financial condition.

a. Financial statements
b. Balance sheet
c. Statement of retained earnings
d. 3M Company

30. _____ is a type of lease - the other being an operating lease. A _____ effectively allows a firm to finance the purchase of an asset, even if, strictly speaking, the firm never acquires the asset. Typically, a _____ will give the lessee control over an asset for a large proportion of the asset's useful life, providing them the benefits and risks of ownership.

a. Debt ratio
b. Finance lease
c. Profitability index
d. 3M Company

31. A _____ is a contract conferring a right on one person to possess property belonging to another person (called a landlord or lessor) to the exclusion of the owner landlord. It is a rental agreement between landlord and tenant. The relationship between the tenant and the landlord is called a tenancy, and the right to possession by the tenant is sometimes called a leasehold interest.

a. Federal Sentencing Guidelines
b. Lease
c. Model Code of Professional Responsibility
d. Robinson-Patman Act

32. A _____ estate is an ownership interest in land in which a lessee or a tenant holds real property by some form of title from a lessor or landlord.

_____ is a form of property tenure where one party buys the right to occupy land or a building for a given length of time. As lease is a legal estate, _____ estate can be bought and sold on the open market.

a. Real Estate Investment Trust
b. Liquidation value
c. 3M Company
d. Leasehold

33. An _____ is a lease whose term is short compared to the useful life of the asset or piece of equipment (an airliner, a ship etc.) being leased. An _____ is commonly used to acquire equipment on a relatively short-term basis.

a. Issued shares
b. Express warranty
c. Employee Retirement Income Security Act
d. Operating lease

Chapter 13. Property, Plant, and Equipment: Depreciation and Depletion

34. _____ is that which is owed; usually referencing assets owed, but the term can also cover moral obligations and other interactions not requiring money. In the case of assets, _____ is a means of using future purchasing power in the present before a summation has been earned. Some companies and corporations use _____ as a part of their overall corporate finance strategy.
   a. Loan
   b. Debenture
   c. Lender
   d. Debt

35. In physics, and more specifically kinematics, _____ is the change in velocity over time. Because velocity is a vector, it can change in two ways: a change in magnitude and/or a change in direction. In one dimension, _____ is the rate at which something speeds up or slows down.
   a. AMEX
   b. AIG
   c. ABC Television Network
   d. Acceleration

36. The _____ is the current method of accelerated asset depreciation required by the United States income tax code. Under _____, all assets are divided into classes which dictate the number of years over which an asset's cost will be recovered.

Prior to the Accelerated Cost Recovery System (ACRS), most capital purchases were depreciated using a straight line technique, that allowed for the depreciation of the asset over its useful life.

   a. Modified Accelerated Cost Recovery System
   b. BMC Software, Inc.
   c. 3M Company
   d. Categorical grants

37. _____ refers to any one of several methods by which a company, for 'financial accounting' and/or tax purposes, depreciates a fixed asset in such a way that the amount of depreciation taken each year is higher during the earlier years of an assete;s life. For financial accounting purposes, _____ is generally used when an asset is expected to be much more productive during its early years, so that depreciation expense will more accurately represent how much of an assete;s usefulness is being used up each year. For tax purposes, _____ provides a way of deferring corporate income taxes by reducing taxable income in current years, in exchange for increased taxable income in future years.
   a. Indirect tax
   b. Effective marginal tax rates
   c. User charge
   d. Accelerated depreciation

38. There are several methods for calculating depreciation, generally based on either the passage of time or the level of activity (or use) of the asset.

_____ is the simplest and most often used technique, in which the company estimates the salvage value of the asset at the end of the period during which it will be used to generate revenues (useful life), and will expense a portion of original cost in equal increments over that period.

   a. Current asset
   b. Closing entries
   c. Pro forma
   d. Straight-line depreciation

39. In economics, business, retail, and accounting, a _____ is the value of money that has been used up to produce something, and hence is not available for use anymore. In economics, a _____ is an alternative that is given up as a result of a decision. In business, the _____ may be one of acquisition, in which case the amount of money expended to acquire it is counted as _____.

a. Cost allocation	b. Prime cost
c. Cost of quality	d. Cost

40. An _____ is a practitioner of accountancy, which is the measurement, disclosure or provision of assurance about financial information that helps managers, investors, tax authorities and other decision makers make resource allocation decisions.

The word '_____' is derived from the French 'Compter' which took its origin from the Latin 'Computare'. The word was formerly written in English as 'Accomptant', but in process of time the word, which was always pronounced by dropping the 'p', became gradually changed both in pronunciation and in orthography to its present form.

a. ABC Television Network	b. AIG
c. Accountant	d. AMEX

41. _____ is the process of increasing, or accounting for, an amount over a period of time. Particular instances of the term include:

- _____, the allocation of a lump sum amount to different time periods, particularly for loans and other forms of finance, including related interest or other finance charges.
    - _____ schedule, a table detailing each periodic payment on a loan (typically a mortgage), as generated by an _____ calculator.
    - Negative _____, an _____ schedule where the loan amount actually increases through not paying the full interest
- Amortized analysis, analyzing the execution cost of algorithms over a sequence of operations.
- _____ of capital expenditures of certain assets under accounting rules, particularly intangible assets, in a manner analogous to depreciation.
- _____

a. Amortization	b. EBIT
c. Annuity	d. Intangible

42. _____ are defined as identifiable non-monetary assets that cannot be seen, touched or physically measured, which are created through time and/or effort and that are identifiable as a separate asset. There are two primary forms of intangibles - legal intangibles (such as trade secrets (e.g., customer lists), copyrights, patents, trademarks, and goodwill) and competitive intangibles (such as knowledge activities (know-how, knowledge), collaboration activities, leverage activities, and structural activities.) Legal intangibles are known under the generic term intellectual property and generate legal property rights defensible in a court of law.

a. AIG	b. Overhead
c. ABC Television Network	d. Intangible assets

43. _____ is concerned with the provisions and use of accounting information to managers within organizations, to provide them with the basis to make informed business decisions that will allow them to be better equipped in their management and control functions.

Chapter 13. Property, Plant, and Equipment: Depreciation and Depletion

In contrast to financial accountancy information, _____ information is:

- usually confidential and used by management, instead of publicly reported;
- forward-looking, instead of historical;
- pragmatically computed using extensive management information systems and internal controls, instead of complying with accounting standards.

This is because of the different emphasis: _____ information is used within an organization, typically for decision-making.

a. Grenzplankostenrechnung
c. Nonassurance services
b. Governmental accounting
d. Management accounting

44. A _____ is a set of exclusive rights granted by a state to an inventor or his assignee for a limited period of time in exchange for a disclosure of an invention.

The procedure for granting _____s, the requirements placed on the _____ee and the extent of the exclusive rights vary widely between countries according to national laws and international agreements. Typically, however, a _____ application must include one or more claims defining the invention which must be new, inventive, and useful or industrially applicable.

a. Trust indenture
c. FLSA
b. Negligence
d. Patent

45. A _____ or trade mark, identified by the symbols â„¢ (not yet registered) and Â® (registered), is a distinctive sign or indicator used by an individual, business organization or other legal entity to identify that the products and/or services to consumers with which the _____ appears originate from a unique source, and to distinguish its products or services from those of other entities. A _____ is a type of intellectual property, and typically a name, word, phrase, logo, symbol, design, image, or a combination of these elements. There is also a range of non-conventional _____s comprising marks which do not fall into these standard categories.

a. Risk management
c. Kanban
b. Trademark
d. FIFO

Chapter 14. Accounts Payable and Other Liabilities

1. In financial accounting, a _____ is defined as an obligation of an entity arising from past transactions or events, the settlement of which may result in the transfer or use of assets, provision of services or other yielding of economic benefits in the future.
   a. False Claims Act
   b. Vested
   c. Corporate governance
   d. Liability

2. _____ is a file or account that contains money that a person or company owes to suppliers, but has not paid yet (a form of debt.) When you receive an invoice you add it to the file, and then you remove it when you pay. Thus, the A/P is a form of credit that suppliers offer to their purchasers by allowing them to pay for a product or service after it has already been received.
   a. Accrual
   b. Earnings before interest, taxes, depreciation and amortization
   c. Accounts payable
   d. Accounts receivable

3. _____ are liabilities which have occurred, but have not been paid or logged under accounts payable during an accounting period; in other words, obligations for goods and services provided to a company for which invoices have not yet been received. Examples would include accrued wages payable, accrued sales tax payable, and accrued rent payable.

There are two general types of _____:

- Routine and recurring
- Infrequent or non-routine

Most companies pay their employees on a predetermined schedule. Let's say that the 'Imaginary company Ltd.' pays its employees each Friday for the hours worked that week.

   a. ABC Television Network
   b. AMEX
   c. Accrued liabilities
   d. AIG

4. _____, in auditing, is the risk that the account or section being audited is materially misstated without considering internal controls due to error; _____ does not include an assessment of the risk of material misstatement due to fraud. The assessment of _____ depends on the professional judgement of the auditor, and it is done after assessing the business environment of the entity being audited.

_____ is typically assessed using a scale, with assessments being either low, medium, or high.

   a. AIG
   b. ABC Television Network
   c. AMEX
   d. Inherent risk

5. In finance, _____ is the process of estimating the potential market value of a financial asset or liability. They can be done on assets (for example, investments in marketable securities such as stocks, options, business enterprises, or intangible assets such as patents and trademarks) or on liabilities (e.g., Bonds issued by a company.) A _____ is required in many contexts including investment analysis, capital budgeting, merger and acquisition transactions, financial reporting, taxable events to determine the proper tax liability, and in litigation.
   a. Vyborg Appeal
   b. Disclosure
   c. Daybook
   d. Valuation

Chapter 14. Accounts Payable and Other Liabilities

6. A _____ is a bond which is worth a certain monetary value and which may only be spent for specific reasons or on specific goods. Examples include -- but are not limited to -- housing, travel and food _____s. The term _____ is also a synonym for receipt, and is often used to refer to receipts used as evidence of, for example, the declaration that a service has been performed or that an expenditure has been made.
   a. 3M Company
   b. BMC Software, Inc.
   c. Source document
   d. Voucher

7. _____ means the giving out of information, either voluntarily or to be in compliance with legal regulations or workplace rules.

   - In Computer security, full _____ means disclosing full information about vulnerabilities.
   - In computing, _____ widget
   - Journalism, full _____ refers to disclosing the interests of the writer which may bear on the subject being written about, for example, if the writer has worked with an interview subject in the past.

   - In law:
     - The law of England and Wales, _____ refers to a process that may form part of legal proceedings, whereby parties inform to other parties the existence of any relevant documents that are, or have been, in their control. This compares with the process known as discovery in the course of legal proceedings in the United States.
     - In U.S. civil procedure (litigation rules for civil cases), _____ is a stage prior to trial. In civil cases, each party must disclose to the opposing party the following: names of witnesses which it may use to support its side, copies of documents (or mere description of these documents) in its control which it may use to support its side, computation of damages claimed, and certain insurance information. _____ is related to, but technically prior to, the discovery stage.
     - In Company law (known as 'corporate law' in the United States), _____ refers to giving out information about public or limited companies or their officers, which might be kept secret if the company was a private company or a partnership.

   - In real property transactions, _____ refers to providing to a buyer information known to the seller or broker/agent concerning the condition or other aspects of real property that would affect the property's value or desirability. These rules regarding what information must be disclosed, and whether the information must be disclosed even if a buyer does not ask, vary from one jurisdiction to the next.

   a. Tax harmonisation
   b. Controlled Foreign Corporations
   c. Trailing
   d. Disclosure

8. _____ is a specific term used in companies' financial reporting from the company-whole point of view. Because that use excludes the effects of changing ownership interest, an economic measure of _____ is necessary for financial analysis from the shareholders' point of view

_____ is defined by the Financial Accounting Standards Board, or FASB, as 'the change in equity [net assets] of a business enterprise during a period from transactions and other events and circumstances from nonowner sources. It includes all changes in equity during a period except those resulting from investments by owners and distributions to owners.'

_____ is the sum of net income and other items that must bypass the income statement because they have not been realized, including items like an unrealized holding gain or loss from available for sale securities and foreign currency translation gains or losses.

    a. BMC Software, Inc.
    b. Comprehensive income
    c. 3M Company
    d. BNSF Railway

9. An _____ is a term used in behavioral economics to describe those types of behaviors that impose costs on a person in the long-run that are not taken into account when making decisions in the present. Classical Economics discourages government from creating legislation that targets internalities, because it is assumed that the consumer takes these personal costs into account when paying for the good that causes the _____. For example, cigarettes should be taxed because of the negative consumption externalities that they impose, such as second-hand smoke, not because the smoker harms him or herself by smoking.

    a. Authorised capital
    b. Operating budget
    c. Inventory turnover ratio
    d. Internality

10. In accounting and organizational theory, _____ is defined as a process effected by an organization's structure, work and authority flows, people and management information systems, designed to help the organization accomplish specific goals or objectives. It is a means by which an organization's resources are directed, monitored, and measured. It plays an important role in preventing and detecting fraud and protecting the organization's resources, both physical (e.g., machinery and property) and intangible (e.g., reputation or intellectual property such as trademarks.)

    a. Audit committee
    b. Auditor independence
    c. Audit risk
    d. Internal control

11. _____ is a concept that denotes the precise probability of specific eventualities. Technically, the notion of _____ is independent from the notion of value and, as such, eventualities may have both beneficial and adverse consequences. However, in general usage the convention is to focus only on potential negative impact to some characteristic of value that may arise from a future event.

    a. Risk adjusted return on capital
    b. Risk
    c. Discount factor
    d. Discounting

12. A _____ is a commercial document issued by a buyer to a seller, indicating types, quantities, and agreed prices for products or services the seller will provide to the buyer. Sending a _____ to a supplier constitutes a legal offer to buy products or services. Acceptance of a _____ by a seller usually forms a once-off contract between the buyer and seller, so no contract exists until the _____ is accepted.

    a. BMC Software, Inc.
    b. Purchase order
    c. Voucher
    d. 3M Company

13. _____ refers to a business or organization attempting to acquire goods or services to accomplish the goals of the enterprise. Though there are several organizations that attempt to set standards in the _____ process, processes can vary greatly between organizations. Typically the word e;_____e; is not used interchangeably with the word e;procuremente;, since procurement typically includes Expediting, Supplier Quality, and Traffic and Logistics (T'L) in addition to _____.

a. Purchasing
b. Consignor
c. Supply chain
d. Free port

14. _____ is the concept of having more than one person required to complete a task. It is alternatively called segregation of duties or, in the political realm, separation of powers.

_____ is one of the key concepts of internal control and is the most difficult and sometimes the most costly one to achieve. The term _____ is already well-known in financial accounting systems. Companies in all sizes understand not to combine roles such as receiving checks (payment on account) and approving write-offs, depositing cash and reconciling bank statements, approving time cards and have custody of pay checks, etc.

a. Separation of duties
b. BMC Software, Inc.
c. Salary
d. 3M Company

15. In accounting, the _____ is a worksheet listing the balance at a certain date, of each ledger account in two columns, namely debit and credit. Under the double-entry system, in any transaction the total of any debits must equal the total of any credits, so in a _____ the total of the debit side should always be equal to the total of the credit side. The _____ thus serves as a tool to detect errors, which can result in the totals not being equal.

a. Current asset
b. Bottom line
c. Depreciation
d. Trial balance

16. The general definition of an _____ is an evaluation of a person, organization, system, process, project or product. _____s are performed to ascertain the validity and reliability of information; also to provide an assessment of a system's internal control. The goal of an _____ is to express an opinion on the person/organization/system (etc) in question, under evaluation based on work done on a test basis.

a. Institute of Chartered Accountants of India
b. Assurance service
c. Audit regime
d. Audit

17. A _____ is a common type of chart, that represents an algorithm or process, showing the steps as boxes of various kinds, and their order by connecting these with arrows. _____s are used in analyzing, designing, documenting or managing a process or program in various fields.

The first structured method for documenting process flow, the 'flow process chart', was introduced by Frank Gilbreth to members of ASME in 1921 as the presentation e;Process Charts--First Steps in Finding the One Best Waye;.

a. BMC Software, Inc.
b. 3M Company
c. BNSF Railway
d. Flowchart

18. _____, in auditing, is the risk that a company's internal controls are insufficient to mitigate or detect errors or fraud.
a. 3M Company
b. BMC Software, Inc.
c. BNSF Railway
d. Control risk

19. _____ or audit log is a chronological sequence of audit records, each of which contains evidence directly pertaining to and resulting from the execution of a business process or system function.

Audit records typically result from activities such as transactions or communications by individual people, systems, accounts or other entities.

Webopedia defines an _____ as 'a record showing who has accessed a computer system and what operations he or she has performed during a given period of time.' ()

In telecommunication, the term means a record of both completed and attempted accesses and service, or data forming a logical path linking a sequence of events, used to trace the transactions that have affected the contents of a record.

a. AMEX
b. ABC Television Network
c. AIG
d. Audit trail

20. As part of an organization's internal financial controls, the accounting department may institute a _____ process to help manage requests for purchases. Requests for the creation of purchase of goods and services are documented and routed for approval within the organization and then delivered to the accounting group.

Typically an accounting staff member is assigned responsibility for purchase order management, referred to commonly as the PO (purchase order) Coordinator.

a. 3M Company
b. Purchase requisition
c. BMC Software, Inc.
d. BNSF Railway

21. An _____ or bill is a commercial document issued by a seller to the buyer, indicating the products, quantities, and agreed prices for products or services the seller has provided the buyer. An _____ indicates the buyer must pay the seller, according to the payment terms.

In the rental industry, an _____ must include a specific reference to the duration of the time being billed, so rather than quantity, price and discount the invoicing amount is based on quantity, price, discount and duration.

a. AMEX
b. AIG
c. ABC Television Network
d. Invoice

22. Discounting is a financial mechanism in which a debtor obtains the right to delay payments to a creditor, for a defined period of time, in exchange for a charge or fee. Essentially, the party that owes money in the present purchases the right to delay the payment until some future date. The _____, or charge, is simply the difference between the original amount owed in the present and the amount that has to be paid in the future to settle the debt.

a. Discount
b. Risk aversion
c. Discount factor
d. Discounting

23. _____ or in-process inventory includes the set at large of unfinished items for products in a production process. These items are not yet completed but either just being fabricated or waiting in a queue for further processing or in a buffer storage. The term is used in production and supply chain management.

Chapter 14. Accounts Payable and Other Liabilities

a. BMC Software, Inc.
b. 3M Company
c. BNSF Railway
d. Work in process

24. _____ is a process where a business physically counts its entire inventory. A _____ may be mandated by financial accounting rules or the tax regulations to place an accurate value on the inventory, or the business may need to count inventory so component parts or raw materials can be restocked. Businesses may use several different tactics to minimize the disruption caused by _____.

a. BNSF Railway
b. BMC Software, Inc.
c. 3M Company
d. Physical inventory

25. In a company, _____ is the sum of all financial records of salaries, wages, bonuses and deductions.

A paycheck, is traditionally a paper document issued by an employer to pay an employee for services rendered. While most commonly used in the United States, recently the physical paycheck has been increasingly replaced by electronic direct deposit to bank accounts.

a. 3M Company
b. Payroll
c. Tax expense
d. Total Expense Ratio

26. A _____ is the pinnacle activity involved in selling products or services in return for money or other compensation. It is an act of completion of a commercial activity.

A _____ is completed by the seller, the owner of the goods.

a. Sale
b. High yield stock
c. Tertiary sector of economy
d. Maturity

27. A _____ is a compensation, usually financial, received by a worker in exchange for their labor.

Compensation in terms of _____s is given to worker and compensation in terms of salary is given to employees. Compensation is a monetary benefits given to employees in returns of the services provided by them.

a. Wage
b. Retirement plan
c. BMC Software, Inc.
d. 3M Company

28. The _____ of 1974 (Pub.L. 93-406, 88 Stat. 829, enacted September 2, 1974) is an American federal statute that establishes minimum standards for pension plans in private industry and provides for extensive rules on the federal income tax effects of transactions associated with employee benefit plans. It was enacted to protect the interests of employee benefit plan participants and their beneficiaries by requiring the disclosure to them of financial and other information concerning the plan; by establishing standards of conduct for plan fiduciaries; and by providing for appropriate remedies and access to the federal courts.

a. Investment Advisers Act of 1940
b. Exclusive right
c. Operating Lease
d. Employee Retirement Income Security Act

29. Employment is a contract between two parties, one being the employer and the other being the _____. An _____ may be defined as: 'A person in the service of another under any contract of hire, express or implied, oral or written, where the employer has the power or right to control and direct the _____ in the material details of how the work is to be performed.' Black's Law Dictionary page 471 (5th ed. 1979.)
   a. ABC Television Network
   b. AMEX
   c. AIG
   d. Employee

30. _____ is any physical or virtual entity that is owned by an individual or jointly by a group of individuals. An owner of _____ has the right to consume, sell, rent, mortgage, transfer and exchange his or her _____. Important widely-recognized types of _____ include real _____, personal _____ (other physical possessions), and intellectual _____ (rights over artistic creations, inventions, etc.), although the latter is not always as widely recognized or enforced.
   a. Fiduciary
   b. Property
   c. Primary authority
   d. Disclosure requirement

31. A _____ is a fungible, negotiable instrument representing financial value. they are broadly categorized into debt securities (such as banknotes, bonds and debentures), and equity securities; e.g., common stocks. The company or other entity issuing the _____ is called the issuer.
   a. 3M Company
   b. BMC Software, Inc.
   c. Security
   d. Tracking stock

32. _____ of something is, in finance, the adding together of interest or different investments over a period of time such as atoms (1 - the act or process of accruing; 2 - the amount that accrues.) It holds specific meanings in accounting and payroll.

_____, in accounting, describes the accounting method known as _____ basis, whereby revenues and expenses are recognized when they are accrued, i.e. accumulated (earned or incurred), regardless when the actual cash is received or paid out.

   a. Accrual
   b. Earnings before interest, taxes, depreciation and amortization
   c. Assets
   d. Accounts receivable

Chapter 14. Accounts Payable and Other Liabilities

33. _____ is evidence obtained during a financial audit and recorded in the audit working papers.

    - In the audit engagement acceptance or reappointment stage, _____ is the information that the auditor is to consider for the appointment. For examples, change in the entity control environment, inherent risk and nature of the entity business, and scope of audit work.

    - In the audit planning stage, _____ is the information that the auditor is to consider for the most effective and efficient audit approach. For examples, reliability of internal control procedures, and analytical review systems.

    - In the control testing stage, _____ is the information that the auditor is to consider for the mix of audit test of control and audit substantive tests.

    - In the substantive testing stage, _____ is the information that the auditor is to make sure the appropriation of financial statement assertions. For examples, existence, rights and obligations, occurrence, completeness, valuation, measurement, presentation and disclosure of a particular transaction or account balance.

    a. Audit
    b. ITGCs
    c. Institute of Chartered Accountants of India
    d. Audit evidence

34. An _____ is a business professional who deals with the financial impact of risk and uncertainty. They have a deep understanding of financial security systems, their reasons for being, their complexity, their mathematics, and the way they work (Trowbridge 1989, p. 7).
    a. AMEX
    b. AIG
    c. ABC Television Network
    d. Actuary

35. The term _____ or superannuation refers to a pension granted upon retirement. They may be set up by employers, insurance companies, the government or other institutions such as employer associations or trade unions.
    a. 3M Company
    b. Wage
    c. BMC Software, Inc.
    d. Retirement plan

36. The _____ is the national, professional association of CPAs in the United States, with more than 330,000 members, including CPAs in business and industry, public practice, government, and education; student affiliates; and international associates. It sets ethical standards for the profession and U.S. auditing standards for audits of private companies; federal, state and local governments; and non-profit organizations.

    Approximately 40% of its members are engaged in the practice of public accounting, in areas such as auditing, accounting, taxation, general business consulting, business valuation, personal financial planning and business technology.

    a. ABC Television Network
    b. AIG
    c. Other postemployment benefits
    d. American Institute of Certified Public Accountants

37. An _____ is a tax levied on the financial income of people, corporations, or other legal entities. Various _____ systems exist, with varying degrees of tax incidence. Income taxation can be progressive, proportional, or regressive.

a. Income tax
b. Ordinary income
c. Implied level of government service
d. Individual Retirement Arrangement

38. In financial accounting, a _____ or statement of financial position is a summary of a person's or organization's balances. Assets, liabilities and ownership equity are listed as of a specific date, such as the end of its financial year. A _____ is often described as a snapshot of a company's financial condition.
a. 3M Company
b. Statement of retained earnings
c. Financial statements
d. Balance sheet

39. The _____ of 1977 (15 U.S.C. ÂÂ§ÂÂ§ 78dd-1, et seq.) is a United States federal law known primarily for two of its main provisions, one that addresses accounting transparency requirements under the Securities Exchange Act of 1934 and another concerning bribery of foreign officials.
a. Foreign Corrupt Practices Act
b. Lease
c. Pre-emption right
d. Competition law

40. An _____ is the buying of one company by another. An _____ may be friendly or hostile. In the former case, the companies cooperate in negotiations; in the latter case, the takeover target is unwilling to be bought or the target's board has no prior knowledge of the offer. _____ usually refers to a purchase of a smaller firm by a larger one. Sometimes, however, a smaller firm will acquire management control of a larger or longer established company and keep its name for the combined entity. This is known as a reverse takeover.
a. AMEX
b. ABC Television Network
c. Acquisition
d. AIG

Chapter 15. Debt and Equity Capital

1. In finance, a _____ is a debt security, in which the authorized issuer owes the holders a debt and, depending on the terms of the _____, is obliged to pay interest (the coupon) and/or to repay the principal at a later date, termed maturity. It is a formal contract to repay borrowed money with interest at fixed intervals.

Thus a _____ is like a loan: the issuer is the borrower, the _____ holder is the lender, and the coupon is the interest.

a. Zero-coupon bond
c. Coupon rate
b. Revenue bonds
d. Bond

2. A _____ is defined as a certificate of agreement of loans which is given under the company's stamp and carries an undertaking that the _____ holder will get a fixed return (fixed on the basis of interest rates) and the principal amount whenever the _____ matures.

In finance, a _____ is a long-term debt instrument used by governments and large companies to obtain funds. It is defined as 'any form of borrowing that commits a firm to pay interest and repay capital.

a. Credit rating
c. Loan to value
b. Debenture
d. Loan

3. _____ is that which is owed; usually referencing assets owed, but the term can also cover moral obligations and other interactions not requiring money. In the case of assets, _____ is a means of using future purchasing power in the present before a summation has been earned. Some companies and corporations use _____ as a part of their overall corporate finance strategy.

a. Loan
c. Debt
b. Debenture
d. Lender

4. The _____ of 1977 (15 U.S.C. §§ 78dd-1, et seq.) is a United States federal law known primarily for two of its main provisions, one that addresses accounting transparency requirements under the Securities Exchange Act of 1934 and another concerning bribery of foreign officials.

a. Competition law
c. Pre-emption right
b. Lease
d. Foreign Corrupt Practices Act

5. _____, in auditing, is the risk that the account or section being audited is materially misstated without considering internal controls due to error; _____ does not include an assessment of the risk of material misstatement due to fraud. The assessment of _____ depends on the professional judgement of the auditor, and it is done after assessing the business environment of the entity being audited.

_____ is typically assessed using a scale, with assessments being either low, medium, or high.

a. AMEX
c. ABC Television Network
b. Inherent risk
d. AIG

6. _____ is a fee paid on borrowed assets. It is the price paid for the use of borrowed money, or, money earned by deposited funds. Assets that are sometimes lent with _____ include money, shares, consumer goods through hire purchase, major assets such as aircraft, and even entire factories in finance lease arrangements. The _____ is calculated upon the value of the assets in the same manner as upon money.

a. AIG
b. ABC Television Network
c. Insolvency
d. Interest

7. _____ relates to the cost of borrowing money. It is the price that a lender charges a borrower for the use of the lender's money. _____ is different from OPEX and CAPEX, for it relates to the capital structure of a company.
   a. AIG
   b. Interest
   c. Interest expense
   d. ABC Television Network

8. A _____ is a fund established by a government agency or business for the purpose of reducing debt.

The _____ was first used in Great Britain in the 18th century to reduce national debt. While used by Robert Walpole in 1716 and effectively in the 1720s and early 1730s, it originated in the commercial tax syndicates of the Italian peninsula of the 14th century to retire redeemable public debt of those cities.

   a. Sinking fund
   b. Treasury company
   c. Payback period
   d. Segregated portfolio company

9. The United States _____ Act of 1939 (Trust indentureA), codified at 15 U.S.C. Â§ 77aaa through 15 U.S.C. Â§ 77bbbb, supplements the Securities Act of 1933 in the case of the distribution of debt securities.
   a. Robinson-Patman Act
   b. Trust indenture
   c. Charter
   d. Covenant

10. In finance, _____ is the process of estimating the potential market value of a financial asset or liability. They can be done on assets (for example, investments in marketable securities such as stocks, options, business enterprises, or intangible assets such as patents and trademarks) or on liabilities (e.g., Bonds issued by a company.) A _____ is required in many contexts including investment analysis, capital budgeting, merger and acquisition transactions, financial reporting, taxable events to determine the proper tax liability, and in litigation.
    a. Vyborg Appeal
    b. Daybook
    c. Disclosure
    d. Valuation

11. _____ is a file or account that contains money that a person or company owes to suppliers, but has not paid yet (a form of debt.) When you receive an invoice you add it to the file, and then you remove it when you pay. Thus, the A/P is a form of credit that suppliers offer to their purchasers by allowing them to pay for a product or service after it has already been received.
    a. Earnings before interest, taxes, depreciation and amortization
    b. Accrual
    c. Accounts payable
    d. Accounts receivable

12. The general definition of an _____ is an evaluation of a person, organization, system, process, project or product. _____s are performed to ascertain the validity and reliability of information; also to provide an assessment of a system's internal control. The goal of an _____ is to express an opinion on the person/organization/system (etc) in question, under evaluation based on work done on a test basis.
    a. Assurance service
    b. Audit regime
    c. Institute of Chartered Accountants of India
    d. Audit

Chapter 15. Debt and Equity Capital

13. Title _____s serve as guarantees to the recipient of property, ensuring that the recipient receives what he or she bargained for. The English _____s of title, sometimes included in deeds to real property, are that the grantor is lawfully seized (in fee simple) of the property, (2) that the grantor has the right to convey the property to the grantee, (3) that the property is conveyed without encumbrances (this _____ is frequently modified to allow for certain encumbrances), (4) that the grantor has done no act to encumber the property, (5) that the grantee shall have quiet possession of the property, and (6) that the grantor will execute such further assurances of the land as may be requisite (Nos. 3 and 4, which overlap significantly, are sometimes treated as one item.)
    a. Patent
    b. Liability
    c. Covenant
    d. Tax patent

14. _____ means the giving out of information, either voluntarily or to be in compliance with legal regulations or workplace rules.

    - In Computer security, full _____ means disclosing full information about vulnerabilities.
    - In computing, _____ widget
    - Journalism, full _____ refers to disclosing the interests of the writer which may bear on the subject being written about, for example, if the writer has worked with an interview subject in the past.

    - In law:
        - The law of England and Wales, _____ refers to a process that may form part of legal proceedings, whereby parties inform to other parties the existence of any relevant documents that are, or have been, in their control. This compares with the process known as discovery in the course of legal proceedings in the United States.
        - In U.S. civil procedure (litigation rules for civil cases), _____ is a stage prior to trial. In civil cases, each party must disclose to the opposing party the following: names of witnesses which it may use to support its side, copies of documents (or mere description of these documents) in its control which it may use to support its side, computation of damages claimed, and certain insurance information. _____ is related to, but technically prior to, the discovery stage.
        - In Company law (known as 'corporate law' in the United States), _____ refers to giving out information about public or limited companies or their officers, which might be kept secret if the company was a private company or a partnership.

    - In real property transactions, _____ refers to providing to a buyer information known to the seller or broker/agent concerning the condition or other aspects of real property that would affect the property's value or desirability. These rules regarding what information must be disclosed, and whether the information must be disclosed even if a buyer does not ask, vary from one jurisdiction to the next.

    a. Tax harmonisation
    b. Trailing
    c. Controlled Foreign Corporations
    d. Disclosure

15. Discounting is a financial mechanism in which a debtor obtains the right to delay payments to a creditor, for a defined period of time, in exchange for a charge or fee. Essentially, the party that owes money in the present purchases the right to delay the payment until some future date. The _____, or charge, is simply the difference between the original amount owed in the present and the amount that has to be paid in the future to settle the debt.

a. Risk aversion
c. Discounting
b. Discount factor
d. Discount

16. In accounting, _____ has a very specific meaning. It is an outflow of cash or other valuable assets from a person or company to another person or company. This outflow of cash is generally one side of a trade for products or services that have equal or better current or future value to the buyer than to the seller.
   a. ABC Television Network
   b. AMEX
   c. AIG
   d. Expense

17. An _____ is a legal contract between two parties, particularly for indentured labour or a term of apprenticeship but also for certain land transactions. The term comes from the medieval English '_____ of retainer' -- a legal contract written in duplicate on the same sheet, with the copies separated by cutting along a jagged line so that the teeth of the two parts could later be refitted to confirm authenticity. Each party to the deed would then retain a part.
   a. Employee Retirement Income Security Act
   b. Impracticability
   c. Operating Lease
   d. Indenture

18. An _____ is a term used in behavioral economics to describe those types of behaviors that impose costs on a person in the long-run that are not taken into account when making decisions in the present. Classical Economics discourages government from creating legislation that targets internalities, because it is assumed that the consumer takes these personal costs into account when paying for the good that causes the _____. For example, cigarettes should be taxed because of the negative consumption externalities that they impose, such as second-hand smoke, not because the smoker harms him or herself by smoking.
   a. Operating budget
   b. Inventory turnover ratio
   c. Authorised capital
   d. Internality

19. In accounting and organizational theory, _____ is defined as a process effected by an organization's structure, work and authority flows, people and management information systems, designed to help the organization accomplish specific goals or objectives. It is a means by which an organization's resources are directed, monitored, and measured. It plays an important role in preventing and detecting fraud and protecting the organization's resources, both physical (e.g., machinery and property) and intangible (e.g., reputation or intellectual property such as trademarks.)
   a. Internal control
   b. Audit risk
   c. Auditor independence
   d. Audit committee

20. In economic models, the _____ time frame assumes no fixed factors of production. Firms can enter or leave the marketplace, and the cost (and availability) of land, labor, raw materials, and capital goods can be assumed to vary. In contrast, in the short-run time frame, certain factors are assumed to be fixed, because there is not sufficient time for them to change.
   a. Short-run
   b. 3M Company
   c. BMC Software, Inc.
   d. Long-run

21. _____ is a concept that denotes the precise probability of specific eventualities. Technically, the notion of _____ is independent from the notion of value and, as such, eventualities may have both beneficial and adverse consequences. However, in general usage the convention is to focus only on potential negative impact to some characteristic of value that may arise from a future event.

Chapter 15. Debt and Equity Capital

a. Risk adjusted return on capital
c. Discount factor
b. Discounting
d. Risk

22. A _____ is a debt security issued by a business entity, such as a corporation, or by a government. It differs from the more common types of investment securities in that it is unregistered - no records are kept of the owner, or the transactions involving ownership. Whoever physically holds the paper on which the bond is issued owns the instrument.
a. Revenue bonds
c. Coupon rate
b. Bearer bond
d. Convertible bond

23. A _____ is a body of elected or appointed members who jointly oversee the activities of a company or organization. The body sometimes has a different name, such as board of trustees, board of governors, board of managers, or executive board. It is often simply referred to as 'the board.'

A board's activities are determined by the powers, duties, and responsibilities delegated to it or conferred on it by an authority outside itself.

a. Consumer protection laws
c. Chief Financial Officers Act of 1990
b. Board of directors
d. Hospital Survey and Construction Act

24. _____ is a legal document issued to lenders and describes key terms such as the interest rate, maturity date, convertibility, pledge, promises, representations, covenants, and other terms of the bond offering. When the Offering Memorandum is prepared in advance of marketing a Bond, the indenture will typically be summarised in the 'Description of Notes' section.
a. Leasing
c. Bond indenture
b. Consumer protection laws
d. Malpractice

25. In marketing a _____ is a ticket or document that can be exchanged for a financial discount or rebate when purchasing a product. Customarily, _____s are issued by manufacturers of consumer packaged goods or by retailers, to be used in retail stores as a part of sales promotions. They are often widely distributed through mail, magazines, newspapers, the Internet, and mobile devices such as cell phones.
a. 3M Company
c. Coupon
b. Merchandising
d. BMC Software, Inc.

26. A _____ is a type of debt Like all debt instruments, a _____ entails the redistribution of financial assets over time, between the lender and the borrower.
a. Lender
c. Debenture
b. Loan to value
d. Loan

27. A _____, also referred to as a note payable in accounting, is a contract where one party (the maker or issuer) makes an unconditional promise in writing to pay a sum of money to the other (the payee), either at a fixed or determinable future time or on demand of the payee, under specific terms. They differ from IOUs in that they contain a specific promise to pay, rather than simply acknowledging that a debt exists.

The terms of a note typically include the principal amount, the interest rate if any, and the maturity date.

Chapter 15. Debt and Equity Capital

a. BNSF Railway
c. BMC Software, Inc.
b. 3M Company
d. Promissory note

28. A _____ is the transfer of wealth from one party (such as a person or company) to another. A _____ is usually made in exchange for the provision of goods, services or both, or to fulfill a legal obligation.

The simplest and oldest form of _____ is barter, the exchange of one good or service for another.

a. Payee
c. Payment
b. 3M Company
d. BMC Software, Inc.

29. _____ is a legal term that refers to a holder of property on behalf of a beneficiary. A trust can be set up either to benefit particular persons, or for any charitable purposes (but not generally for non-charitable purposes): typical examples are a will trust for the testator's children and family, a pension trust (to confer benefits on employees and their families), and a charitable trust. In all cases, the _____ may be a person or company, whether or not they are a prospective beneficiary.

a. Trustee
c. Cash cow
b. Performance measurement
d. Management by exception

30. In financial accounting, a _____ is defined as an obligation of an entity arising from past transactions or events, the settlement of which may result in the transfer or use of assets, provision of services or other yielding of economic benefits in the future.

a. Vested
c. Corporate governance
b. False Claims Act
d. Liability

31. A _____ is the transfer of an interest in property (or the equivalent in law - a charge) to a lender as a security for a debt - usually a loan of money. While a _____ in itself is not a debt, it is the lender's security for a debt. It is a transfer of an interest in land (or the equivalent) from the owner to the _____ lender, on the condition that this interest will be returned to the owner when the terms of the _____ have been satisfied or performed.

a. Mortgage
c. BMC Software, Inc.
b. 3M Company
d. BNSF Railway

Chapter 15. Debt and Equity Capital

32. _____ is evidence obtained during a financial audit and recorded in the audit working papers.

- In the audit engagement acceptance or reappointment stage, _____ is the information that the auditor is to consider for the appointment. For examples, change in the entity control environment, inherent risk and nature of the entity business, and scope of audit work.

- In the audit planning stage, _____ is the information that the auditor is to consider for the most effective and efficient audit approach. For examples, reliability of internal control procedures, and analytical review systems.

- In the control testing stage, _____ is the information that the auditor is to consider for the mix of audit test of control and audit substantive tests.

- In the substantive testing stage, _____ is the information that the auditor is to make sure the appropriation of financial statement assertions. For examples, existence, rights and obligations, occurrence, completeness, valuation, measurement, presentation and disclosure of a particular transaction or account balance.

a. Institute of Chartered Accountants of India
b. Audit
c. ITGCs
d. Audit evidence

33. A _____ is a habit, a preparation, a state of readiness, or a tendency to act in a specified way.

The terms dispositional belief and occurrent belief refer, in the former case, to a belief that is held in the mind but not currently being considered, and in the latter case, to a belief that is currently being considered by the mind.

In Bourdieu's theory of fields _____s are the natural tendencies of each individual to take on a certain position in any field.

a. 3M Company
b. Disposition
c. BNSF Railway
d. BMC Software, Inc.

34. A _____ is a fungible, negotiable instrument representing financial value. they are broadly categorized into debt securities (such as banknotes, bonds and debentures), and equity securities; e.g., common stocks. The company or other entity issuing the _____ is called the issuer.

a. BMC Software, Inc.
b. 3M Company
c. Tracking stock
d. Security

35. Congress enacted the _____, in the aftermath of the stock market crash of 1929 and during the ensuing Great Depression.

a. Securities Act of 1933
b. Bookkeeping
c. Monte Carlo methods
d. Sustainability measurement

36. In business and accounting, _____ are everything of value that is owned by a person or company. It is a claim on the property your income of a borrower. The balance sheet of a firm records the monetary value of the _____ owned by the firm.

a. Accrual basis accounting
b. Assets
c. Accounts receivable
d. Earnings before interest, taxes, depreciation and amortization

37. In accounting, _____ are considered liabilities of the business that are to be settled in cash within the fiscal year or the operating cycle, whichever period is longer.

For example accounts payable for goods, services or supplies that were purchased for use in the operation of the business and payable within a normal period of time would be _____.

Bonds, mortgages and loans that are payable over a term exceeding one year would be fixed liabilities.

a. Treasury stock
b. Closing entries
c. Current liabilities
d. Payroll

38. _____ in law is the planning and desire to perform an act, to fail to do so (i.e. an omission) or to achieve a state of affairs in psychological view it may mean a different thing.

In criminal law, for a given actus reus ('guilty act'), the required element to prove _____ consists of showing mens rea (mental state, 'guilty mind'.)

The requirements for the proof of _____ in tort law are generally simpler than criminal law.

a. ABC Television Network
b. Intent
c. AMEX
d. AIG

39. _____ that may or may not be incurred by an entity depending on the outcome of a future event such as a court case. These liabilities are recorded in a company's accounts and shown in the balance sheet when both probable and reasonably estimable. A footnote to the balance sheet describes the nature and extent of the _____.

a. Tangible
b. Nonacquiescence
c. Contingent Liabilities
d. Headnote

40. In economics, _____ or _____ goods or real _____ refers to factors of production used to create goods or services that are not themselves significantly consumed (though they may depreciate) in the production process. _____ goods may be acquired with money or financial _____. In finance and accounting, _____ generally refers to financial wealth, especially that used to start or maintain a business.

a. Disclosure
b. Screening
c. Capital
d. Vyborg Appeal

41. _____ is the concept of having more than one person required to complete a task. It is alternatively called segregation of duties or, in the political realm, separation of powers.

_____ is one of the key concepts of internal control and is the most difficult and sometimes the most costly one to achieve. The term _____ is already well-known in financial accounting systems. Companies in all sizes understand not to combine roles such as receiving checks (payment on account) and approving write-offs, depositing cash and reconciling bank statements, approving time cards and have custody of pay checks, etc.

a. BMC Software, Inc.
c. Salary

b. Separation of duties
d. 3M Company

42. _____ is a specific term used in companies' financial reporting from the company-whole point of view. Because that use excludes the effects of changing ownership interest, an economic measure of _____ is necessary for financial analysis from the shareholders' point of view

_____ is defined by the Financial Accounting Standards Board, or FASB, as 'the change in equity [net assets] of a business enterprise during a period from transactions and other events and circumstances from nonowner sources. It includes all changes in equity during a period except those resulting from investments by owners and distributions to owners.'

_____ is the sum of net income and other items that must bypass the income statement because they have not been realized, including items like an unrealized holding gain or loss from available for sale securities and foreign currency translation gains or losses.

a. BMC Software, Inc.
c. 3M Company

b. BNSF Railway
d. Comprehensive income

43. Companies that have publicly traded securities typically use _____s to keep track of the individuals and entities that own their stocks and bonds. Most _____s are banks or trust companies, but sometimes a company acts as its own _____.

_____s perform three main functions:

1. Issue and cancel certificates to reflect changes in ownership. For example, when a company declares a stock dividend or stock split, the _____ issues new shares. _____s keep records of who owns a company's stocks and bonds and how those stocks and bonds are held--whether by the owner in certificate form, by the company in book-entry form, or by the investor's brokerage firm in street name. They also keep records of how many shares or bonds each investor owns.
2. Act as an intermediary for the company. A _____ may also serve as the company's paying agent to pay out interest, cash and stock dividends, or other distributions to stock- and bondholders. In addition, _____s act as proxy agent (sending out proxy materials), exchange agent (exchanging a company's stock or bonds in a merger), tender agent (tendering shares in a tender offer), and mailing agent (mailing the company's quarterly, annual, and other reports.)
3. Handle lost, destroyed, or stolen certificates. _____s help shareholders and bondholders when a stock or bond certificate has been lost, destroyed, or stolen.

In many cases, you can find out which _____ a company uses by visiting the investor relations section of the companye;s website.

a. Market price
c. Mark-to-market

b. Transfer agent
d. Financial market

Chapter 15. Debt and Equity Capital

44. _____ are payments made by a corporation to its shareholder members. It is the portion of corporate profits paid out to stockholders. When a corporation earns a profit or surplus, that money can be put to two uses: it can either be re-invested in the business (called retained earnings), or it can be paid to the shareholders as a dividend.

   a. Dividend payout ratio
   b. Dividend stripping
   c. Dividend yield
   d. Dividends

45. _____ is an equity (stock) exchange located at 11 Wall Street in lower Manhattan, New York, USA.) It is the largest stock exchange in the world by dollar value of its listed companies' securities. As of October 2008, the combined capitalization of all domestic _____ listed companies was US$10.1 trillion.

   a. 3M Company
   b. BNSF Railway
   c. New York Stock Exchange
   d. BMC Software, Inc.

46. A _____, (formerly a securities exchange) is a corporation or mutual organization which provides 'trading' facilities for stock brokers and traders, to trade stocks and other securities. _____s also provide facilities for the issue and redemption of securities as well as other financial instruments and capital events including the payment of income and dividends. The securities traded on a _____ include: shares issued by companies, unit trusts, derivatives, pooled investment products and bonds.

   a. Stock Exchange
   b. BNSF Railway
   c. BMC Software, Inc.
   d. 3M Company

47. In corporate law, a _____ is a legal document that certifies ownership of a specific number of stock shares in a corporation. In large corporations, buying shares does not always lead to a _____

   Usually only shareholders with _____s can vote in a shareholders' general meeting.

   a. 3M Company
   b. Stock certificate
   c. BNSF Railway
   d. BMC Software, Inc.

48. A mutual shareholder or _____ is an individual or company (including a corporation) that legally owns one or more shares of stock in a joint stock company. A company's shareholders collectively own that company. Thus, the typical goal of such companies is to enhance shareholder value.

   a. 3M Company
   b. Stockholder
   c. Growth investing
   d. Stock split

49. A _____ is a common type of chart, that represents an algorithm or process, showing the steps as boxes of various kinds, and their order by connecting these with arrows. _____s are used in analyzing, designing, documenting or managing a process or program in various fields.

   The first structured method for documenting process flow, the 'flow process chart', was introduced by Frank Gilbreth to members of ASME in 1921 as the presentation e;Process Charts--First Steps in Finding the One Best Waye;.

   a. 3M Company
   b. BMC Software, Inc.
   c. BNSF Railway
   d. Flowchart

Chapter 15. Debt and Equity Capital

50. The _____ are the primary rules governing the management of a corporation in the United States and Canada, and are filed with a state or other regulatory agency. The equivalent in the United Kingdom and various other countries is Articles of Association.

A corporation's _____ generally provide information such as:

- The corporation's name, which has to be unique from any other corporation in that jurisdiction. As part of the corporation's name, certain words such as 'incorporated', 'limited', 'corporation', (or their abbreviations) or some equivalent term in countries whose language is not English, are usually required as part of the name as a 'flag' to indicate to persons doing business with the organization that it is a corporation as opposed to an individual or partnership (with unlimited liability.) In some cases, certain types of names are prohibited except by special permission, such as words implying the corporation is a government agency or has powers to act in ways it is not otherwise allowed.
- The name of the person(s) organizing the corporation (usually members of the board of directors.)
- Whether the corporation is a stock corporation or a non-stock corporation.
- Whether the corporation's existence is permanent or limited for a specific period of time. Generally the rule is that a corporation existence is forever, or until (1) it stops paying the yearly corporate renewal fees or otherwise fails to do something required to continue its existence such as file certain paperwork each year; or (2) it files a request to 'wind up and dissolve.'
- In some cases, a corporation must state the purposes for which it is formed. Some jurisdictions permit a general statement such as 'any lawful purpose' but some require explicit specifications.
- If a non-stock corporation, whether it is for profit or non-profit. However, some jurisdictions differentiate by 'for profit' or 'non profit' and some by 'stock or non-stock'.
- In the United States, if a corporation is to be organized as a non-profit, to be recognized as such by the Internal Revenue Service, such as for eligibility for tax exemption, certain specific wording must be included stating no part of the assets of the corporation are to benefit the members.
- If a stock corporation, the number of shares the corporation is authorized to issue, or the maximum amount in a specific currency of stock that may be issued, e.g. a maximum of $25,000.
- The number and names of the corporation's initial Board of Directors (though this is optional in most cases.)
- The initial director(s) of the corporation (in some cases the incorporator or the registered agent must be a director, if not an attorney or another corporation.)
- The location of the corporation's 'registered office' - the location at which legal papers can be served to the corporation if necessary. Some states further require the designation of a Registered Agent: a person to whom such papers could be delivered.

Most states permit a corporation to be formed by one person; in some cases (such as non-profit corporations) it may require three or five or more. This change has come about as a result of Delaware liberalizing its corporation rules to allow corporations to be formed by one person, and states not wanting to lose corporate charters to Delaware had to revise their rules as a result.

a. Articles of incorporation
b. Exclusive right
c. Employee Retirement Income Security Act
d. Express warranty

Chapter 15. Debt and Equity Capital

51. _____ can refer to a law of local or limited application, passed under the authority of a higher law specifying what things may be regulated by the _____, or it can refer to the internal rules of a company or organisation.
    a. Scottish Poor Laws
    b. Lease
    c. Bylaw
    d. Letter of credit

52. _____ is subcontracting a process, such as product design or manufacturing, to a third-party company. The decision to outsource is often made in the interest of lowering cost or making better use of time and energy costs, redirecting or conserving energy directed at the competencies of a particular business, or to make more efficient use of land, labor, capital, (information) technology and resources. _____ became part of the business lexicon during the 1980s.
    a. Economic Growth and Tax Relief Reconciliation Act of 2001
    b. US Airways, Inc.
    c. USA Today
    d. Outsourcing

53. A _____ or reacquired stock is stock which is bought back by the issuing company, reducing the amount of outstanding stock on the open market ('open market' including insiders' holdings).

    Stock repurchases are often used as a tax-efficient method to put cash into shareholders' hands, rather than pay dividends. Sometimes, companies do this when they feel that their stock is undervalued on the open market.

    a. Matching principle
    b. Net profit
    c. Cost of goods sold
    d. Treasury stock

54. Employment is a contract between two parties, one being the employer and the other being the _____. An _____ may be defined as: 'A person in the service of another under any contract of hire, express or implied, oral or written, where the employer has the power or right to control and direct the _____ in the material details of how the work is to be performed.' Black's Law Dictionary page 471 (5th ed. 1979).
    a. AIG
    b. Employee
    c. AMEX
    d. ABC Television Network

55. _____, also called fair price (in a commonplace conflation of the two distinct concepts), is a concept used in finance and economics, defined as a rational and unbiased estimate of the potential market price of a good, service, or asset, taking into account such objective factors as:

    - acquisition/production/distribution costs, replacement costs, or costs of close substitutes
    - actual utility at a given level of development of social productive capability
    - supply vs. demand

    and subjective factors such as

    - risk characteristics
    - cost of capital
    - individually perceived utility

Chapter 15. Debt and Equity Capital

In accounting, _____ is used as an estimate of the market value of an asset (or liability) for which a market price cannot be determined (usually because there is no established market for the asset.) Under GAAP (FAS 157), _____ is the amount at which the asset could be bought or sold in a current transaction between willing parties, or transferred to an equivalent party, other than in a liquidation sale. This is used for assets whose carrying value is based on mark-to-market valuations; for assets carried at historical cost, the _____ of the asset is not used. One example of where _____ is an issue is a College kitchen with a cost of $2 million which was built 5 years ago.

a. 3M Company
c. BMC Software, Inc.
b. Fair Value
d. BNSF Railway

56. In finance, an _____ is a contract between a buyer and a seller that gives the buyer the right--but not the obligation-- to buy or to sell a particular asset (the underlying asset) at a later time at an agreed price. In return for granting the _____, the seller collects a payment (the premium) from the buyer. A call _____ gives the buyer the right to buy the underlying asset; a put _____ gives the buyer of the _____ the right to sell the underlying asset.

a. ABC Television Network
c. AIG
b. AMEX
d. Option

57. In finance, a _____ is a type of bond that can be converted into shares of stock in the issuing company, usually at some pre-announced ratio. It is a hybrid security with debt- and equity-like features. Although it typically has a low coupon rate, the holder is compensated with the ability to convert the bond to common stock, usually at a substantial discount to the stock's market value.

a. Zero-coupon
c. Zero-coupon bond
b. Convertible bond
d. Coupon rate

58. A _____ is a type of business entity in which partners (owners) share with each other the profits or losses of the business undertaking in which all have invested. _____s are often favored over corporations for taxation purposes, as the _____ structure does not generally incur a tax on profits before it is distributed to the partners (i.e. there is no dividend tax levied.) However, depending on the _____ structure and the jurisdiction in which it operates, owners of a _____ may be exposed to greater personal liability than they would as shareholders of a corporation.

a. National Information Infrastructure Protection Act
c. Corporate governance
b. Partnership
d. Resource Conservation and Recovery Act

59. A _____, or simply proprietorship is a type of business entity which legally has no separate existence from its owner. Hence, the limitations of liability enjoyed by a corporation and limited liability partnerships do not apply to sole proprietors. All debts of the business are debts of the owner.

a. Free cash flow
c. Sole proprietorship
b. Customer satisfaction
d. Time to market

60. A sole _____, or simply _____ is a type of business entity which legally has no separate existence from its owner. Hence, the limitations of liability enjoyed by a corporation and limited liability partnerships do not apply to sole proprietors. All debts of the business are debts of the owner.

a. Proprietorship
c. Free cash flow
b. Pre-determined overhead rate
d. Safety stock

Chapter 16. Auditing Operations and Completing the Audit

1. The general definition of an _____ is an evaluation of a person, organization, system, process, project or product. _____s are performed to ascertain the validity and reliability of information; also to provide an assessment of a system's internal control. The goal of an _____ is to express an opinion on the person/organization/system (etc) in question, under evaluation based on work done on a test basis.

   a. Assurance service
   b. Audit regime
   c. Institute of Chartered Accountants of India
   d. Audit

2. _____ is a political and social term from the Latin verb conservare meaning to save or preserve. As the name suggests it usually indicates support for tradition and traditional values though the meaning has changed in different countries and time periods. The modern political term conservative was used by French politician Chateaubriand in 1819.

   a. Politicized issue
   b. 3M Company
   c. Conservatism
   d. BMC Software, Inc.

3. _____ is a term used in accounting, economics and finance to spread the cost of an asset over the span of several years.

   In simple words we can say that _____ is the reduction in the value of an asset due to usage, passage of time, wear and tear, technological outdating or obsolescence, depletion, inadequacy, rot, rust, decay or other such factors.

   In accounting, _____ is a term used to describe any method of attributing the historical or purchase cost of an asset across its useful life, roughly corresponding to normal wear and tear.

   a. Current asset
   b. Depreciation
   c. General ledger
   d. Net profit

4. The _____ of 1977 (15 U.S.C. ÂÂ§ÂÂ§ 78dd-1, et seq.) is a United States federal law known primarily for two of its main provisions, one that addresses accounting transparency requirements under the Securities Exchange Act of 1934 and another concerning bribery of foreign officials.

   a. Foreign Corrupt Practices Act
   b. Pre-emption right
   c. Competition law
   d. Lease

5. _____, in auditing, is the risk that the account or section being audited is materially misstated without considering internal controls due to error; _____ does not include an assessment of the risk of material misstatement due to fraud. The assessment of _____ depends on the professional judgement of the auditor, and it is done after assessing the business environment of the entity being audited.

   _____ is typically assessed using a scale, with assessments being either low, medium, or high.

   a. AIG
   b. ABC Television Network
   c. AMEX
   d. Inherent risk

6. In finance, _____ is the process of estimating the potential market value of a financial asset or liability. They can be done on assets (for example, investments in marketable securities such as stocks, options, business enterprises, or intangible assets such as patents and trademarks) or on liabilities (e.g., Bonds issued by a company.) A _____ is required in many contexts including investment analysis, capital budgeting, merger and acquisition transactions, financial reporting, taxable events to determine the proper tax liability, and in litigation.

Chapter 16. Auditing Operations and Completing the Audit 149

a. Disclosure
b. Valuation
c. Daybook
d. Vyborg Appeal

7. _____ is a file or account that contains money that a person or company owes to suppliers, but has not paid yet (a form of debt.) When you receive an invoice you add it to the file, and then you remove it when you pay. Thus, the A/P is a form of credit that suppliers offer to their purchasers by allowing them to pay for a product or service after it has already been received.

a. Accrual
b. Earnings before interest, taxes, depreciation and amortization
c. Accounts payable
d. Accounts receivable

8. In accounting, _____ has a very specific meaning. It is an outflow of cash or other valuable assets from a person or company to another person or company. This outflow of cash is generally one side of a trade for products or services that have equal or better current or future value to the buyer than to the seller.

a. AMEX
b. Expense
c. ABC Television Network
d. AIG

9. _____ is a concept that denotes the precise probability of specific eventualities. Technically, the notion of _____ is independent from the notion of value and, as such, eventualities may have both beneficial and adverse consequences. However, in general usage the convention is to focus only on potential negative impact to some characteristic of value that may arise from a future event.

a. Discounting
b. Risk
c. Discount factor
d. Risk adjusted return on capital

10. In business and accounting, _____ are everything of value that is owned by a person or company. It is a claim on the property your income of a borrower. The balance sheet of a firm records the monetary value of the _____ owned by the firm.

a. Earnings before interest, taxes, depreciation and amortization
b. Accrual basis accounting
c. Accounts receivable
d. Assets

11. In financial accounting, a _____ or statement of financial position is a summary of a person's or organization's balances. Assets, liabilities and ownership equity are listed as of a specific date, such as the end of its financial year. A _____ is often described as a snapshot of a company's financial condition.

a. Financial statements
b. Statement of retained earnings
c. 3M Company
d. Balance sheet

12. The term _____ describes a reduction in recognized value. In accounting terminology, it refers to recognition of the reduced or zero value of an asset. In income tax statements, it refers to a reduction of taxable income as recognition of certain expenses required to produce the income.

a. Salvage value
b. Current asset
c. Payroll
d. Write-off

13. _____ means the giving out of information, either voluntarily or to be in compliance with legal regulations or workplace rules.

- In Computer security, full _____ means disclosing full information about vulnerabilities.
- In computing, _____ widget
- Journalism, full _____ refers to disclosing the interests of the writer which may bear on the subject being written about, for example, if the writer has worked with an interview subject in the past.

- In law:
    - The law of England and Wales, _____ refers to a process that may form part of legal proceedings, whereby parties inform to other parties the existence of any relevant documents that are, or have been, in their control. This compares with the process known as discovery in the course of legal proceedings in the United States.
    - In U.S. civil procedure (litigation rules for civil cases), _____ is a stage prior to trial. In civil cases, each party must disclose to the opposing party the following: names of witnesses which it may use to support its side, copies of documents (or mere description of these documents) in its control which it may use to support its side, computation of damages claimed, and certain insurance information. _____ is related to, but technically prior to, the discovery stage.
    - In Company law (known as 'corporate law' in the United States), _____ refers to giving out information about public or limited companies or their officers, which might be kept secret if the company was a private company or a partnership.

- In real property transactions, _____ refers to providing to a buyer information known to the seller or broker/agent concerning the condition or other aspects of real property that would affect the property's value or desirability. These rules regarding what information must be disclosed, and whether the information must be disclosed even if a buyer does not ask, vary from one jurisdiction to the next.

a. Trailing
c. Tax harmonisation
b. Controlled Foreign Corporations
d. Disclosure

14. A _____ has several related meanings:

- a daily record of events or business; a private _____ is usually referred to as a diary.
- a newspaper or other periodical, in the literal sense of one published each day;
- many publications issued at stated intervals, such as magazines, or scholarly academic _____s, or the record of the transactions of a society, are often called _____s. Although _____ is sometimes used, erroneously, as a synonym for 'magazine,' in academic use, a _____ refers to a serious, scholarly publication, most often peer-reviewed. A non-scholarly magazine written for an educated audience about an industry or an area of professional activity is usually called a professional magazine.

The word 'journalist' for one whose business is writing for the public press has been in use since the end of the 17th century.

Open access _____s are scholarly _____s that are available to the reader without financial or other barrier other than access to the internet itself. Some are subsidized, and some require payment on behalf of the author. Subsidized _____s are financed by an academic institution or a government information center.

Chapter 16. Auditing Operations and Completing the Audit

a. BMC Software, Inc.
c. Journal

b. 3M Company
d. BNSF Railway

15. A _____ is the pinnacle activity involved in selling products or services in return for money or other compensation. It is an act of completion of a commercial activity.

A _____ is completed by the seller, the owner of the goods.

a. High yield stock
c. Tertiary sector of economy

b. Sale
d. Maturity

16. _____ is a company's financial statement that indicates how the revenue is transformed into the net income The purpose of the _____ is to show managers and investors whether the company made or lost money during the period being reported.

The important thing to remember about an _____ is that it represents a period of time.

a. AIG
c. AMEX

b. Income statement
d. ABC Television Network

17. Book Value = Original Cost - _____

Book value at the end of year becomes book value at the beginning of next year. The asset is depreciated until the book value equals scrap value.

If the vehicle were to be sold and the sales price exceeded the depreciated value (net book value) then the excess would be considered a gain and subject to depreciation recapture.

a. ABC Television Network
c. Accumulated depreciation

b. AMEX
d. AIG

18. In economics, business, retail, and accounting, a _____ is the value of money that has been used up to produce something, and hence is not available for use anymore. In economics, a _____ is an alternative that is given up as a result of a decision. In business, the _____ may be one of acquisition, in which case the amount of money expended to acquire it is counted as _____.

a. Prime cost
c. Cost of quality

b. Cost allocation
d. Cost

19. In financial accounting, _____ or cost of sales includes the direct costs attributable to the production of the goods sold by a company. This amount includes the materials cost used in creating the goods along with the direct labor costs used to produce the good. It excludes indirect expenses such as distribution costs and sales force costs.

a. Cost of goods sold
c. FIFO and LIFO accounting

b. Reorder point
d. 3M Company

20. The _____ of 1938 (_____, ch. 676, 52 Stat. 1060, June 25, 1938, 29 U.S.C.

Chapter 16. Auditing Operations and Completing the Audit

a. FCPA
b. Fair Labor Standards Act
c. National Information Infrastructure Protection Act
d. Jenkins Committee

21. An _____ is a tax levied on the financial income of people, corporations, or other legal entities. Various _____ systems exist, with varying degrees of tax incidence. Income taxation can be progressive, proportional, or regressive.
    a. Ordinary income
    b. Individual Retirement Arrangement
    c. Implied level of government service
    d. Income tax

22. In a company, _____ is the sum of all financial records of salaries, wages, bonuses and deductions.

A paycheck, is traditionally a paper document issued by an employer to pay an employee for services rendered. While most commonly used in the United States, recently the physical paycheck has been increasingly replaced by electronic direct deposit to bank accounts.

   a. Payroll
   b. Tax expense
   c. 3M Company
   d. Total Expense Ratio

23. _____ is an increasingly broadening term with which an organization knowledge and experience, Employee Relations and resource planning at various levels. The field draws upon concepts developed in Industrial/Organizational Psychology and System Theory. _____ has at least two related interpretations depending on context.
    a. BMC Software, Inc.
    b. Separation of duties
    c. 3M Company
    d. Human resources

24. An _____ is a term used in behavioral economics to describe those types of behaviors that impose costs on a person in the long-run that are not taken into account when making decisions in the present. Classical Economics discourages government from creating legislation that targets internalities, because it is assumed that the consumer takes these personal costs into account when paying for the good that causes the _____. For example, cigarettes should be taxed because of the negative consumption externalities that they impose, such as second-hand smoke, not because the smoker harms him or herself by smoking.
    a. Inventory turnover ratio
    b. Authorised capital
    c. Operating budget
    d. Internality

25. In accounting and organizational theory, _____ is defined as a process effected by an organization's structure, work and authority flows, people and management information systems, designed to help the organization accomplish specific goals or objectives. It is a means by which an organization's resources are directed, monitored, and measured. It plays an important role in preventing and detecting fraud and protecting the organization's resources, both physical (e.g., machinery and property) and intangible (e.g., reputation or intellectual property such as trademarks.)
    a. Audit committee
    b. Auditor independence
    c. Audit risk
    d. Internal control

26. In financial accounting, a _____ is defined as an obligation of an entity arising from past transactions or events, the settlement of which may result in the transfer or use of assets, provision of services or other yielding of economic benefits in the future.

Chapter 16. Auditing Operations and Completing the Audit   153

a. Vested
c. False Claims Act
b. Corporate governance
d. Liability

27. A _____ is a type of debt Like all debt instruments, a _____ entails the redistribution of financial assets over time, between the lender and the borrower.

a. Lender
c. Loan
b. Debenture
d. Loan to value

28. _____s are the recurring expenses which are related to the operation of a business component, piece of equipment or facility.

For a commercial enterprise, _____s fall into two broad categories:

- fixed costs, which are the same whether the operation is closed or running at 100% capacity
- variable costs, which may increase depending on whether more production is done, and how it is done (producing 100 items of product might require 10 days of normal time or take 7 days if overtime is used. It may be more or less expensive to use overtime production depending on whether faster production means the product can be more profitable.)

Overhead costs for a business are the cost of resources used by an organization just to maintain its existence. Overhead costs are usually measured in monetary terms, but non-monetary overhead is possible in the form of time required to accomplish tasks.

Examples of overhead costs include:

- payment of rent on the office space a business occupies
- cost of electricity for the office lights
- some office personnel wages

Non-overhead costs are incremental costs, such as the cost of raw materials used in the goods a business sells.

In the case of a device, component, piece of equipment or facility (for the rest of this article, all of these items will be referred to in general as equipment), it is the regular, usual and customary recurring costs of operating the equipment.

a. AMEX
c. ABC Television Network
b. AIG
d. Operating cost

29. _____ generally refers to two kinds of taxes: Taxes which employers are required to withhold from employees' pay Pay-As-You-Earn or Pay-As-You-Go tax; and taxes which are paid from the employer's own funds and which are directly related to employing a worker, which may be either fixed charges or proportionally linked to an employee's pay.

In Australia, the _____ is a specific tax which is paid to states and territories by employers, not by employees. The tax is not deducted from the worker's pay.

Chapter 16. Auditing Operations and Completing the Audit

a. Passive foreign investment company
c. Federal Unemployment Tax Act
b. Nonbusiness Energy Property Tax Credit
d. Payroll tax

30. Employment is a contract between two parties, one being the employer and the other being the _____. An _____ may be defined as: 'A person in the service of another under any contract of hire, express or implied, oral or written, where the employer has the power or right to control and direct the _____ in the material details of how the work is to be performed.' Black's Law Dictionary page 471 (5th ed. 1979.)

a. ABC Television Network
c. AIG
b. AMEX
d. Employee

31. _____, in auditing, is the risk that a company's internal controls are insufficient to mitigate or detect errors or fraud.

a. BNSF Railway
c. 3M Company
b. BMC Software, Inc.
d. Control risk

32. _____ is a specific term used in companies' financial reporting from the company-whole point of view. Because that use excludes the effects of changing ownership interest, an economic measure of _____ is necessary for financial analysis from the shareholders' point of view

_____ is defined by the Financial Accounting Standards Board, or FASB, as 'the change in equity [net assets] of a business enterprise during a period from transactions and other events and circumstances from nonowner sources. It includes all changes in equity during a period except those resulting from investments by owners and distributions to owners.'

_____ is the sum of net income and other items that must bypass the income statement because they have not been realized, including items like an unrealized holding gain or loss from available for sale securities and foreign currency translation gains or losses.

a. BNSF Railway
c. 3M Company
b. BMC Software, Inc.
d. Comprehensive income

33. A _____ is a common type of chart, that represents an algorithm or process, showing the steps as boxes of various kinds, and their order by connecting these with arrows. _____s are used in analyzing, designing, documenting or managing a process or program in various fields.

The first structured method for documenting process flow, the 'flow process chart', was introduced by Frank Gilbreth to members of ASME in 1921 as the presentation e;Process Charts--First Steps in Finding the One Best Waye;.

a. 3M Company
c. BNSF Railway
b. BMC Software, Inc.
d. Flowchart

34. A _____ is a compensation, usually financial, received by a worker in exchange for their labor.

Compensation in terms of _____s is given to worker and compensation in terms of salary is given to employees. Compensation is a monetary benefits given to employees in returns of the services provided by them.

a. Wage
b. BMC Software, Inc.
c. Retirement plan
d. 3M Company

35. In financial accounting, a _____ or Statement of cash flows is a financial statement that shows a company's flow of cash. The money coming into the business is called cash inflow, and money going out from the business is called cash outflow. The statement shows how changes in balance sheet and income accounts affect cash and cash equivalents, and breaks the analysis down to operating, investing, and financing activities.

a. BNSF Railway
b. BMC Software, Inc.
c. 3M Company
d. Cash flow statement

36. _____ is the balance of the amounts of cash being received and paid by a business during a defined period of time, sometimes tied to a specific project. Measurement of _____ can be used

- to evaluate the state or performance of a business or project.
- to determine problems with liquidity. Being profitable does not necessarily mean being liquid. A company can fail because of a shortage of cash, even while profitable.
- to project rate of returns. The time of _____s into and out of projects are used as inputs to financial models such as internal rate of return, and net present value.
- to examine income or growth of a business when it is believed that accrual accounting concepts do not represent economic realities. Alternately, _____ can be used to 'validate' the net income generated by accrual accounting.

_____ as a generic term may be used differently depending on context, and certain _____ definitions may be adapted by analysts and users for their own uses. Common terms include operating _____ and free _____.

a. Cash flow
b. Flow-through entity
c. Controlling interest
d. Commercial paper

37. _____ is one of financial audit skill which help an auditor understand the client's business and changes in the business, to identify potential risk areas and to plan other audit procedures.

_____ include comparison of financial information (data in financial statement) with

1. prior periods
2. budgets
3. forecasts
4. similar industries and so on.

It also includes consideration of predictable relationships, such as:

1. gross profit to sales,
2. payroll costs to employees,
3. financial information and non-financial information, for examples the CEO's reports and the industry news.

possible sources of information about the client include:

1. interim financial information
2. Budgets
3. Management accounts
4. Non-Financial information
5. Bank and cash records
6. VAT returns
7. Board minutes
8. Discussion or correspondance with the client at they year-end

a. External auditor
b. Assurance service
c. International Federation of Audit Bureaux of Circulations
d. Analytical procedures

38. In economic models, the _____ time frame assumes no fixed factors of production. Firms can enter or leave the marketplace, and the cost (and availability) of land, labor, raw materials, and capital goods can be assumed to vary. In contrast, in the short-run time frame, certain factors are assumed to be fixed, because there is not sufficient time for them to change.
a. Short-run
b. 3M Company
c. BMC Software, Inc.
d. Long-run

39. _____ is that which is owed; usually referencing assets owed, but the term can also cover moral obligations and other interactions not requiring money. In the case of assets, _____ is a means of using future purchasing power in the present before a summation has been earned. Some companies and corporations use _____ as a part of their overall corporate finance strategy.
a. Loan
b. Debenture
c. Debt
d. Lender

40. _____ is one of a series of accounting transactions dealing with the billing of customers who owe money to a person, company or organization for goods and services that have been provided to the customer. In most business entities this is typically done by generating an invoice and mailing or electronically delivering it to the customer, who in turn must pay it within an established timeframe called credit or payment terms.

An example of a common payment term is Net 30, meaning payment is due in the amount of the invoice 30 days from the date of invoice.

a. Accrual
b. Accrued revenue
c. Accounts receivable
d. Adjusting entries

Chapter 16. Auditing Operations and Completing the Audit 157

41. The _____ is the United States federal government agency that collects taxes and enforces the internal revenue laws. It is an agency within the U.S. Dept of the treasury responsible for interpretation and application of Federal tax law. The official U.S. Treasury regulations provide (in part):

The _____ is a bureau of the Department of the Treasury under the immediate direction of the Commissioner of Internal Revenue.

a. Internal Revenue Service
c. Use tax
b. Indirect tax
d. Income tax

42. _____ is a term that is commonly used in relation to the audit of the financial statements of an entity. (.
a. Audit working paper
c. Auditor independence
b. Engagement Letter
d. Audit Risk

43. The U.S. _____ is an independent agency of the United States government which holds primary responsibility for enforcing the federal securities laws and regulating the securities industry, the nation's stock and options exchanges, and other electronic securities markets. The SEC was created by section 4 of the Securities Exchange Act of 1934 (now codified as 15 U.S.C. ÅÂ§ 78d and commonly referred to as the 1934 Act.)
a. 3M Company
c. BNSF Railway
b. Securities and Exchange Commission
d. BMC Software, Inc.

44. The term _____ is a term applied to practices that are perfunctory, or seek to satisfy the minimum requirements or to conform to a convention or doctrine. It has different meanings in different fields.

In accounting, _____ earnings are those earnings of companies in addition to actual earnings calculated under the Generally Accepted Accounting Principles (GAAP) in their quarterly and yearly financial reports.

a. Payroll
c. Treasury stock
b. Bottom line
d. Pro forma

45. A _____, or simply proprietorship is a type of business entity which legally has no separate existence from its owner. Hence, the limitations of liability enjoyed by a corporation and limited liability partnerships do not apply to sole proprietors. All debts of the business are debts of the owner.
a. Customer satisfaction
c. Free cash flow
b. Time to market
d. Sole proprietorship

46. A sole _____, or simply _____ is a type of business entity which legally has no separate existence from its owner. Hence, the limitations of liability enjoyed by a corporation and limited liability partnerships do not apply to sole proprietors. All debts of the business are debts of the owner.
a. Proprietorship
c. Safety stock
b. Free cash flow
d. Pre-determined overhead rate

Chapter 16. Auditing Operations and Completing the Audit

47. _____ is systematic determination of merit, worth, and significance of something or someone using criteria against a set of standards. _____ often is used to characterize and appraise subjects of interest in a wide range of human enterprises, including the arts, criminal justice, foundations and non-profit organizations, government, health care, and other human services.

Depending on the topic of interest, there are professional groups which look to the quality and rigor of the _____ process.

a. AMEX
b. ABC Television Network
c. Evaluation
d. AIG

48. In accounting/accountancy, _____ are journal entries usually made at the end of an accounting period to allocate income and expenditure to the period in which they actually occurred. The revenue recognition principle is the basis of making _____ that pertain to unearned and accrued revenues under accrual-basis accounting. They are sometimes called Balance Day adjustments because they are made on balance day.

a. Adjusting entries
b. Accrued expense
c. Earnings before interest, taxes, depreciation and amortization
d. Accrual

49. In mathematics _____s are numbers or other things that get multiplied. In particular, see:

- Factorization, the decomposition of an object into a product of other objects
- Integer factorization, the process of breaking down a composite number into smaller non-trivial divisors
- A coefficient
- A divisor of a particular number, or of an element of a monoid
- A von Neumann algebra with a trivial center

In statistics

- _____ analysis is the study of how _____s or certain variables affect variables.

In technology:

- Human _____s, a profession that focuses on how people interact with products, tools, or procedures
- 'Functionality, Application domain, Conditions, Technology, Objects and Responsibility;', In object-oriented programming

In computer science and information technology:

- Authentication _____, a piece of information used to verify a person's identity for security purposes
- _____, a Unix command for numbers factorization
- _____ (programming language), an experimental Forth-like programming language

Chapter 16. Auditing Operations and Completing the Audit   159

In television:

- The O'Reilly _____, an American talk show hosted by Bill O'Reilly on Fox News.
- The Krypton _____, a British game show hosted by Gordon Burns, formally on ITV. Also had an American version.

a. The Goodyear Tire ' Rubber Company
c. Merck ' Co., Inc.
b. Valuation
d. Factor

50. In economics, _____ or _____ goods or real _____ refers to factors of production used to create goods or services that are not themselves significantly consumed (though they may depreciate) in the production process. _____ goods may be acquired with money or financial _____. In finance and accounting, _____ generally refers to financial wealth, especially that used to start or maintain a business.
  a. Vyborg Appeal
  b. Disclosure
  c. Screening
  d. Capital

51. _____ is an umbrella term which refers to the various accounting systems used by various public sector entities. In the United States, for instance, there are two levels of government which follow different accounting standards set forth by independent, private sector boards. At the federal level, the Federal Accounting Standards Advisory Board (FASAB) sets forth the accounting standards to follow.
  a. Nonassurance services
  b. Product control
  c. Management accounting
  d. Governmental Accounting

52. The _____ is currently the source of generally accepted accounting principles (GAAP) used by State and Local governments in the [[United States of America]]. As with most of the entities involved in creating GAAP in the United States, it is a private, non-governmental organization.

The _____ is subject to oversight by the Financial Accounting Foundation (FAF), which selects the members of the _____ and the Financial Accounting Standards Board, and funds both organizations.

  a. Multinational corporation
  b. National Conference of Commissioners on Uniform State Laws
  c. Fannie Mae
  d. Governmental Accounting Standards Board

53. A _____ is a fungible, negotiable instrument representing financial value. they are broadly categorized into debt securities (such as banknotes, bonds and debentures), and equity securities; e.g., common stocks. The company or other entity issuing the _____ is called the issuer.
  a. 3M Company
  b. Tracking stock
  c. BMC Software, Inc.
  d. Security

54. _____ are formal records of a business' financial activities.

In British English, including United Kingdom company law, _____ are often referred to as accounts, although the term _____ is also used, particularly by accountants.

_____ provide an overview of a business' financial condition in both short and long term.

a. 3M Company
c. Notes to the financial statements
b. Financial Statements
d. Statement of retained earnings

55. _____ is the term used to refer to the standard framework of guidelines for financial accounting used in any given jurisdiction. _____ includes the standards, conventions, and rules accountants follow in recording and summarizing transactions, and in the preparation of financial statements.

Financial accounting information must be assembled and reported objectively.

a. General ledger
c. Long-term liabilities
b. Current asset
d. Generally accepted accounting principles

56. The _____ extends the concept of auditing holistically from a traditional scope of accounting and finance to the organisational information management system. Information is representative of a resource which requires effective management and this led to the development of interest in the use of an _____.

Prior the 1990's and the methodologies of Orna, Henczel, Wood, Buchanan and Gibb, _____ approaches and methodologies focused mainly upon an identification of formal information resources (IR.)

a. External auditor
c. Assurance service
b. International Federation of Audit Bureaux of Circulations
d. Information Audit

57. In a publicly-held company, an _____ is an operating committee of the Board of Directors, typically charged with oversight of financial reporting and disclosure. Committee members are drawn from members of the Company's board of directors, with a Chairperson selected from among the members. An _____ of a publicly-traded company in the United States is composed of independent and outside directors referred to as non-executive directors, at least one of which is typically a financial expert.

a. Audit working paper
c. Event data
b. Audit Committee
d. External auditor

Chapter 17. Auditors' Reports

1. In financial accounting, a _____ or statement of financial position is a summary of a person's or organization's balances. Assets, liabilities and ownership equity are listed as of a specific date, such as the end of its financial year. A _____ is often described as a snapshot of a company's financial condition.
   a. 3M Company
   b. Balance sheet
   c. Financial statements
   d. Statement of retained earnings

2. The _____ is a private, not-for-profit organization whose primary purpose is to develop generally accepted accounting principles (GAAP) within the United States in the public's interest. The Securities and Exchange Commission (SEC) designated the _____ as the organization responsible for setting accounting standards for public companies in the U.S. It was created in 1973, replacing the Accounting Principles Board and the Committee on Accounting Procedure of the American Institute of Certified Public Accountants. The _____'s mission is 'to establish and improve standards of financial accounting and reporting for the guidance and education of the public, including issuers, auditors, and users of financial information.'

   The _____ is not a governmental body.

   a. Public company
   b. Governmental Accounting Standards Board
   c. Fannie Mae
   d. Financial Accounting Standards Board

3. _____ is a company's financial statement that indicates how the revenue is transformed into the net income The purpose of the _____ is to show managers and investors whether the company made or lost money during the period being reported.

   The important thing to remember about an _____ is that it represents a period of time.

   a. AMEX
   b. Income statement
   c. ABC Television Network
   d. AIG

4. In financial accounting, a _____ or Statement of cash flows is a financial statement that shows a company's flow of cash. The money coming into the business is called cash inflow, and money going out from the business is called cash outflow. The statement shows how changes in balance sheet and income accounts affect cash and cash equivalents, and breaks the analysis down to operating, investing, and financing activities.
   a. Cash flow statement
   b. BMC Software, Inc.
   c. 3M Company
   d. BNSF Railway

5. The _____ is one of the basic financial statements as per Generally Accepted Accounting Principles, and it explains the changes in a company's retained earnings over the reporting period. It breaks down changes affecting the account, such as profits or losses from operations, dividends paid, and any other items charged or credited to retained earnings. A retained earnings statement is required by Generally Accepted Accounting Principles whenever comparative balance sheets and income statements are presented.
   a. 3M Company
   b. Statement of retained earnings
   c. Financial statements
   d. Notes to the financial statements

Chapter 17. Auditors' Reports

6. _____ is the balance of the amounts of cash being received and paid by a business during a defined period of time, sometimes tied to a specific project. Measurement of _____ can be used

- to evaluate the state or performance of a business or project.
- to determine problems with liquidity. Being profitable does not necessarily mean being liquid. A company can fail because of a shortage of cash, even while profitable.
- to project rate of returns. The time of _____s into and out of projects are used as inputs to financial models such as internal rate of return, and net present value.
- to examine income or growth of a business when it is believed that accrual accounting concepts do not represent economic realities. Alternately, _____ can be used to 'validate' the net income generated by accrual accounting.

_____ as a generic term may be used differently depending on context, and certain _____ definitions may be adapted by analysts and users for their own uses. Common terms include operating _____ and free _____.

a. Flow-through entity
b. Commercial paper
c. Controlling interest
d. Cash flow

7. _____ means the giving out of information, either voluntarily or to be in compliance with legal regulations or workplace rules.

- In Computer security, full _____ means disclosing full information about vulnerabilities.
- In computing, _____ widget
- Journalism, full _____ refers to disclosing the interests of the writer which may bear on the subject being written about, for example, if the writer has worked with an interview subject in the past.

- In law:
    - The law of England and Wales, _____ refers to a process that may form part of legal proceedings, whereby parties inform to other parties the existence of any relevant documents that are, or have been, in their control. This compares with the process known as discovery in the course of legal proceedings in the United States.
    - In U.S. civil procedure (litigation rules for civil cases), _____ is a stage prior to trial. In civil cases, each party must disclose to the opposing party the following: names of witnesses which it may use to support its side, copies of documents (or mere description of these documents) in its control which it may use to support its side, computation of damages claimed, and certain insurance information. _____ is related to, but technically prior to, the discovery stage.
    - In Company law (known as 'corporate law' in the United States), _____ refers to giving out information about public or limited companies or their officers, which might be kept secret if the company was a private company or a partnership.

- In real property transactions, _____ refers to providing to a buyer information known to the seller or broker/agent concerning the condition or other aspects of real property that would affect the property's value or desirability. These rules regarding what information must be disclosed, and whether the information must be disclosed even if a buyer does not ask, vary from one jurisdiction to the next.

a. Disclosure
b. Controlled Foreign Corporations
c. Trailing
d. Tax harmonisation

8. Most patent law systems require that a patent application disclose a claimed invention in sufficient detail for the notional person skilled in the art to carry out that claimed invention. This requirement is often known as sufficiency of disclosure or enablement, depending on the jurisdiction.

The _____ lies at the heart and origin of patent law. A state or government grants an inventor, or the inventor's assignee, a monopoly for a given period of time in exchange for the inventor disclosing to the public how to make or practice his or her invention. If a patent fails to contain such information, then the bargain is violated, and the patent is unenforceable.

a. Disclosure requirement
b. False Claims Act
c. Pre-emption right
d. Tax patent

9. _____ is a specific term used in companies' financial reporting from the company-whole point of view. Because that use excludes the effects of changing ownership interest, an economic measure of _____ is necessary for financial analysis from the shareholders' point of view

_____ is defined by the Financial Accounting Standards Board, or FASB, as 'the change in equity [net assets] of a business enterprise during a period from transactions and other events and circumstances from nonowner sources. It includes all changes in equity during a period except those resulting from investments by owners and distributions to owners.'

_____ is the sum of net income and other items that must bypass the income statement because they have not been realized, including items like an unrealized holding gain or loss from available for sale securities and foreign currency translation gains or losses.

a. Comprehensive income
b. 3M Company
c. BMC Software, Inc.
d. BNSF Railway

10. _____ is the term used to refer to the standard framework of guidelines for financial accounting used in any given jurisdiction. _____ includes the standards, conventions, and rules accountants follow in recording and summarizing transactions, and in the preparation of financial statements.

Financial accounting information must be assembled and reported objectively.

a. Generally accepted accounting principles
b. Current asset
c. General ledger
d. Long-term liabilities

11. _____ are formal records of a business' financial activities.

In British English, including United Kingdom company law, _____ are often referred to as accounts, although the term _____ is also used, particularly by accountants.

_____ provide an overview of a business' financial condition in both short and long term.

a. 3M Company
b. Notes to the financial statements
c. Statement of retained earnings
d. Financial statements

12. The general definition of an _____ is an evaluation of a person, organization, system, process, project or product. _____s are performed to ascertain the validity and reliability of information; also to provide an assessment of a system's internal control. The goal of an _____ is to express an opinion on the person/organization/system (etc) in question, under evaluation based on work done on a test basis.

a. Audit
b. Assurance service
c. Institute of Chartered Accountants of India
d. Audit regime

13. An _____ is a term used in behavioral economics to describe those types of behaviors that impose costs on a person in the long-run that are not taken into account when making decisions in the present. Classical Economics discourages government from creating legislation that targets internalities, because it is assumed that the consumer takes these personal costs into account when paying for the good that causes the _____. For example, cigarettes should be taxed because of the negative consumption externalities that they impose, such as second-hand smoke, not because the smoker harms him or herself by smoking.

a. Internality
b. Inventory turnover ratio
c. Authorised capital
d. Operating budget

14. In accounting and organizational theory, _____ is defined as a process effected by an organization's structure, work and authority flows, people and management information systems, designed to help the organization accomplish specific goals or objectives. It is a means by which an organization's resources are directed, monitored, and measured. It plays an important role in preventing and detecting fraud and protecting the organization's resources, both physical (e.g., machinery and property) and intangible (e.g., reputation or intellectual property such as trademarks.)

a. Auditor independence
b. Audit committee
c. Audit risk
d. Internal Control

15. The term _____ usually refers to a company that is permitted to offer its registered securities (stock, bonds, etc.) for sale to the general public, typically through a stock exchange, or occasionally a company whose stock is traded over the counter (OTC) via market makers who use non-exchange quotation services.

The term '_____' may also refer to a company owned by the government.

a. Professional association
b. Governmental Accounting Standards Board
c. MicroStrategy
d. Public Company

16. The _____ (sometimes called 'Peekaboo') is a private-sector, non-profit corporation created by the Sarbanes-Oxley Act, a 2002 United States federal law, to oversee the auditors of public companies. Its stated purpose is to 'protect the interests of investors and further the public interest in the preparation of informative, fair, and independent audit reports'. Although a private entity, the _____ has many government-like regulatory functions, making it in some ways similar to the private Self Regulatory Organizations (SROs) that regulate stock markets and other aspects of the financial markets in the United States.

Chapter 17. Auditors' Reports

a. Pension Benefit Guaranty Corporation
b. Public Company Accounting Oversight Board
c. Financial Crimes Enforcement Network
d. 3M Company

17. A _____ is a business that functions without the intention or threat of liquidation for the foreseeable future, usually regarded as at least within 12 months.

In accounting, '_____' refers to a company's ability to continue functioning as a business entity. It is the responsibility of the directors to assess whether the _____ assumption is appropriate when preparing the financial statements.

a. 3M Company
b. Payment
c. BMC Software, Inc.
d. Going Concern

18. The _____ is the former authoritative body of the American Institute of Certified Public Accountants (AICPA.) It was created by the American Institute of Certified Public Accountants in 1959 and issued pronouncements on accounting principles until 1973, when it was replaced by the Financial Accounting Standards Board (FASB.)

The _____ was disbanded in the hopes that the smaller, fully-independent FASB could more effectively create accounting standards.

a. Institute of Management Accountants
b. International Federation of Accountants
c. American Payroll Association
d. Accounting Principles Board

19. The _____ is currently the source of generally accepted accounting principles (GAAP) used by State and Local governments in the [[United States of America]]. As with most of the entities involved in creating GAAP in the United States, it is a private, non-governmental organization.

The _____ is subject to oversight by the Financial Accounting Foundation (FAF), which selects the members of the _____ and the Financial Accounting Standards Board, and funds both organizations.

a. Fannie Mae
b. Multinational corporation
c. National Conference of Commissioners on Uniform State Laws
d. Governmental Accounting Standards Board

20. _____ is an umbrella term which refers to the various accounting systems used by various public sector entities. In the United States, for instance, there are two levels of government which follow different accounting standards set forth by independent, private sector boards. At the federal level, the Federal Accounting Standards Advisory Board (FASAB) sets forth the accounting standards to follow.
a. Nonassurance services
b. Management accounting
c. Product control
d. Governmental Accounting

21. A _____ is a type of debt Like all debt instruments, a _____ entails the redistribution of financial assets over time, between the lender and the borrower.
a. Debenture
b. Lender
c. Loan to value
d. Loan

Chapter 17. Auditors' Reports

22. A _____ is an annual report required by the U.S. Securities and Exchange Commission (SEC), that gives a comprehensive summary of a public company's performance. Although similarly named, the annual report on _____ is distinct from the often glossy 'annual report to shareholders', which a company must send to its shareholders when it holds an annual meeting to elect directors (though some companies combine the annual report and the 10-K into one document.) The 10-K includes information such as company history, organizational structure, executive compensation, equity, subsidiaries, and audited financial statements, among other information.
   a. Form 8-K
   b. Form 10-K
   c. 3M Company
   d. Form 10-Q

23. _____, Quarterly Report Pursuant to Section 13 or 15(d) of the Securities Exchange Act of 1934, is an SEC filing that must be filed quarterly with the US Securities and Exchange Commission. It contains similar information to the annual form 10-K, however the information is generally less detailed, and the financial statements are generally unaudited. Information for the final quarter of a firm's fiscal year is included in the 10-K, so only three 10-Q filings are made each year.
   a. Form 8-K
   b. Form 20-F
   c. 3M Company
   d. Form 10-Q

24. _____ is a report required to be filed by public companies with the United States Securities and Exchange Commission pursuant to the Securities Exchange Act of 1934, as amended. After a significant event like bankruptcy or departure of a CEO, a public company generally must file a Current Report on _____ within four business days to provide an update to previously filed quartely reports on Form 10-Q and/or Annual Reports on Form 10-K. _____ is a very broad form used to notify investors of any unscheduled material event that is important to shareholders or the SEC.
   a. Form 10-Q
   b. Form 20-F
   c. Form 8-K
   d. 3M Company

25. The U.S. _____ is an independent agency of the United States government which holds primary responsibility for enforcing the federal securities laws and regulating the securities industry, the nation's stock and options exchanges, and other electronic securities markets. The SEC was created by section 4 of the Securities Exchange Act of 1934 (now codified as 15 U.S.C. §§ 78d and commonly referred to as the 1934 Act.)
   a. 3M Company
   b. BNSF Railway
   c. Securities and Exchange Commission
   d. BMC Software, Inc.

26. A _____ is a fungible, negotiable instrument representing financial value. they are broadly categorized into debt securities (such as banknotes, bonds and debentures), and equity securities; e.g., common stocks. The company or other entity issuing the _____ is called the issuer.
   a. Tracking stock
   b. 3M Company
   c. BMC Software, Inc.
   d. Security

27. The _____ of 1934 is a law governing the secondary trading of securities (stocks, bonds, and debentures) in the United States of America. The Act, 48 Stat. 881 (enacted June 6, 1934), codified at 15 U.S.C.
   a. Securities Exchange Act
   b. 3M Company
   c. BMC Software, Inc.
   d. BNSF Railway

28. The _____ is a law governing the secondary trading of securities (stocks, bonds, and debentures) in the United States of America. The Act, 48 Stat. 881 (enacted June 6, 1934), codified at 15 U.S.C.

a. BNSF Railway
b. 3M Company
c. Securities Exchange Act of 1934
d. BMC Software, Inc.

Chapter 18. Integrated Audits of Public Companies

1. The general definition of an _____ is an evaluation of a person, organization, system, process, project or product. _____s are performed to ascertain the validity and reliability of information; also to provide an assessment of a system's internal control. The goal of an _____ is to express an opinion on the person/organization/system (etc) in question, under evaluation based on work done on a test basis.
   a. Institute of Chartered Accountants of India
   b. Audit regime
   c. Assurance service
   d. Audit

2. _____ are formal records of a business' financial activities.

   In British English, including United Kingdom company law, _____ are often referred to as accounts, although the term _____ is also used, particularly by accountants.

   _____ provide an overview of a business' financial condition in both short and long term.

   a. Statement of retained earnings
   b. 3M Company
   c. Notes to the financial statements
   d. Financial Statements

3. A _____ is an annual report required by the U.S. Securities and Exchange Commission (SEC), that gives a comprehensive summary of a public company's performance. Although similarly named, the annual report on _____ is distinct from the often glossy 'annual report to shareholders', which a company must send to its shareholders when it holds an annual meeting to elect directors (though some companies combine the annual report and the 10-K into one document.) The 10-K includes information such as company history, organizational structure, executive compensation, equity, subsidiaries, and audited financial statements, among other information.
   a. Form 10-K
   b. Form 8-K
   c. Form 10-Q
   d. 3M Company

4. An _____ is a term used in behavioral economics to describe those types of behaviors that impose costs on a person in the long-run that are not taken into account when making decisions in the present. Classical Economics discourages government from creating legislation that targets internalities, because it is assumed that the consumer takes these personal costs into account when paying for the good that causes the _____. For example, cigarettes should be taxed because of the negative consumption externalities that they impose, such as second-hand smoke, not because the smoker harms him or herself by smoking.
   a. Operating budget
   b. Internality
   c. Inventory turnover ratio
   d. Authorised capital

5. In accounting and organizational theory, _____ is defined as a process effected by an organization's structure, work and authority flows, people and management information systems, designed to help the organization accomplish specific goals or objectives. It is a means by which an organization's resources are directed, monitored, and measured. It plays an important role in preventing and detecting fraud and protecting the organization's resources, both physical (e.g., machinery and property) and intangible (e.g., reputation or intellectual property such as trademarks.)
   a. Audit committee
   b. Auditor independence
   c. Audit risk
   d. Internal Control

6. The U.S. _____ is an independent agency of the United States government which holds primary responsibility for enforcing the federal securities laws and regulating the securities industry, the nation's stock and options exchanges, and other electronic securities markets. The SEC was created by section 4 of the Securities Exchange Act of 1934 (now codified as 15 U.S.C. §§ 78d and commonly referred to as the 1934 Act).

Chapter 18. Integrated Audits of Public Companies 169

a. 3M Company
c. Securities and Exchange Commission
b. BNSF Railway
d. BMC Software, Inc.

7. _____ is a file or account that contains money that a person or company owes to suppliers, but has not paid yet (a form of debt.) When you receive an invoice you add it to the file, and then you remove it when you pay. Thus, the A/P is a form of credit that suppliers offer to their purchasers by allowing them to pay for a product or service after it has already been received.

a. Accrual
c. Earnings before interest, taxes, depreciation and amortization
b. Accounts receivable
d. Accounts payable

8. _____ is systematic determination of merit, worth, and significance of something or someone using criteria against a set of standards. _____ often is used to characterize and appraise subjects of interest in a wide range of human enterprises, including the arts, criminal justice, foundations and non-profit organizations, government, health care, and other human services.

Depending on the topic of interest, there are professional groups which look to the quality and rigor of the _____ process.

a. ABC Television Network
c. AMEX
b. AIG
d. Evaluation

9. _____ is a concept that denotes the precise probability of specific eventualities. Technically, the notion of _____ is independent from the notion of value and, as such, eventualities may have both beneficial and adverse consequences. However, in general usage the convention is to focus only on potential negative impact to some characteristic of value that may arise from a future event.

a. Risk adjusted return on capital
c. Discount factor
b. Discounting
d. Risk

10. _____ is the world's largest professional services firm. It was formed in 1998 from a merger between Price Waterhouse and Coopers ' Lybrand, both formed in London.

_____ earned aggregated worldwide revenues of $28 billion for fiscal 2008, and employed over 146,000 people in 150 countries.

a. Daybook
c. Serial bonds
b. PricewaterhouseCoopers
d. Total-factor productivity

11. In mathematics _____s are numbers or other things that get multiplied. In particular, see:

- Factorization, the decomposition of an object into a product of other objects
- Integer factorization, the process of breaking down a composite number into smaller non-trivial divisors
- A coefficient
- A divisor of a particular number, or of an element of a monoid
- A von Neumann algebra with a trivial center

Chapter 18. Integrated Audits of Public Companies

In statistics

- _____ analysis is the study of how _____s or certain variables affect variables.

In technology:

- Human _____s, a profession that focuses on how people interact with products, tools, or procedures
- 'Functionality, Application domain, Conditions, Technology, Objects and Responsibility;', In object-oriented programming

In computer science and information technology:

- Authentication _____, a piece of information used to verify a person's identity for security purposes
- _____, a Unix command for numbers factorization
- _____ (programming language), an experimental Forth-like programming language

In television:

- The O'Reilly _____, an American talk show hosted by Bill O'Reilly on Fox News.
- The Krypton _____, a British game show hosted by Gordon Burns, formally on ITV. Also had an American version.

a. The Goodyear Tire ' Rubber Company
b. Valuation
c. Merck ' Co., Inc.
d. Factor

12. _____ is the calculated approximation of a result which is usable even if input data may be incomplete or uncertain.

In statistics, see _____ theory, estimator.

In mathematics, approximation or _____ typically means finding upper or lower bounds of a quantity that cannot readily be computed precisely and is also an educated guess .

a. Estimation
b. AMEX
c. ABC Television Network
d. AIG

Chapter 18. Integrated Audits of Public Companies 171

13. _____, commonly abbreviated as SAS, provide guidance to external auditors on generally accepted auditing standards in regards to auditing an entity and issuing a report. They are usually issued by the certified public accountant authoritative body in the region where the standards apply, such as the American Institute of Certified Public Accountants in the United States.

- _____
- _____ (Taiwan)

a. Financial Instruments and Exchange Law
b. GASB 45
c. RSM International
d. Statements on Auditing Standards

14. In a publicly-held company, an _____ is an operating committee of the Board of Directors, typically charged with oversight of financial reporting and disclosure. Committee members are drawn from members of the Company's board of directors, with a Chairperson selected from among the members. An _____ of a publicly-traded company in the United States is composed of independent and outside directors referred to as non-executive directors, at least one of which is typically a financial expert.

a. External auditor
b. Event data
c. Audit working paper
d. Audit committee

15. _____ is a profession and activity involved in helping organisations achieve their stated objectives. It does this by using a systematic methodology for analyzing business processes, procedures and activities with the goal of highlighting organizational problems and recommending solutions. Professionals called internal auditors are employed by organizations to perform the _____ activity.

a. ITGCs
b. Assurance service
c. Information audit
d. Internal auditing

16. _____ is one of a series of accounting transactions dealing with the billing of customers who owe money to a person, company or organization for goods and services that have been provided to the customer. In most business entities this is typically done by generating an invoice and mailing or electronically delivering it to the customer, who in turn must pay it within an established timeframe called credit or payment terms.

An example of a common payment term is Net 30, meaning payment is due in the amount of the invoice 30 days from the date of invoice.

a. Accounts receivable
b. Accrued revenue
c. Accrual
d. Adjusting entries

17. _____ is one of financial audit skill which help an auditor understand the client's business and changes in the business, to identify potential risk areas and to plan other audit procedures.

Chapter 18. Integrated Audits of Public Companies

_____ include comparison of financial information (data in financial statement) with

1. prior periods
2. budgets
3. forecasts
4. similar industries and so on.

It also includes consideration of predictable relationships, such as:

1. gross profit to sales,
2. payroll costs to employees,
3. financial information and non-financial information, for examples the CEO's reports and the industry news.

possible sources of information about the client include:

1. interim financial information
2. Budgets
3. Management accounts
4. Non-Financial information
5. Bank and cash records
6. VAT returns
7. Board minutes
8. Discussion or correspondance with the client at they year-end

a. External auditor

b. International Federation of Audit Bureaux of Circulations

c. Assurance service

d. Analytical procedures

18. _____ is that part of statistical practice concerned with the selection of individual observations intended to yield some knowledge about a population of concern, especially for the purposes of statistical inference. Each observation measures one or more properties (weight, location, etc.) of an observable entity enumerated to distinguish objects or individuals.
   a. Alan Greenspan
   b. Abby Joseph Cohen
   c. Arthur Betz Laffer
   d. Sampling

19. The _____ (sometimes called 'Peekaboo') is a private-sector, non-profit corporation created by the Sarbanes-Oxley Act, a 2002 United States federal law, to oversee the auditors of public companies. Its stated purpose is to 'protect the interests of investors and further the public interest in the preparation of informative, fair, and independent audit reports'. Although a private entity, the _____ has many government-like regulatory functions, making it in some ways similar to the private Self Regulatory Organizations (SROs) that regulate stock markets and other aspects of the financial markets in the United States.

a. 3M Company
c. Pension Benefit Guaranty Corporation
b. Financial Crimes Enforcement Network
d. Public Company Accounting Oversight Board

Chapter 19. Additional Assurance Services: Historical Financial Information

1. _____s have been defined by the American Institute of Certified Public Accountants (AICPA) as 'Independent Professional Services that improve information quality or its context'. _____s reduce the information risk; risk that the information provided is incorrect, on more than just financial data. The major purpose of _____s is to provide independent and professional opinions that improve the quality of information to management as well as other decision makers within a given firm.

   a. Auditor independence
   b. ITGCs
   c. Assurance service
   d. Institute of Chartered Accountants of India

2. An _____ is a practitioner of accountancy, which is the measurement, disclosure or provision of assurance about financial information that helps managers, investors, tax authorities and other decision makers make resource allocation decisions.

   The word '_____' is derived from the French 'Compter' which took its origin from the Latin 'Computare'. The word was formerly written in English as 'Accomptant', but in process of time the word, which was always pronounced by dropping the 'p', became gradually changed both in pronunciation and in orthography to its present form.

   a. AMEX
   b. AIG
   c. ABC Television Network
   d. Accountant

3. The general definition of an _____ is an evaluation of a person, organization, system, process, project or product. _____s are performed to ascertain the validity and reliability of information; also to provide an assessment of a system's internal control. The goal of an _____ is to express an opinion on the person/organization/system (etc) in question, under evaluation based on work done on a test basis.

   a. Audit
   b. Institute of Chartered Accountants of India
   c. Audit regime
   d. Assurance service

4. The _____ (sometimes called 'Peekaboo') is a private-sector, non-profit corporation created by the Sarbanes-Oxley Act, a 2002 United States federal law, to oversee the auditors of public companies. Its stated purpose is to 'protect the interests of investors and further the public interest in the preparation of informative, fair, and independent audit reports'. Although a private entity, the _____ has many government-like regulatory functions, making it in some ways similar to the private Self Regulatory Organizations (SROs) that regulate stock markets and other aspects of the financial markets in the United States.

   a. Public Company Accounting Oversight Board
   b. Financial Crimes Enforcement Network
   c. 3M Company
   d. Pension Benefit Guaranty Corporation

5. The U.S. _____ is an independent agency of the United States government which holds primary responsibility for enforcing the federal securities laws and regulating the securities industry, the nation's stock and options exchanges, and other electronic securities markets. The SEC was created by section 4 of the Securities Exchange Act of 1934 (now codified as 15 U.S.C. ÂÂ§ 78d and commonly referred to as the 1934 Act.)

   a. BNSF Railway
   b. Securities and Exchange Commission
   c. BMC Software, Inc.
   d. 3M Company

6. _____ are formal records of a business' financial activities.

   In British English, including United Kingdom company law, _____ are often referred to as accounts, although the term _____ is also used, particularly by accountants.

Chapter 19. Additional Assurance Services: Historical Financial Information

_____ provide an overview of a business' financial condition in both short and long term.

a. 3M Company
b. Statement of retained earnings
c. Notes to the financial statements
d. Financial statements

7. An _____ is a term used in behavioral economics to describe those types of behaviors that impose costs on a person in the long-run that are not taken into account when making decisions in the present. Classical Economics discourages government from creating legislation that targets internalities, because it is assumed that the consumer takes these personal costs into account when paying for the good that causes the _____. For example, cigarettes should be taxed because of the negative consumption externalities that they impose, such as second-hand smoke, not because the smoker harms him or herself by smoking.

a. Authorised capital
b. Operating budget
c. Inventory turnover ratio
d. Internality

8. In accounting and organizational theory, _____ is defined as a process effected by an organization's structure, work and authority flows, people and management information systems, designed to help the organization accomplish specific goals or objectives. It is a means by which an organization's resources are directed, monitored, and measured. It plays an important role in preventing and detecting fraud and protecting the organization's resources, both physical (e.g., machinery and property) and intangible (e.g., reputation or intellectual property such as trademarks.)

a. Audit committee
b. Auditor independence
c. Audit risk
d. Internal control

9. _____ is a legally declared inability or impairment of ability of an individual or organization to pay its creditors. Creditors may file a _____ petition against a debtor ('involuntary _____') in an effort to recoup a portion of what they are owed or initiate a restructuring. In the majority of cases, however, _____ is initiated by the debtor (a 'voluntary _____' that is filed by the bankrupt individual or organization.)

a. Bankruptcy protection
b. BMC Software, Inc.
c. Bankruptcy
d. 3M Company

10. A _____, also client, buyer or purchaser is the buyer or user of the paid products of an individual or organization, mostly called the supplier or seller. This is typically through purchasing or renting goods or services.

a. BMC Software, Inc.
b. BNSF Railway
c. 3M Company
d. Customer

11. Method used by the Certified Public Accountant to assure various parties, such as bankers and stockbrokers, that financial data under review by them is correct. _____ tells the data user that nothing has come to the CPA's attention of an adverse nature or character regarding the financial data reviewed. This type of assurance is normally given to investment bankers and the SEC when the financial data are being used for stock and bond issuance.

a. SOFT audit
b. Financial audit
c. Continuous auditing
d. Negative assurance

12. _____ is that which is owed; usually referencing assets owed, but the term can also cover moral obligations and other interactions not requiring money. In the case of assets, _____ is a means of using future purchasing power in the present before a summation has been earned. Some companies and corporations use _____ as a part of their overall corporate finance strategy.

a. Loan
b. Lender
c. Debenture
d. Debt

13. Title _____s serve as guarantees to the recipient of property, ensuring that the recipient receives what he or she bargained for. The English _____s of title, sometimes included in deeds to real property, are that the grantor is lawfully seized (in fee simple) of the property, (2) that the grantor has the right to convey the property to the grantee, (3) that the property is conveyed without encumbrances (this _____ is frequently modified to allow for certain encumbrances), (4) that the grantor has done no act to encumber the property, (5) that the grantee shall have quiet possession of the property, and (6) that the grantor will execute such further assurances of the land as may be requisite (Nos. 3 and 4, which overlap significantly, are sometimes treated as one item.)
   a. Liability
   b. Tax patent
   c. Patent
   d. Covenant

14. A _____ is a type of debt Like all debt instruments, a _____ entails the redistribution of financial assets over time, between the lender and the borrower.
   a. Lender
   b. Debenture
   c. Loan to value
   d. Loan

15. In business, _____ is the total assets minus total outside liabilities of an individual or a company. For a company, this is called shareholders' equity and may be referred to as book value. _____ is stated as at a particular point in time.
   a. Debtor
   b. Creditor
   c. Restructuring
   d. Net worth

16. In business and accounting, _____ are everything of value that is owned by a person or company. It is a claim on the property your income of a borrower. The balance sheet of a firm records the monetary value of the _____ owned by the firm.
   a. Earnings before interest, taxes, depreciation and amortization
   b. Accrual basis accounting
   c. Accounts receivable
   d. Assets

17. The _____ of 1977 (15 U.S.C. §§ 78dd-1, et seq.) is a United States federal law known primarily for two of its main provisions, one that addresses accounting transparency requirements under the Securities Exchange Act of 1934 and another concerning bribery of foreign officials.
   a. Competition law
   b. Lease
   c. Pre-emption right
   d. Foreign Corrupt Practices Act

18. _____, Quarterly Report Pursuant to Section 13 or 15(d) of the Securities Exchange Act of 1934, is an SEC filing that must be filed quarterly with the US Securities and Exchange Commission. It contains similar information to the annual form 10-K, however the information is generally less detailed, and the financial statements are generally unaudited. Information for the final quarter of a firm's fiscal year is included in the 10-K, so only three 10-Q filings are made each year.
   a. Form 10-Q
   b. Form 8-K
   c. Form 20-F
   d. 3M Company

19. _____ is one of financial audit skill which help an auditor understand the client's business and changes in the business, to identify potential risk areas and to plan other audit procedures.

Chapter 19. Additional Assurance Services: Historical Financial Information 177

_____ include comparison of financial information (data in financial statement) with

1. prior periods
2. budgets
3. forecasts
4. similar industries and so on.

It also includes consideration of predictable relationships, such as:

1. gross profit to sales,
2. payroll costs to employees,
3. financial information and non-financial information, for examples the CEO's reports and the industry news.

possible sources of information about the client include:

1. interim financial information
2. Budgets
3. Management accounts
4. Non-Financial information
5. Bank and cash records
6. VAT returns
7. Board minutes
8. Discussion or correspondance with the client at they year-end

a. Assurance service

c. External auditor

b. Analytical procedures

d. International Federation of Audit Bureaux of Circulations

20. _____ is a specific term used in companies' financial reporting from the company-whole point of view. Because that use excludes the effects of changing ownership interest, an economic measure of _____ is necessary for financial analysis from the shareholders' point of view

_____ is defined by the Financial Accounting Standards Board, or FASB, as 'the change in equity [net assets] of a business enterprise during a period from transactions and other events and circumstances from nonowner sources. It includes all changes in equity during a period except those resulting from investments by owners and distributions to owners.'

_____ is the sum of net income and other items that must bypass the income statement because they have not been realized, including items like an unrealized holding gain or loss from available for sale securities and foreign currency translation gains or losses.

a. 3M Company
b. BMC Software, Inc.
c. Comprehensive income
d. BNSF Railway

21. _____ is the statutory title of qualified accountants in the United States who have passed the Uniform _____ Examination and have met additional state education and experience requirements for certification as a _____. Individuals who have passed the Exam but have not either accomplished the required on-the-job experience or have previously met it but in the meantime have lapsed their continuing professional education are, in many states, permitted the designation '_____ Inactive' or an equivalent phrase. In most U.S. states, only _____s who are licensed are able to provide to the public attestation (including auditing) opinions on financial statements.

a. Chartered Accountant
b. Certified General Accountant
c. Chartered Certified Accountant
d. Certified public accountant

22. In accounting/accountancy, _____ are journal entries usually made at the end of an accounting period to allocate income and expenditure to the period in which they actually occurred. The revenue recognition principle is the basis of making _____ that pertain to unearned and accrued revenues under accrual-basis accounting. They are sometimes called Balance Day adjustments because they are made on balance day.

a. Accrued expense
b. Earnings before interest, taxes, depreciation and amortization
c. Adjusting entries
d. Accrual

23. _____ is a concept that denotes the precise probability of specific eventualities. Technically, the notion of _____ is independent from the notion of value and, as such, eventualities may have both beneficial and adverse consequences. However, in general usage the convention is to focus only on potential negative impact to some characteristic of value that may arise from a future event.

a. Risk adjusted return on capital
b. Discount factor
c. Discounting
d. Risk

24. The _____ is the national, professional association of CPAs in the United States, with more than 330,000 members, including CPAs in business and industry, public practice, government, and education; student affiliates; and international associates. It sets ethical standards for the profession and U.S. auditing standards for audits of private companies; federal, state and local governments; and non-profit organizations.

Approximately 40% of its members are engaged in the practice of public accounting, in areas such as auditing, accounting, taxation, general business consulting, business valuation, personal financial planning and business technology.

a. Other postemployment benefits
b. ABC Television Network
c. American Institute of Certified Public Accountants
d. AIG

25. Accounting _____ define the basic standards for representing attestation engagements. Attestation is defined as an engagement in which a practitioner is hired to issue written communication that expresses a conclusion about the reliability of written assertions prepared by a separate party. The American Institute of Certified Public Accountants identified a number of different engagements that fall under the scope of _____, including: examining financial forecasts and projections, examining pro forma financial statements, evaluating internal control, assessing compliance with rules, regulations, and contractual obligations, as well as evaluating management discussions and analysis of financial results.

Chapter 19. Additional Assurance Services: Historical Financial Information 179

a. Attestation standards
c. Audit working paper

b. Institute of Chartered Accountants of India
d. Audit management

26. In financial accounting, a _____ is defined as an obligation of an entity arising from past transactions or events, the settlement of which may result in the transfer or use of assets, provision of services or other yielding of economic benefits in the future.

a. Liability
c. Vested

b. False Claims Act
d. Corporate governance

27. An _____ defines the legal relationship (or engagement) between a professional firm (e.g., law, investment banking, consulting, advisory or accountancy firm) and its client(s.) This letter states the terms and conditions of the engagement, principally addressing the scope of the engagement and the terms of compensation for the firm.

Most _____s follow a standard format.

a. Audit evidence
c. Internal control

b. Audit risk
d. Engagement letter

28. _____, in general, is the investigation of a great number of something (for instance, people) looking for those with a particular problem or feature. One example is at an airport, where many bags get x-rayed to try to detect any which may contain weapons or explosives. People are also screened going through a metal detector.

a. Capital
c. Pay-as-you-go

b. General partner
d. Screening

29. _____ is the term used to refer to the standard framework of guidelines for financial accounting used in any given jurisdiction. _____ includes the standards, conventions, and rules accountants follow in recording and summarizing transactions, and in the preparation of financial statements.

Financial accounting information must be assembled and reported objectively.

a. General ledger
c. Current asset

b. Generally accepted accounting principles
d. Long-term liabilities

30. A _____ is an annual report required by the U.S. Securities and Exchange Commission (SEC), that gives a comprehensive summary of a public company's performance. Although similarly named, the annual report on _____ is distinct from the often glossy 'annual report to shareholders', which a company must send to its shareholders when it holds an annual meeting to elect directors (though some companies combine the annual report and the 10-K into one document.) The 10-K includes information such as company history, organizational structure, executive compensation, equity, subsidiaries, and audited financial statements, among other information.

a. Form 8-K
c. Form 10-Q

b. 3M Company
d. Form 10-K

31. A _____ is a fungible, negotiable instrument representing financial value. they are broadly categorized into debt securities (such as banknotes, bonds and debentures), and equity securities; e.g., common stocks. The company or other entity issuing the _____ is called the issuer.

a. BMC Software, Inc.
c. Tracking stock
b. Security
d. 3M Company

32. Congress enacted the _____, in the aftermath of the stock market crash of 1929 and during the ensuing Great Depression.
   a. Securities Act of 1933
   b. Sustainability measurement
   c. Bookkeeping
   d. Monte Carlo methods

33. An _____ is a comprehensive report on a company's activities throughout the preceding year. _____s are intended to give shareholders and other interested persons information about the company's activities and financial performance. Most jurisdictions require companies to prepare and disclose _____s, and many require the _____ to be filed at the company's registry.
   a. AIG
   b. AMEX
   c. ABC Television Network
   d. Annual report

34. _____ means the giving out of information, either voluntarily or to be in compliance with legal regulations or workplace rules.

   - In Computer security, full _____ means disclosing full information about vulnerabilities.
   - In computing, _____ widget
   - Journalism, full _____ refers to disclosing the interests of the writer which may bear on the subject being written about, for example, if the writer has worked with an interview subject in the past.

   - In law:
     o The law of England and Wales, _____ refers to a process that may form part of legal proceedings, whereby parties inform to other parties the existence of any relevant documents that are, or have been, in their control. This compares with the process known as discovery in the course of legal proceedings in the United States.
     o In U.S. civil procedure (litigation rules for civil cases), _____ is a stage prior to trial. In civil cases, each party must disclose to the opposing party the following: names of witnesses which it may use to support its side, copies of documents (or mere description of these documents) in its control which it may use to support its side, computation of damages claimed, and certain insurance information. _____ is related to, but technically prior to, the discovery stage.
     o In Company law (known as 'corporate law' in the United States), _____ refers to giving out information about public or limited companies or their officers, which might be kept secret if the company was a private company or a partnership.

   - In real property transactions, _____ refers to providing to a buyer information known to the seller or broker/agent concerning the condition or other aspects of real property that would affect the property's value or desirability. These rules regarding what information must be disclosed, and whether the information must be disclosed even if a buyer does not ask, vary from one jurisdiction to the next.

   a. Tax harmonisation
   b. Controlled Foreign Corporations
   c. Disclosure
   d. Trailing

Chapter 20. Additional Assurance Services: Other Information

1. _____s have been defined by the American Institute of Certified Public Accountants (AICPA) as 'Independent Professional Services that improve information quality or its context'. _____s reduce the information risk; risk that the information provided is incorrect, on more than just financial data. The major purpose of _____s is to provide independent and professional opinions that improve the quality of information to management as well as other decision makers within a given firm.

   a. Assurance Service
   b. Auditor independence
   c. Institute of Chartered Accountants of India
   d. ITGCs

2. Accounting _____ define the basic standards for representing attestation engagements. Attestation is defined as an engagement in which a practitioner is hired to issue written communication that expresses a conclusion about the reliability of written assertions prepared by a separate party. The American Institute of Certified Public Accountants identified a number of different engagements that fall under the scope of _____, including: examining financial forecasts and projections, examining pro forma financial statements, evaluating internal control, assessing compliance with rules, regulations, and contractual obligations, as well as evaluating management discussions and analysis of financial results.

   a. Attestation standards
   b. Audit management
   c. Institute of Chartered Accountants of India
   d. Audit working paper

3. _____ is a concept that denotes the precise probability of specific eventualities. Technically, the notion of _____ is independent from the notion of value and, as such, eventualities may have both beneficial and adverse consequences. However, in general usage the convention is to focus only on potential negative impact to some characteristic of value that may arise from a future event.

   a. Discounting
   b. Risk adjusted return on capital
   c. Risk
   d. Discount factor

4. _____ that may or may not be incurred by an entity depending on the outcome of a future event such as a court case. These liabilities are recorded in a company's accounts and shown in the balance sheet when both probable and reasonably estimable. A footnote to the balance sheet describes the nature and extent of the _____.

   a. Contingent liabilities
   b. Tangible
   c. Nonacquiescence
   d. Headnote

5. In financial accounting, a _____ is defined as an obligation of an entity arising from past transactions or events, the settlement of which may result in the transfer or use of assets, provision of services or other yielding of economic benefits in the future.

   a. False Claims Act
   b. Corporate governance
   c. Vested
   d. Liability

6. The _____ is the national, professional association of CPAs in the United States, with more than 330,000 members, including CPAs in business and industry, public practice, government, and education; student affiliates; and international associates. It sets ethical standards for the profession and U.S. auditing standards for audits of private companies; federal, state and local governments; and non-profit organizations.

Approximately 40% of its members are engaged in the practice of public accounting, in areas such as auditing, accounting, taxation, general business consulting, business valuation, personal financial planning and business technology.

a. ABC Television Network
b. AIG
c. Other postemployment benefits
d. American Institute of Certified Public Accountants

7. _____ is a term that is commonly used in relation to the audit of the financial statements of an entity. (.
a. Auditor independence
b. Audit working paper
c. Engagement Letter
d. Audit risk

8. _____, in auditing, is the risk that a company's internal controls are insufficient to mitigate or detect errors or fraud.
a. BMC Software, Inc.
b. BNSF Railway
c. 3M Company
d. Control risk

9. _____, in auditing, is the risk that the auditing procedures used will not find a material misstatement in the financial statements of the company being audited. .
a. 3M Company
b. BMC Software, Inc.
c. BNSF Railway
d. Detection risk

10. _____, in auditing, is the risk that the account or section being audited is materially misstated without considering internal controls due to error; _____ does not include an assessment of the risk of material misstatement due to fraud. The assessment of _____ depends on the professional judgement of the auditor, and it is done after assessing the business environment of the entity being audited.

_____ is typically assessed using a scale, with assessments being either low, medium, or high.

a. ABC Television Network
b. AMEX
c. Inherent risk
d. AIG

11. The general definition of an _____ is an evaluation of a person, organization, system, process, project or product. _____s are performed to ascertain the validity and reliability of information; also to provide an assessment of a system's internal control. The goal of an _____ is to express an opinion on the person/organization/system (etc) in question, under evaluation based on work done on a test basis.
a. Institute of Chartered Accountants of India
b. Audit
c. Audit regime
d. Assurance service

12. Method used by the Certified Public Accountant to assure various parties, such as bankers and stockbrokers, that financial data under review by them is correct. _____ tells the data user that nothing has come to the CPA's attention of an adverse nature or character regarding the financial data reviewed. This type of assurance is normally given to investment bankers and the SEC when the financial data are being used for stock and bond issuance.
a. Continuous auditing
b. SOFT audit
c. Financial audit
d. Negative assurance

13. An _____ is a term used in behavioral economics to describe those types of behaviors that impose costs on a person in the long-run that are not taken into account when making decisions in the present. Classical Economics discourages government from creating legislation that targets internalities, because it is assumed that the consumer takes these personal costs into account when paying for the good that causes the _____. For example, cigarettes should be taxed because of the negative consumption externalities that they impose, such as second-hand smoke, not because the smoker harms him or herself by smoking.

a. Authorised capital
c. Inventory turnover ratio
b. Internality
d. Operating budget

14. In accounting and organizational theory, _____ is defined as a process effected by an organization's structure, work and authority flows, people and management information systems, designed to help the organization accomplish specific goals or objectives. It is a means by which an organization's resources are directed, monitored, and measured. It plays an important role in preventing and detecting fraud and protecting the organization's resources, both physical (e.g., machinery and property) and intangible (e.g., reputation or intellectual property such as trademarks.)
a. Internal control
c. Auditor independence
b. Audit risk
d. Audit committee

15. The _____ of 1977 (15 U.S.C. §§ 78dd-1, et seq.) is a United States federal law known primarily for two of its main provisions, one that addresses accounting transparency requirements under the Securities Exchange Act of 1934 and another concerning bribery of foreign officials.
a. Foreign Corrupt Practices Act
c. Competition law
b. Pre-emption right
d. Lease

16. _____ are formal records of a business' financial activities.

In British English, including United Kingdom company law, _____ are often referred to as accounts, although the term _____ is also used, particularly by accountants.

_____ provide an overview of a business' financial condition in both short and long term.

a. Financial statements
c. 3M Company
b. Notes to the financial statements
d. Statement of retained earnings

17. A _____ is an annual report required by the U.S. Securities and Exchange Commission (SEC), that gives a comprehensive summary of a public company's performance. Although similarly named, the annual report on _____ is distinct from the often glossy 'annual report to shareholders', which a company must send to its shareholders when it holds an annual meeting to elect directors (though some companies combine the annual report and the 10-K into one document.) The 10-K includes information such as company history, organizational structure, executive compensation, equity, subsidiaries, and audited financial statements, among other information.
a. Form 8-K
c. 3M Company
b. Form 10-Q
d. Form 10-K

18. _____, Quarterly Report Pursuant to Section 13 or 15(d) of the Securities Exchange Act of 1934, is an SEC filing that must be filed quarterly with the US Securities and Exchange Commission. It contains similar information to the annual form 10-K, however the information is generally less detailed, and the financial statements are generally unaudited. Information for the final quarter of a firm's fiscal year is included in the 10-K, so only three 10-Q filings are made each year.
a. Form 20-F
c. Form 8-K
b. 3M Company
d. Form 10-Q

Chapter 20. Additional Assurance Services: Other Information

19. The U.S. _____ is an independent agency of the United States government which holds primary responsibility for enforcing the federal securities laws and regulating the securities industry, the nation's stock and options exchanges, and other electronic securities markets. The SEC was created by section 4 of the Securities Exchange Act of 1934 (now codified as 15 U.S.C. ÂÂ§ 78d and commonly referred to as the 1934 Act.)
   - a. Securities and Exchange Commission
   - b. 3M Company
   - c. BNSF Railway
   - d. BMC Software, Inc.

20. An _____ is a practitioner of accountancy, which is the measurement, disclosure or provision of assurance about financial information that helps managers, investors, tax authorities and other decision makers make resource allocation decisions.

    The word '_____' is derived from the French 'Compter' which took its origin from the Latin 'Computare'. The word was formerly written in English as 'Accomptant', but in process of time the word, which was always pronounced by dropping the 'p', became gradually changed both in pronunciation and in orthography to its present form.
    - a. ABC Television Network
    - b. AMEX
    - c. AIG
    - d. Accountant

21. The _____ is the umbrella body for the Chartered Accountant profession in Canada and Bermuda. Membership of the CICA totals 70,000 Chartered Accountants and 8,500 students.

    Canadian chartered accountants use the designation CA.
    - a. BMC Software, Inc.
    - b. 3M Company
    - c. BNSF Railway
    - d. Canadian Institute of Chartered Accountants

22. _____ is the title used by members of certain professional accountancy associations in the British Commonwealth countries and Ireland. The term chartered comes from the Royal Charter granted to the world's first professional body of accountants upon their establishment in 1854. The Edinburgh Society of Accountants (formed 1854), the Glasgow Institute of Accountants and Actuaries (1854) and the Aberdeen Society of Accountants (1867) were each granted a royal charter almost from their inception.
    - a. Certified General Accountant
    - b. Certified public accountant
    - c. Chartered Certified Accountant
    - d. Chartered Accountant

23. A _____ is a fungible, negotiable instrument representing financial value. they are broadly categorized into debt securities (such as banknotes, bonds and debentures), and equity securities; e.g., common stocks. The company or other entity issuing the _____ is called the issuer.
    - a. Tracking stock
    - b. Security
    - c. BMC Software, Inc.
    - d. 3M Company

24. In business and accounting, _____ are everything of value that is owned by a person or company. It is a claim on the property your income of a borrower. The balance sheet of a firm records the monetary value of the _____ owned by the firm.

Chapter 20. Additional Assurance Services: Other Information

a. Earnings before interest, taxes, depreciation and amortization
b. Accrual basis accounting
c. Accounts receivable
d. Assets

25. _____ describes commerce transactions between businesses, such as between a manufacturer and a wholesaler, or between a wholesaler and a retailer. Contrasting terms are business-to-consumer (B2C) and business-to-government (B2G.)

The volume of B2B transactions is much higher than the volume of B2C transactions.

a. Value chain
b. Market segment
c. Market share
d. Business-to-business

26. _____ is an electronic commerce business model in which consumers (individuals) offer products and services to companies and the companies pay them. This business model is a complete reversal of traditional business model where companies offer goods and services to consumers (business-to-consumer = B2C.)

This kind of economic relationship is qualified as an inverted business type.

a. Redemption value
b. Fund accounting
c. Refunding
d. Consumer-to-business

27. _____, commonly known as e-commerce or eCommerce, consists of the buying and selling of products or services over electronic systems such as the Internet and other computer networks. The amount of trade conducted electronically has grown extraordinarily since the spread of the Internet. A wide variety of commerce is conducted in this way, spurring and drawing on innovations in electronic funds transfer, supply chain management, Internet marketing, online transaction processing, electronic data interchange (EDI), inventory management systems, and automated data collection systems.

a. Electronic commerce
b. AIG
c. Electronic data interchange
d. ABC Television Network

28. _____ is the process whereby an organization establishes the parameters within which programs, investments, and acquisitions are reaching the desired results. Performance Reference Model of the Federal Enterprise Architecture, 2005.

This process of measuring performance often requires the use of statistical evidence to determine progress toward specific defined organizational objectives.

There are many types of measurements.

a. Trustee
b. Performance measurement
c. Management by objectives
d. Management by exception

Chapter 21. Internal, Operational, and Compliance Auditing

1. The _____ of 1977 (15 U.S.C. §§ 78dd-1, et seq.) is a United States federal law known primarily for two of its main provisions, one that addresses accounting transparency requirements under the Securities Exchange Act of 1934 and another concerning bribery of foreign officials.
   a. Lease
   b. Competition law
   c. Pre-emption right
   d. Foreign Corrupt Practices Act

2. An _____ is a term used in behavioral economics to describe those types of behaviors that impose costs on a person in the long-run that are not taken into account when making decisions in the present. Classical Economics discourages government from creating legislation that targets internalities, because it is assumed that the consumer takes these personal costs into account when paying for the good that causes the _____. For example, cigarettes should be taxed because of the negative consumption externalities that they impose, such as second-hand smoke, not because the smoker harms him or herself by smoking.
   a. Inventory turnover ratio
   b. Operating budget
   c. Authorised capital
   d. Internality

3. _____ is a profession and activity involved in helping organisations achieve their stated objectives. It does this by using a systematic methodology for analyzing business processes, procedures and activities with the goal of highlighting organizational problems and recommending solutions. Professionals called internal auditors are employed by organizations to perform the _____ activity.
   a. Assurance service
   b. Information audit
   c. ITGCs
   d. Internal auditing

4. The general definition of an _____ is an evaluation of a person, organization, system, process, project or product. _____s are performed to ascertain the validity and reliability of information; also to provide an assessment of a system's internal control. The goal of an _____ is to express an opinion on the person/organization/system (etc) in question, under evaluation based on work done on a test basis.
   a. Institute of Chartered Accountants of India
   b. Audit regime
   c. Audit
   d. Assurance service

5. In a publicly-held company, an _____ is an operating committee of the Board of Directors, typically charged with oversight of financial reporting and disclosure. Committee members are drawn from members of the Company's board of directors, with a Chairperson selected from among the members. An _____ of a publicly-traded company in the United States is composed of independent and outside directors referred to as non-executive directors, at least one of which is typically a financial expert.
   a. Audit working paper
   b. Event data
   c. External auditor
   d. Audit Committee

6. _____ is subcontracting a process, such as product design or manufacturing, to a third-party company. The decision to outsource is often made in the interest of lowering cost or making better use of time and energy costs, redirecting or conserving energy directed at the competencies of a particular business, or to make more efficient use of land, labor, capital, (information) technology and resources. _____ became part of the business lexicon during the 1980s.
   a. US Airways, Inc.
   b. USA Today
   c. Economic Growth and Tax Relief Reconciliation Act of 2001
   d. Outsourcing

Chapter 21. Internal, Operational, and Compliance Auditing

7. The _____ of 2002 (Pub.L. 107-204, 116 Stat. 745, enacted July 30, 2002), also known as the Public Company Accounting Reform and Investor Protection Act of 2002, is a United States federal law enacted on July 30, 2002 in response to a number of major corporate and accounting scandals including those affecting Enron, Tyco International, Adelphia, Peregrine Systems and WorldCom. The legislation establishes new or enhanced standards for all U.S. public company boards, management, and public accounting firms. It does not apply to privately held companies.
   a. Sarbanes-Oxley Act
   b. FCPA
   c. Lease
   d. Fair Labor Standards Act

8. _____ are formal records of a business' financial activities.

   In British English, including United Kingdom company law, _____ are often referred to as accounts, although the term _____ is also used, particularly by accountants.

   _____ provide an overview of a business' financial condition in both short and long term.

   a. 3M Company
   b. Notes to the financial statements
   c. Statement of retained earnings
   d. Financial Statements

9. In accounting and organizational theory, _____ is defined as a process effected by an organization's structure, work and authority flows, people and management information systems, designed to help the organization accomplish specific goals or objectives. It is a means by which an organization's resources are directed, monitored, and measured. It plays an important role in preventing and detecting fraud and protecting the organization's resources, both physical (e.g., machinery and property) and intangible (e.g., reputation or intellectual property such as trademarks.)
   a. Auditor independence
   b. Audit risk
   c. Audit committee
   d. Internal Control

10. _____ is a demonstration of a process -- such as a variable, term, or object -- relative in terms of the specific process or set of validation tests used to determine its presence and quantity. Properties described in this manner must be sufficiently accessible, so that persons other than the definer may independently measure or test for them at will. An _____ is generally designed to model a conceptual definition.
    a. ABC Television Network
    b. AMEX
    c. Operational definition
    d. AIG

11. A _____ an audit of financial statements, is the review of the financial statements of a company or any other legal entity (including governments), resulting in the publication of an independent opinion on whether or not those financial statements are relevant, accurate, complete, and fairly presented. _____s are typically performed by firms of practicing accountants due to the specialist financial reporting knowledge they require. The _____ is one of many assurance or attestation functions provided by accounting and auditing firms, whereby the firm provides an independent opinion on published information.
    a. Lead Auditor
    b. Mainframe audit
    c. Management representation
    d. Financial audit

12. Internal auditing is a profession and activity involved in helping organisations achieve their stated objectives. It does this by utilizing a systematic methodology for analyzing business processes, procedures and activities with the goal of highlighting organizational problems and recommending solutions. Professionals called _____ are employed by organizations to perform the internal auditing activity.

a. Internal Auditing
b. Internal auditors
c. Auditor independence
d. Auditing Standards Board

13. _____ refers to the confirmation of certain characteristics of an object, person, or organization. This confirmation is often, but not always, provided by some form of external review, education, or assessment. One of the most common types of _____ in modern society is professional _____, where a person is certified as being able to competently complete a job or task, usually by the passing of an examination.
   a. 3M Company
   b. BNSF Railway
   c. BMC Software, Inc.
   d. Certification

14. _____ is a concept that denotes the precise probability of specific eventualities. Technically, the notion of _____ is independent from the notion of value and, as such, eventualities may have both beneficial and adverse consequences. However, in general usage the convention is to focus only on potential negative impact to some characteristic of value that may arise from a future event.
   a. Discount factor
   b. Discounting
   c. Risk
   d. Risk adjusted return on capital

15. A _____ is a type of debt Like all debt instruments, a _____ entails the redistribution of financial assets over time, between the lender and the borrower.
   a. Loan to value
   b. Debenture
   c. Lender
   d. Loan

16. A _____ is a common type of chart, that represents an algorithm or process, showing the steps as boxes of various kinds, and their order by connecting these with arrows. _____s are used in analyzing, designing, documenting or managing a process or program in various fields.

The first structured method for documenting process flow, the 'flow process chart', was introduced by Frank Gilbreth to members of ASME in 1921 as the presentation e;Process Charts--First Steps in Finding the One Best Waye;.

   a. BMC Software, Inc.
   b. Flowchart
   c. 3M Company
   d. BNSF Railway

17. Accounting _____ define the basic standards for representing attestation engagements. Attestation is defined as an engagement in which a practitioner is hired to issue written communication that expresses a conclusion about the reliability of written assertions prepared by a separate party. The American Institute of Certified Public Accountants identified a number of different engagements that fall under the scope of _____, including: examining financial forecasts and projections, examining pro forma financial statements, evaluating internal control, assessing compliance with rules, regulations, and contractual obligations, as well as evaluating management discussions and analysis of financial results.
   a. Attestation Standards
   b. Audit management
   c. Institute of Chartered Accountants of India
   d. Audit working paper

18. _____, in law and economics, is a form of risk management primarily used to hedge against the risk of a contingent loss. _____ is defined as the equitable transfer of the risk of a loss, from one entity to another, in exchange for a premium, and can be thought of as a guaranteed small loss to prevent a large, possibly devastating loss. An insurer is a company selling the _____; an insured is the person or entity buying the _____.

| a. AMEX | b. ABC Television Network |
| c. Insurance | d. AIG |

19. _____ are ten auditing standards, developed by the AICPA, consisting of general standards, standards of field work, and standards of reporting, along with interpretations. They were developed by the AICPA in 1947 and have undergone minor changes since then.

The _____ are as follows:

1. The auditor must have adequate technical training and proficiency to perform the audit
2. The auditor must maintain independence in mental attitude in all matters related to the audit.
3. The auditor must use due professional care during the performance of the audit and the preparation of the report.

1. The auditor must adequately plan the work and must properly supervise any assistants.
2. The auditor must obtain a sufficient understanding of the entity and its environment, including its internal control, to assess the risk of material misstatement of the financial statements whether due to error or fraud, and to design the nature, timing, and extent of further audit procedures.
3. The auditor must obtain sufficient appropriate audit evidence by performing audit procedures to afford a reasonable basis for an opinion regarding the financial statements under audit.

The new standards are in effect for audits of financial statements for periods beginning on or after December 15, 2006.

1. The auditor must state in the auditor's report whether the financial statements are in accordance with generally accepted accounting principles (GAAP.)
2. The auditor must identify in the auditor's report those circumstances in which such principles have not been consistently observed in the current period in relation to the preceding period.
3. When the auditor determines that informative disclosures are not reasonably adequate, the auditor must so state in the auditor's report.
4. The auditor must either express an opinion regarding the financial statements, taken as a whole the auditor should state the reasons therefore in the auditor's report. In all cases where the auditor's name is associated with the financial statements, the auditor should clearly indicate the character of the auditor's work, if any, and the degree of responsibility the auditor is taking, in the auditor's report.

| a. Negative assurance | b. Continuous auditing |
| c. Generally accepted auditing standards | d. Joint audit |

20. The _____ (GAO) is the audit, evaluation, and investigative arm of the United States Congress. It is located in the Legislative branch of the United States government.

The _____ was established as the _____ by the Budget and Accounting Act of 1921 (Pub.L.

a. 3M Company
c. GAO
b. General Accounting Office
d. BMC Software, Inc.

21. Title _____s serve as guarantees to the recipient of property, ensuring that the recipient receives what he or she bargained for. The English _____s of title, sometimes included in deeds to real property, are that the grantor is lawfully seized (in fee simple) of the property, (2) that the grantor has the right to convey the property to the grantee, (3) that the property is conveyed without encumbrances (this _____ is frequently modified to allow for certain encumbrances), (4) that the grantor has done no act to encumber the property, (5) that the grantee shall have quiet possession of the property, and (6) that the grantor will execute such further assurances of the land as may be requisite (Nos. 3 and 4, which overlap significantly, are sometimes treated as one item.)

a. Liability
c. Tax patent
b. Patent
d. Covenant

22. _____ is that which is owed; usually referencing assets owed, but the term can also cover moral obligations and other interactions not requiring money. In the case of assets, _____ is a means of using future purchasing power in the present before a summation has been earned. Some companies and corporations use _____ as a part of their overall corporate finance strategy.

a. Debenture
c. Lender
b. Loan
d. Debt

23. In the United States, _____ federal benefits is defined as any federal program, project, service, and activity provided by the federal government that directly assists or benefits the American public in the areas of education, health, public safety, public welfare, and public works, among others. The assistance, which can reach to over $400 billion dollars annually, is provided and administered by federal government agencies, such as the U.S. Department of Housing and Urban Development and the U.S. Department of Health and Human Services, through special programs to recipients.

The term assistance is defined by the federal government as:

In order to provide _____ in an organized manner, the federal government provides assistance through federal agencies.

a. Federal assistance
c. BMC Software, Inc.
b. BNSF Railway
d. 3M Company

24. _____, in auditing, is the risk that a company's internal controls are insufficient to mitigate or detect errors or fraud.

a. Control risk
c. 3M Company
b. BNSF Railway
d. BMC Software, Inc.

25. _____ is systematic determination of merit, worth, and significance of something or someone using criteria against a set of standards. _____ often is used to characterize and appraise subjects of interest in a wide range of human enterprises, including the arts, criminal justice, foundations and non-profit organizations, government, health care, and other human services.

Depending on the topic of interest, there are professional groups which look to the quality and rigor of the _____ process.

a. AIG
b. ABC Television Network
c. Evaluation
d. AMEX

26. In economics, business, retail, and accounting, a _____ is the value of money that has been used up to produce something, and hence is not available for use anymore. In economics, a _____ is an alternative that is given up as a result of a decision. In business, the _____ may be one of acquisition, in which case the amount of money expended to acquire it is counted as _____.
a. Cost of quality
b. Prime cost
c. Cost allocation
d. Cost

27. _____ is that part of statistical practice concerned with the selection of individual observations intended to yield some knowledge about a population of concern, especially for the purposes of statistical inference. Each observation measures one or more properties (weight, location, etc.) of an observable entity enumerated to distinguish objects or individuals.
a. Arthur Betz Laffer
b. Abby Joseph Cohen
c. Alan Greenspan
d. Sampling

Chapter 1
1. a	2. a	3. c	4. a	5. b	6. b	7. a	8. d	9. c	10. c
11. b	12. d	13. d	14. d	15. d	16. d	17. d	18. d	19. c	20. d
21. d	22. d	23. d	24. a	25. a	26. a	27. d	28. d	29. c	30. c
31. d	32. d	33. b	34. b	35. b	36. d	37. a	38. d	39. b	40. b
41. d	42. a	43. a	44. c	45. d	46. d	47. d	48. a	49. d	50. d
51. c	52. d	53. d	54. d	55. b	56. d	57. d	58. b	59. c	60. d

Chapter 2
1. d	2. d	3. c	4. c	5. a	6. b	7. a	8. b	9. b	10. b
11. c	12. a	13. a	14. d	15. c	16. a	17. b	18. b	19. d	20. d
21. d	22. d	23. d	24. c	25. d	26. d	27. a	28. c	29. d	30. d
31. d	32. a	33. c	34. d						

Chapter 3
1. a	2. b	3. d	4. d	5. d	6. b	7. a	8. d	9. b	10. d
11. a	12. a	13. c	14. c	15. d	16. a	17. d	18. c	19. d	20. d
21. d	22. b	23. d	24. d	25. d	26. d	27. d	28. b	29. a	30. d
31. a	32. a	33. d	34. c	35. c	36. d	37. a	38. d	39. d	40. b
41. d	42. d	43. a	44. c	45. b	46. a	47. c			

Chapter 4
1. c	2. d	3. c	4. a	5. c	6. d	7. b	8. c	9. d	10. d
11. d	12. c	13. c	14. d	15. b	16. c	17. d	18. a	19. d	20. d

Chapter 5
1. d	2. d	3. d	4. a	5. d	6. b	7. b	8. d	9. d	10. b
11. d	12. d	13. d	14. d	15. c	16. d	17. c	18. a	19. c	20. d
21. d	22. b	23. a	24. c	25. b	26. d	27. a	28. d	29. b	30. d
31. d	32. d	33. a	34. a	35. d	36. a	37. d	38. b	39. d	40. d
41. c	42. d	43. b	44. b	45. d					

Chapter 6
1. a	2. a	3. d	4. d	5. b	6. d	7. d	8. a	9. d	10. d
11. c	12. d	13. d	14. d	15. c	16. d	17. d	18. a	19. c	20. c
21. b	22. a	23. b	24. a	25. d	26. d	27. b	28. a	29. a	30. c
31. b	32. d	33. b	34. d	35. c	36. d	37. d	38. b	39. d	40. d
41. d	42. b	43. d	44. c	45. c	46. d	47. a	48. c	49. d	50. d
51. d	52. c	53. b	54. c	55. b	56. d	57. d	58. a	59. d	60. d
61. b	62. d	63. d							

ANSWER KEY

Chapter 7
1. a	2. c	3. d	4. d	5. a	6. d	7. d	8. b	9. c	10. b
11. d	12. d	13. d	14. c	15. d	16. d	17. a	18. d	19. a	20. c
21. d	22. d	23. a	24. b	25. a	26. d	27. c	28. d	29. a	30. a
31. a	32. b	33. b	34. b	35. d	36. a	37. b	38. b	39. c	40. b
41. d	42. d	43. d	44. c	45. b	46. d	47. b			

Chapter 8
1. d	2. b	3. d	4. d	5. d	6. a	7. d	8. a	9. b	10. d
11. d	12. a	13. d	14. d	15. d	16. d	17. c	18. c	19. b	20. d
21. a	22. d	23. c	24. d	25. a	26. c	27. d	28. c	29. b	30. b
31. c									

Chapter 9
1. c	2. a	3. c	4. d	5. d	6. b	7. a	8. d	9. c	10. d
11. a	12. d	13. a	14. d	15. b	16. b	17. d	18. c		

Chapter 10
1. b	2. d	3. d	4. d	5. c	6. a	7. d	8. a	9. b	10. c
11. d	12. b	13. c	14. b	15. d	16. d	17. a	18. a	19. a	20. b
21. a	22. d	23. d	24. c	25. d	26. a	27. d	28. c	29. d	30. d
31. d	32. c	33. d	34. d	35. d	36. c	37. d	38. d	39. b	40. d

Chapter 11
1. d	2. d	3. d	4. b	5. c	6. d	7. c	8. d	9. d	10. b
11. d	12. d	13. a	14. d	15. b	16. d	17. a	18. d	19. d	20. b
21. b	22. b	23. d	24. a	25. d	26. c	27. b	28. c	29. c	30. b
31. d	32. d	33. c	34. d	35. d	36. c	37. b	38. d	39. c	40. c
41. d	42. d	43. b	44. d	45. a	46. d	47. d	48. a		

Chapter 12
1. d	2. a	3. a	4. b	5. b	6. a	7. c	8. d	9. a	10. b
11. d	12. c	13. c	14. c	15. d	16. c	17. d	18. a	19. d	20. b
21. a	22. a	23. a	24. d	25. a	26. d	27. d	28. d	29. d	30. d
31. b	32. b	33. d	34. d	35. d	36. d	37. a	38. a	39. d	40. d
41. c	42. a	43. d	44. d	45. d	46. d	47. c	48. d	49. a	

Chapter 13
1. d	2. b	3. c	4. a	5. c	6. a	7. d	8. b	9. d	10. c
11. d	12. d	13. a	14. d	15. d	16. d	17. b	18. a	19. c	20. c
21. d	22. c	23. c	24. c	25. d	26. b	27. d	28. d	29. b	30. b
31. b	32. d	33. d	34. d	35. d	36. a	37. d	38. d	39. d	40. c
41. a	42. d	43. d	44. d	45. b					

Chapter 14

1. d	2. c	3. c	4. d	5. d	6. d	7. d	8. b	9. d	10. d
11. b	12. b	13. a	14. a	15. d	16. d	17. d	18. d	19. d	20. b
21. d	22. a	23. d	24. d	25. b	26. a	27. a	28. d	29. d	30. b
31. c	32. a	33. d	34. d	35. d	36. d	37. a	38. d	39. a	40. c

Chapter 15

1. d	2. b	3. c	4. d	5. b	6. d	7. c	8. a	9. b	10. d
11. c	12. d	13. c	14. d	15. d	16. d	17. d	18. d	19. a	20. d
21. d	22. b	23. b	24. c	25. c	26. d	27. d	28. c	29. a	30. d
31. a	32. d	33. b	34. d	35. a	36. b	37. c	38. b	39. c	40. c
41. b	42. d	43. b	44. d	45. c	46. a	47. b	48. b	49. d	50. a
51. c	52. d	53. d	54. b	55. b	56. d	57. b	58. b	59. c	60. a

Chapter 16

1. d	2. c	3. b	4. a	5. d	6. b	7. c	8. b	9. b	10. d
11. d	12. d	13. d	14. c	15. b	16. b	17. c	18. d	19. a	20. b
21. d	22. a	23. d	24. d	25. d	26. d	27. c	28. d	29. d	30. d
31. d	32. d	33. d	34. a	35. d	36. a	37. d	38. d	39. c	40. c
41. a	42. d	43. b	44. d	45. d	46. a	47. c	48. a	49. d	50. d
51. d	52. d	53. d	54. b	55. d	56. d	57. b			

Chapter 17

1. b	2. d	3. b	4. a	5. b	6. d	7. a	8. a	9. a	10. a
11. d	12. a	13. a	14. d	15. d	16. b	17. d	18. d	19. d	20. d
21. d	22. b	23. d	24. c	25. c	26. d	27. a	28. c		

Chapter 18

| 1. d | 2. d | 3. a | 4. b | 5. d | 6. c | 7. d | 8. d | 9. d | 10. b |
| 11. d | 12. a | 13. d | 14. d | 15. d | 16. a | 17. d | 18. d | 19. d | |

Chapter 19

1. c	2. d	3. a	4. a	5. b	6. d	7. d	8. d	9. c	10. d
11. d	12. d	13. d	14. d	15. d	16. d	17. d	18. a	19. b	20. c
21. d	22. c	23. d	24. c	25. a	26. a	27. d	28. d	29. b	30. d
31. b	32. a	33. d	34. c						

Chapter 20

1. a	2. a	3. c	4. a	5. d	6. d	7. d	8. d	9. d	10. c
11. b	12. d	13. b	14. a	15. a	16. a	17. d	18. d	19. a	20. d
21. d	22. d	23. b	24. d	25. d	26. d	27. a	28. b		

ANSWER KEY

Chapter 21

1. d	2. d	3. d	4. c	5. d	6. d	7. a	8. d	9. d	10. c
11. d	12. b	13. d	14. c	15. d	16. b	17. a	18. c	19. c	20. c
21. d	22. d	23. a	24. a	25. c	26. d	27. d			

www.ingramcontent.com/pod-product-compliance
Lightning Source LLC
Chambersburg PA
CBHW081352230426
43667CB00017B/2813